MW01091954

NECESSARY CONDITIONS

GEOFF KRALL

NECESSARY
CONDITIONS

TEACHING SECONDARY MATH WITH ACADEMIC SAFETY,

QUALITY TASKS, AND EFFECTIVE FACILITATION

FOREWORD BY FAWN NGUYEN

Stenhouse
PUBLISHERS

www.stenhouse.com

Stenhouse Publishers
www.stenhouse.com

Copyright © 2018 by Geoff Krall

All rights reserved. Except for pages in the appendix, which can be photocopied for classroom use, no part of this publication may be reproduced or transmitted in any form or by any means, electronic or mechanical, including photocopy, or any information storage and retrieval system, without permission from the publisher.

Every effort has been made to contact copyright holders and students for permission to reproduce borrowed material. We regret any oversights that may have occurred and will be pleased to rectify them in subsequent reprints of the work.

Some of the schools' and teachers' names in this book appear as a pseudonym by choice and for the ease of the reader. Other teachers' and schools' names appear authentically when given permissions and where appropriate.

Figure 10.10. © The Regents of the University of California. The publishing of this information does not represent an endorsement of the book, *Necessary Conditions*.

Library of Congress Cataloging-in-Publication Data

Names: Krall, Geoff, 1980—author.
Title: Necessary conditions : teaching secondary math with academic safety, quality tasks, and effective facilitation.
Other titles: Teaching secondary math with academic safety, quality tasks, and effective facilitation
Description: Portsmouth, New Hampshire : Stenhouse Publishers, [2018] | Includes bibliographical references and index.
Identifiers: LCCN 2018013696 (print) | LCCN 2018017188 (ebook)
    | ISBN 9781625311467 (ebook) | ISBN 9781625311450 (pbk. : alk. paper)
Subjects: LCSH: Mathematics--Study and teaching (Secondary) | Mathematics teachers—In-service training. | Curriculum planning.
Classification: LCC QA11.2 (ebook) | LCC QA11.2 .K725 2018 (print)
    | DDC 510.71/2--dc23
LC record available at https://lccn.loc.gov/2018013696

Cover design, interior design, and typesetting by Gina Poirier, Gina Poirier Design

Manufactured in the United States of America

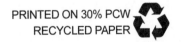
PRINTED ON 30% PCW RECYCLED PAPER

23 22 21 20 19 18   9 8 7 6 5 4 3 2 1

For Addy, whose creativity
inspires me, and for Jude,
whose caring sustains me

CONTENTS

FOREWORD

When Geoff Krall asked me to consider writing a foreword for his upcoming book about secondary teaching, adding, "You *do* the stuff I put forth in the book," I was equally honored and terrified. I told him that he was making a mistake because I haven't published anything, and foreword writers ought to be well-established authors. I even gave him three names of authors whom he should ask instead. He wrote back and gave me four bulleted reasons why he'd still like me to write the foreword.

Six months later I was sent the full manuscript. I read the first chapter and immediately understood why Geoff had reached out to me. I was overwhelmed with pride for *Necessary Conditions*. Geoff's honest storytelling pays diligence to what actually goes on in secondary mathematics classrooms. This important book, full of actionable content, will empower teachers to make math learning more authentic, more relevant, more joyful for all students.

Geoff Krall's three elements of pedagogy—academic safety, quality tasks, and effective teacher facilitation—belong in every math classroom. They form a pedagogical triangle that is the strongest shape and inherently stable and can withstand the ever-changing education landscape and its slew of jargons. Like a three-legged stool, all three elements must be present and given equal weight to uphold what we value so much in mathematics learning, that which is the "social ecosystem of math."

Everything that we know about mathematics learning tells us that productive struggle is necessary and that engaging in mathematical discourse is crucial to learning. We can't squeeze out productive struggle from a low-quality task or one with low cognitive demand, nor can we extract mathematical discourse from it. Geoff shares many examples of quality tasks that must be accessible to all students, including quality warm-ups and a rubric for selecting them. Geoff also understands how incredibly busy teachers are, so he suggests practical ways that we may adapt existing tasks instead.

Being equipped with a quality task but without effective teacher facilitation is like having quality ingredients and not knowing how to assemble them into a meal. Geoff has observed many secondary classrooms and shares classroom vignettes; we see the intentional teacher moves, including the well-planned questions, the in-the-moment adaptations, and the equally important next steps. Geoff believes we need to plan thoroughly so we may deviate from the lesson plan to accommodate students' contributions and challenges, because that's how creative work is done well.

Academic safety. I hold these two words sacred in my own classroom. We can place a high-quality task in the hands of an experienced teacher with ninja facilitation, but if the students in the room have academic stigma plagued with race and gender threats, then it's all for naught. Of the three elements, Geoff writes about academic safety first because he believes it is "the most permanent." He tells a story about Heather's early years in math education, and it all sounds sadly familiar, how she was not invited into an accelerated class because she did not finish some math packets fast enough. Luckily, Heather's story has a happy ending. Geoff understands the critical role of academic safety: "It's one thing if a teacher gives students specific mathematical praise, but to achieve a truly academically safe classroom, students must actively participate in the passing along of academic status."

While each chapter in *Necessary Conditions* is about a particular element or pillar of pedagogy, Geoff never fails to remind us how one is vitally connected to the other two. He also never fails to acknowledge how challenging our teaching craft is, that it takes years of intentional and sustained collaboration, along with organic implementation, to make school mathematics resemble the discipline that mathematicians practice in their field. He reminds us of self-care. Small doable steps, bite-sized implementation.

I also invite administrators to read this book because it weaves together an important and vibrant story about what mathematics learning and teaching should embody with specific ways schools can support that vision. From crafting assessments to buying furniture, from structuring PDs to having a common vocabulary, from aligning to improving academic safety, quality tasks, and teacher facilitation, administrators are essential.

I've been in the classroom for the last twenty-six years, yet *Necessary Conditions* inspires me and energizes me toward another school year. I still have much to learn, and there's more important work ahead. I do plenty of "passive caring," as Geoff points out in his book, but I surely can turn many of my cares into "active caring." I want to implement some sort of restorative circle. I can slow down in how I launch a task. I always need to rethink homework. My assessments remain dreary, but Geoff has reminded me of using portfolios. Whether you are a new teacher or a veteran teacher, or somewhere in between, I hope you find this book all too necessary as I did.

—Fawn Nguyen

PREFACE

I Keep My Math Everywhere

"I keep my math everywhere." What a peculiar phrase, I thought.

We're sitting at a table outside on an overcast Southern California day. I'm asking Karyn about her math experience up to and including her time with her teachers here at Samueli Academy in Santa Ana. Karyn tells me that teachers always had low expectations for her in elementary and middle school. She tells me that in elementary and middle school her math teachers would tell her that she was "no good at math" and that she didn't "belong here." She remembers a teacher asking her, point-blank, "What are you even doing here?" The conviction and clarity with which she quotes this teacher suggests she didn't make this up.

Karyn was never offered challenging work. Having been placed in remedial courses because of her performance, behavior, and ADHD diagnosis, she tells me that all she'd ever done in math was packets. Packet after packet. Her mathematical life was an exercise in digging through her backpack or overturning her bedroom trying to find a missing math packet. This is what she means by "I keep my math everywhere."

Karyn admits she's a tough student. She tells me she was always out of her seat and defiantly wandering around the classroom. "I get so frustrated, I have to walk around to cool off." The way she describes it, it's understandable that a teacher would get upset at her. It's understandable that a teacher would give her unchallenging work: she failed to complete or turn in the work she was given. Because it was everywhere. Truly, it was also nowhere.

Let's not mince words: Karyn hated math and felt that math hated her. She carried that with her for years. Although she struggled in all her classes, math was the class that seemed to yield the most trauma. Her experience in remedial math courses communicated to her that she was not an academically gifted student, not a mathematician. She then carried this self-image with her throughout the school day.

Then she entered Kala's ninth-grade math class.

The two butted heads initially. "I was so *frustrated* by Ms. [Kala] Gabler at first." There's that word again: *frustrated*. "She would get on me day after day about turning in my work and working hard. If I didn't have my work, she would ask me, 'Where's your work?' She gave me hard problems, too. I was used to getting the easiest work in the class or the least amount of work. Because of my ADHD, teachers would modify my assignment to give me five homework problems instead of ten. But now I was getting the same hard problems as the rest of the kids. And she would get upset at me if I didn't have it! She didn't just give me a zero; she would work with me during lunch to make sure I completed it."

"But now I was getting the same hard problems as the rest of the kids. And she would get upset at me if I didn't have it! She didn't just give me a zero; she would work with me during lunch to make sure I completed it."

I'm cross-examining Karyn's story with Kala. "Karyn probably had four or five blowups throughout the first semester of her freshman year. We had to go toe-to-toe a few times." Kala gives Karyn a knowing look with a smirk of affection. It sounds like it was more than a few times, and it sounds like it was a long time before the confrontations subsided.

It took the entire school year of consistently high expectations and direct communication that Karyn was an adept mathematician before Karyn accepted it. It took daily conversations, explicit confidence building, and countless lunch hours.

Now? "I'm really good at explaining mathematical ideas," Karyn tells me. She used to dread coming to math class (so much that she would intentionally try to get kicked out); now it's her refuge. With Kala's help, she's learned to better regulate her emotions. She's learned to keep track of her work. She's learned to celebrate her maturity. What's more, these dispositions have aided her in the rest of her schooling. She's learned to work in groups with students who look and sound different from her. She's passing all her classes—something that had never happened before this year. She has a plan for what she's going to do after she graduates, whereas before it didn't seem like she would graduate.

Karyn's success in math unlocked her academic potential. She still struggles, but now she's better able to persist through challenges. The hard road that she and Kala traveled together is paying dividends. The lessons she learned in math class are being transferred to other classes. Because, after all, she keeps her math everywhere.

▲ ▲ ▲

This book is about students like Karyn and teachers like Kala. How do students experience math? How can teachers provide the best possible experience in math? As challenging as it is to teach math, a high-quality mathematical schooling experience can unlock a person's academic identity. In this book, I've synthesized what we know from research and what I've seen in successful classrooms into a coherent framework for a secondary math pedagogy. As schools jump from curricula to curricula, from initiative to initiative, I've found that the biggest drivers of a high-quality math experience are teachers dedicated to their craft and to their students. Teachers who adhere to three crucial elements (which we'll get into shortly) will be successful, regardless of their context. Join me as we eavesdrop in the classrooms of such teachers.

ACKNOWLEDGMENTS

I never expected to write a book. Truth be told, I couldn't have written a book without a plethora of support at my side. I would like to extend thanks that I can never fully repay.

To Stenhouse Publishers, who allowed me this opportunity I never thought I'd have. And specifically, to my editor, Tracy Zager, who helped the words in this book become the best version of themselves. This book is here because Tracy encouraged me to write it; it's coherent because she edited it.

To my colleagues—you took up my slack as I spent time writing every week. I'm grateful to work at New Tech Network, which allowed and encouraged me to give this a shot.

To Megan Pacheco, who supported me when I was a teacher and who supports me now as a colleague and a friend. From the very beginning, she provided me with books about math instruction that we would discuss at length. I hope she'll hand this book to someone to enhance their own learning.

To Kevin Gant, who helped me refine my ideas as a young teacher and continues to sharpen them to this day.

To Rick Lear, who took a chance on me and never ceased to ensure that I was happy and well-fed.

To Zac Wheatcroft, who made this book come alive with his beautiful photography that accurately captured the best of teaching and learning, and also supplied the diagrams that made it clear what I was trying to say. To the incredible and patient production and design teams at Stenhouse—Stephanie Levy, Jay Kilburn, Gina Poirier, Grace Makley—thank you for delivering such a beautiful physical book for such a persnickety author.

To my dad, who would prompt me to iteratively double numbers in my head until I couldn't go any higher or I fell asleep.

To my mom, who somehow raised three boys and made each of us feel safe and important.

To my wonderful wife, Stephanie, who helps me see the endless colored ways. She makes it possible for me to experience these great classrooms and keeps me sane as I try to figure out what it all means.

To Fawn Nguyen, who has the luckiest students in the world and whose writing clarifies my own thinking.

To the educators that I consistently observed and leaned on as my "brain trust:" Dina Mahmood, Kala Gabler, Kate Byers, Brett Eberly, Brette Woessner, Desé Zuberi, Jeff de Varona, Lea Blair, Hilary Preston, and Missy Tydlacka.

To the students who opened up their academic and personal lives to me. They were honest and inspirational. In particular, one young woman from Southern California described how much she's grown over the past couple years. Throughout the writing of this book, I can only hope I've grown too.

Welcome to Math Class

Damien is at once my favorite kind of student and the student who makes me question everything. We're sitting together for an informal conversation about his educational experiences at Humbolt Early College High School. Humbolt is a public school right outside Detroit, tucked away behind a lake just off I-94.

Currently a senior, Damien has big plans for the future—his own and the community's. After receiving a degree in political science, he's going to devote his life to those less fortunate than himself. This is especially remarkable considering that his own upbringing wasn't terribly privileged.

Damien is quick to talk about his favorite classes. Last year he helped organize a zombie 5K fun run as part of a community project. The year before that, he participated in a political debate in which students developed their own political platform in advance of the midterm elections. His favorite class was a combination sophomore-level English–social studies course creatively titled Money, Power, and the American Dream.

Our conversation turns to math instruction. Or rather, I turn it to math instruction, probably against Damien's will. I ask, year by year, about his experiences in math. As a freshman in algebra, he recalls mostly working through packets, which he did diligently. He received decent grades, but when I press a bit further, he isn't able to identify any concepts he learned that year. "I remember you always had to get x on the left side. . . . If a number or letter is over another letter, you can cross them out. . . . On a graph the x-axis is the horizontal one and the y-axis is the one that goes up and down." For some reason, he can remember that the multiple-choice final exam for the year had exactly eighty questions on it.

For an education environment that strives to standardize instruction and student outcomes, there is remarkably little consensus about what a quality secondary math classroom looks like. Students progress through learning environments that may look nothing like one another: worksheets, instructional software, groupwork.

Sophomore year he took geometry. The teacher was young and enthusiastic. Gone were the days of packets. His teacher, Ms. Fisher, tried to make things more interactive and dynamic. Damien recalls going outside to measure the length of a shadow (but doesn't remember exactly why). They had a project where they designed a floor plan of a house. Each student had to use "one of every shape" and calculate the square footage. I ask Damien if he liked this approach better than his freshman algebra experience. "I don't know." He pauses. "I liked the hands-on stuff, but my grades weren't as good. I wasn't always sure what I was supposed to be doing." His grades suffered a bit, though his standardized test scores were about on par with what they were for algebra. Damien also didn't like the groupwork when it was assigned. He recalls a mixture of groupwork and groups not working.

Junior year brought about Algebra 2. Humbolt Early College High School, concerned by its low test scores, invested heavily in instructional software and the corresponding curriculum. The entire math department at Humbolt was now to teach using the curriculum provided by the developers. In practice, this meant that Algebra 2 was now taught in a computer lab, each kid at a computer. Damien dutifully clocked in every day and progressed through whatever the software had him doing for that session. If he needed help with something, there was a little icon or button he could push and it would give him a hint. Once he answered enough questions in a row correctly, he could progress to the next topic.

Deciding what senior math to take was difficult for Damien. The counselors at the school encouraged him to take a higher-level math course, presumably pre-calculus and/or Advanced Placement Stats because it looks good on a transcript. He had to balance the understanding that universities like higher-level math courses against the presupposition that his GPA might suffer in those classes. He also didn't really like math at this point. When it wasn't boring, it was confusing. When it was doable, it was uninviting. To him, math was a series of steps to follow, with regular tests just to make sure he was following them correctly. I ask him point-blank, yes or no, if he'd describe math as recipe-following, knowing full well it is a terrible interview question. He confirmed and added, "That's exactly what it is. It's these things you have to do in the right order. It's more like baking than cooking. With baking you have to get everything exactly precise." He holds his thumb and index finger close together as if he's describing something very small. I had no idea he was—among his many talents—a kitchen aficionado. "You have to do it just like this at the right time or it all falls apart." He smiles and chuckles. "But there's no cake at the end."

"What about geometry? What about in Ms. Fisher's class? Wasn't that fun?" At this point, I am really digging.

"It was pretty good. Now that I think about it, I probably did learn a lot in that class, but it's hard to place it."

To recap, in his freshman year Damien worked mostly on packets. Sophomore year he had a young teacher with classroom management issues struggling to promote groupwork and hands-on experiences. Junior year he sat at a computer and received hints from the instructional software program.

Damien wouldn't tell you he was "damaged" by his high school math education experience. Going into senior year, he had completed three courses, all taught by credentialed teachers with training and supporting resources. He didn't fail any of the courses; in fact he got mostly Bs and As throughout his time in math. This isn't one of those horror stories you read in a Jonathan Kozol essay where a student has a permanent substitute teacher for ten months or the facilities are rotting from mold or a student goes two years with provisionally credentialed teachers. This is a good student having a relatively par-for-the-course math experience, and he emerges from it hoping to take as little math in the future as possible. The tasks he performed were of middling or varying quality. The instruction was misaligned or spotty. His view of himself as a mathematician was flagging, and his view of math was that it's something you do without agency, in isolation.

Ultimately, he decided to go with pre-calculus for his senior-level math course. It'll look good for college applications. And he had heard the teacher was nice.

▲   ▲   ▲

Walking down the halls of the math wing at Francis Valley High School, just north of the Bay Area in California, I can see the varied, haphazard approaches Damien described in Michigan. What Damien experienced in three wildly different pedagogical models over the course of his high school career, I can see playing out here at exactly the same time. In room 201, kids are all at computers dutifully typing and clicking away. In 202, students are working on poster paper (well, most are). In 204, several kids have their heads on their desks.

For an education environment that strives to standardize instruction and student outcomes, there is remarkably little consensus about what a quality secondary math classroom looks like. Students progress through learning environments that may look nothing like one another: worksheets, instructional software, groupwork. If we think about a learning environment as an ecosystem, it would be like asking a species to adapt and thrive in a rain forest, a desert, and tundra.

Even in schools where practice is aligned, it's often done so with the bludgeon of a prescriptive curriculum that gives students false ideas around what mathematics is and serves to erode their identities as young mathematicians.

It occurs to me as I'm driving away from the Francis Valley campus: *we don't have a secondary math pedagogy*. If teachers are lucky, upon becoming certified they might be equipped with a few successful strategies and some classroom management techniques, and then happen to get hired by a school with a strong culture. There isn't a theme or theory of action when it comes to secondary math.

I wonder if that's in part because of the significant gap between what mathematicians do and what students in math class do. As I recall Damien describing math-as-baking, my heart sinks. I feel the need to apologize to him. I want to apologize for his math instruction having been all over the map. I want to apologize for the fact that math is the course he'll struggle with the most once he gets to college, if it's not actually the barrier to his acceptance into college. I want to apologize for the false message he's received that he's "not good at math." I didn't teach Damien, yet I taught many students like Damien and often taught with the haphazardness that Damien described.

I also recall Ms. Fisher. From Damien's description, it sounds like she's *trying* to engage kids with mathematics in an interesting way. It also sounds like she's quite green and isn't receiving much support from her school or district. Having subsequently been in her classroom and interviewed her, my suspicion has been confirmed. She's trying her best to instill excitement and curiosity through tasks, but it's barely moving the needle toward higher student engagement, equitable groupwork, or content learning.

What's particularly troubling is that none of Damien's high school teachers were derelict in their duty. They all want to see their students succeed and don't intend to harm students. But with no common understanding of what high-quality math instruction looks like or what students are experiencing in their classrooms, gaps in learning and in attitudes toward math will continue to widen. The message that Damien is "not good at math" surely didn't come from any of his teachers' mouths. Rather, it's the accumulation of his experiences and the tasks he's been given in math.

Every boring packet of practice problems, every lesson where he was told exactly what shortcuts to follow, every homework assignment where he had to do problems two through thirty-six (evens) slowly siphoned away his perception that math is a thought-provoking and creative discipline and that his unique talents and passions are welcome at its table.

Students like Damien shake me to the core. He makes me question things because he's an excellent student and will contribute great things to this world. Would it have been better to just stop requiring him to take math after, say, sixth grade? What if math were treated as an elective or presented as a menu of mathematical disciplines? Would Damien have found his mathematical niche there and wound up pursuing the field? Did his high school math education make him hate math? Or become indifferent to it?

These are the questions that trouble me. I'm saddened because Damien will miss out on the world of mathematics, and the world of mathematics will miss out on him. And he's not alone. Moreover, Damien is a great kid. He's everything a teacher would want in a student: diligent, respectful, helpful. He's just—in his words, words that have been repeated countless times by students and adults—"not a math person."

Adding urgency and magnifying the issue is that math is often the biggest—sometimes the only—hurdle to an otherwise prosperous educational career. The lack of a sufficient math background can be the death knell for students once they reach university. In high school, students can often get by well enough with additional support, classwork, remediation, and devoted teachers; students at postsecondary institutions cannot expect such hands-on mentorship. We know that if a student enters postsecondary education requiring remediation (most typically in math), that student is much less likely to graduate. Of students who require remedial courses at four-year universities, only 35 percent go on to graduate within six years (Complete College America 2012). That's the tension we're exploring here: we want kids to like math, we want kids to be mathematical thinkers, and we all want them to lead happy lives. Yet math is often the barrier that prevents students from having a rich secondary or postsecondary experience.

While districts, municipalities, and politicians reinvent the "math wars" of the 1980s and 1990s via Common Core State Standards, the problem of pedagogy remains. Although new, research-based standards are worthy of discussion, standards tell a teacher *what* to teach, not *how* to teach. Or what question to ask to dig just a bit deeper. Or how to ask that question in a way that elicits responses from other students. Or

I'm sitting in the back of an overcrowded classroom in rural Arkansas. Leanne is greeting kids as they walk in. Every single student is acknowledged at the door and welcomed into the room, sometimes with a high five, sometimes with a reprimand for a missing assignment, often both. All receive a smile from Leanne, even the reprimandees. Especially the reprimandees.

how to reveal misconceptions through student work. Or how to build buy-in from students that they (yes, they!) are mathematicians in their own right and have value and voice to bring to the mathematical world.

▲ ▲ ▲

I'm sitting in the back of an overcrowded classroom in rural Arkansas. Leanne is greeting kids as they walk in. Every single student is acknowledged at the door and welcomed into the room, sometimes with a high five, sometimes with a reprimand for a missing assignment, often both. All receive a smile from Leanne, even the reprimandees. Especially the reprimandees.

A few minutes after the bell signals the start of class and after Leanne has connected with every student by name, she finds her way up to the northwest corner of the room.

"All right, guys, I have quite a problem for you today. Check it." Leanne flicks a switch on her computer's projector. We're looking at what appears to be an overhead view of a map of a neighborhood. An orange dot is in the center-north of the map, a blue dot is on the east side of the map, and a purple dot is labeled "Jack in the box" toward the west of the map (Figure 1.1).

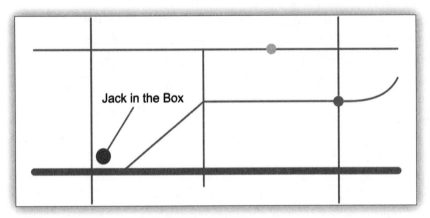

FIGURE 1.1 Map for Jack in the Box task

Leanne pushes a button on her computer and the dots start moving. Her voice is narrating the video. "Two students decide to go to Jack in the Box after school. The orange student decides he's going to walk. However, the blue student decides he's going to jog to Jack in the Box." The two dots begin moving along different roads toward the destination, the blue dot moving slightly faster. The entire video takes fifteen seconds.

"Okay," Leanne says. "I want you to write down the first question that you were thinking as you were watching that video and hearing me describe the problem."

Immediately almost everyone's hand shoots up, apparently neglecting Leanne's direction to write their question down. After playfully rolling her eyes, Leanne goes along with it: "Hannah?"

"Which student is going to get to the Jack in the Box first?"

"All right. That's the question I want y'all to find the answer to. Now, in your groups, I want you to make a list of what you know about the situation that'll help you solve this problem, and a list of things you'll need to know to solve it."

I'm stationed in the back of the classroom, but I'm really more a part of one of the groups of desks, because there isn't room for an additional chair. The desks in Leanne's room are the kind with the chairs firmly affixed to the desktop. They make for an awkward foursome of desks, more of a pinwheel formation than a quadrilateral.

Being strategically located in one of these groups, I'm able to overhear my group-mates brainstorming. As one is brainstorming aloud, another quickly makes a two-column table on a blank piece of paper. One says "*K*," and the other says "*NTK*." Eventually, I pick up that *K* stands for "know" and *NTK* stands for "need to know."

Before the first student even finishes making the table, his partner is armed with a felt-tip marker and adding to each column.

"We know that the blue guy is jogging, so he's probably faster."

"We need to know how far it is to the Jack in the Box."

"We know that the orange dot is closer."

"We need to know how fast both are going."

And so on.

Pretty soon, my group has a list of four or five things they know and four or five things they'd need to know to answer the question Hannah asked. Most groups appear to have lists of about the same length.

What's most striking about this classroom is that every student is engaged in the process. When I was starting out in teaching, I remember my fellow teachers and even some education professors telling me, "There's always going to be a kid or two in class who just won't engage," or something to that effect. "There's always one," they say, accompanied by a sneer or a raised eyebrow. There is not a single one of those "ones" in this class, as far as I can tell. I take sixty seconds to survey the room and see exactly who's participating. By my count, every single student in the room says something during those sixty seconds, mostly to their peers. I can't be certain they are all discussing the math at hand, but the concentration in their faces suggests they are.

Also, there's something about the way these students are saying the phrase "need to know." They're saying it like it's a noun: a need-to-know. Sure enough, as Leanne is moving around the room, I can overhear her ask, "So what are your group's need-to-knows?" This "need-to-know" is clearly a turn of phrase that's been used a lot in this class. It seems like a bit of an aside, but as I'll find later, it's germane to the success of Leanne's students.

Leanne gets everyone's attention again and they start aggregating the lists of "knows" and "need-to-knows." Many of them are similar: How fast are the students traveling? How far do they need to go?

Once those have been voiced, Leanne reveals additional information with the press of a button on the slide deck from which she's working. The orange student is traveling at three miles per hour, the blue student at seven miles per hour. She then reveals the distances of the roads the students are traveling on. Before Leanne even finishes the question, "Now do you have enough information to solve the problem?," students have already grabbed another piece of blank paper and begun solving it.

While Leanne is bouncing from group to group to check on students' progress or ask additional questions, I'm eavesdropping on my group-mates. The level of discourse is astounding—partially because their description of their methods is adept and clear, but also because they are willing to ask questions of one another, give praise to one another, and explore new possibilities at the drop of a hat. They even ask one another to justify their solutions, and they ask probing questions:

"Can you convince me of that?"

"Could we have done this a different way?"

"Does this answer make sense?"

"When would the orange guy have to have started to make it a tie?"

Leanne hadn't made it back to our group yet before my group-mates were asking these questions. Her room is rather hard to negotiate, between the awkward desk pinwheels and the recessed A/C unit. Once she finally makes it back to our group, she glances over the work they've put on paper so far.

"Looks like we've got an answer here. I want you to check it with that group over there, and then I want you and the other group to come up with a question about this scenario that you could all answer together."

As the students shift out of their chairs and combine groups, I happen to glance toward my right to see Leanne's bookshelf, full of math textbooks. It has cobwebs on it.

▲   ▲   ▲

Leanne's classroom is in Weirmont Secondary Academy in a very small town in Arkansas. Weirmont has been recognized by the state for their high math achievement scores in a district with high numbers of students living in households below the poverty line. Weirmont has achieved this recognition multiple years in a row. Beyond the test scores, though, I'm more impressed with the conversations I have with students and that students have with one another. It feels safe. Not "safe" in the sense of being unworried about the threat of physical harm, but "safe" in the sense that everyone is welcome, everyone has something to contribute (and is expected to), and everyone is learning and experimenting.

I adore being in Leanne's classroom. I've had the opportunity to visit and see her in action several times, and every time I do, I'm struck by the depth of mathematical knowledge, the high expectations, the social and emotional safety, and the fun. Leanne's classroom is always a mixture of safety, curiosity, professionalism, high expectations, and—as a result—high levels of student achievement. The discourse students have in this class is remarkable. The students are all in it together. Whatever challenge Leanne puts in front of them, they're up to it. Whatever mathematical ideas students have, the class is able to explore them more fully. It's a self-sustaining ecosystem.

So what is it about Leanne's class that makes it all work? Is it the tasks that she's giving? Is it the stellar facilitation? Is it the safe environment?

It is all three. It is all three working in concert and for a sustained period of time: the task, the facilitation, and the academic safety of Leanne's classroom. And it is the system that sustains them.

Students do not experience math in a vacuum. The curriculum, the students' social and emotional well-being, and the teacher's expertise as a facilitator must all be attended to, and each interacts with the others. Students' perceptions of math and themselves as mathematicians is an accumulation of all these experiences. This is the secondary math pedagogy that I propose in this book (Figure 1.2).

In Leanne's lesson, I see evidence in the academic safety of her students as she's greeting kids by name before the bell rings, looking them in the eye and making sure they feel welcome. I see residue of effective

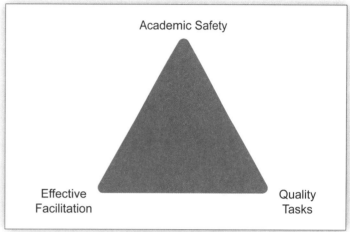

FIGURE 1.2 Our secondary pedagogy

facilitation in the way students are collaborating and testing out ideas. I experience the quality task in the way that students are immediately hooked into the problem. I'm a witness to this triad of elements and their overlap.

Of course, teachers do not teach in a vacuum. Although Leanne is certainly a highly skilled teacher, she's not alone at her school. Weirmont educators share a similar vision in mathematics, grades seven–twelve. In other words, it's not only by the sheer force of Leanne's excellent teaching that students are achieving at high levels. It's the cumulative efforts of the entire district and the Weirmont math team.

I'm interested in how Weirmont got to be that way. What is it about Leanne and about the school that created and nurtured an environment where students were fully engaged in the task, working together equitably, conversing mathematically, asking questions of one another, and then solving those questions together? How did this come to be? What can the rest of us learn from their work?

There are other secondary mathematical ecosystems like Weirmont where learning is thriving—both teacher learning and student learning. In these classrooms and systems of classrooms, which I will describe and analyze in detail so that we can learn from them, students are self-confident in mathematics and demonstrate high achievement. The common thread in these classrooms is that the teachers are implementing high-quality mathematical tasks, facilitating effectively, and attending to the students' social and emotional well-being and self-regard in math.

To that end, let us define our terms briefly here so that we may go in depth in succeeding chapters.

Academic Safety

Academic safety is the most hidden of the three elements of a successful math classroom, yet it is crucial to a student's readiness to learn. It encompasses the social and emotional safety of the student as well as the student's perception of his or her own mathematical ability. How students view themselves, each other, and the very discipline of mathematics is well calcified by the time they approach the secondary grades. Being proactive about academic safety is as critical to a student's success in math as it is in any curriculum, and micro-messages that students receive about their ability to perform mathematics (from teachers, peers, family, and society) can be more powerful than any task or teaching move.

FIGURE 1.3 Academic safety is a student's sense of mathematical identity. It encompasses the social and emotional aspect of learning as well as one's understanding of him- or herself as a mathematician.

This book will provide tools to understand and recognize issues of academic safety when they occur, as well as guidelines to treat these problems. We'll look at how teachers successfully establish and nurture safe climates for adolescent students. We'll examine how the system of school helps or hinders academic safety. When students receive a grade on a quiz or a six-weeks report card, what are the messages they are receiving?

We'll also look at how academic safety interacts with facilitation, because the facilitator is the one who establishes the operating conditions of the mathematical classroom. Do students have the allowance to ask questions, make a mistake, or try something new? How does the teacher create the environment to make such conditions possible? What are the daily routines and teaching moves that fertilize the soil for these endeavors?

Academic safety also relates to the tasks. If students are given low-quality, rote tasks, we lose out on the creativity that they have to offer. To develop self-worth and social status for budding mathematicians, we have to give them tasks worthy of their intellects. Finally, engaging tasks won't fly very far if students view themselves as deficient in the discipline of math. A greater treatment of academic safety resides in Chapters 2 and 3, and we'll discuss the interplay among academic safety, effective facilitation, and quality tasks throughout.

Quality Tasks

Tasks are the items that students are working on—what you can see students doing. A quality task is one that is intrinsically interesting and allows all students to access it. Often a quality task will have multiple solution paths, if not multiple solutions. Quality tasks elicit complex thought and problem solving and engender perseverance and discourse. A fuller discussion of what makes for a quality task awaits you in Chapter 4, and more additional examples and generalized models of quality tasks reside in Chapter 5.

Quality tasks are essential to both academic safety and effective facilitation. For students to build and develop their own mathematical identity they need to hone it with worthy problems and activities. Students cannot realize their mathematical potential without being provided opportunities to demonstrate it. Similarly, effective facilitation becomes possible—or at least easier—when the task is engaging and of sufficient complexity.

FIGURE 1.4 Quality tasks allow students to acquire and demonstrate deep mathematical thinking.

Effective Facilitation

Effective facilitation refers to the series of teacher moves that allow students to construct, enhance, and communicate their mathematical insight to a task. It is the question that pushes the student to think more deeply or with more complexity about a mathematical topic. It is the way that the classroom is oriented to allow for groupwork or the sharing of solutions. It is the way that tasks are rolled out to students or discussed afterward to promote sense making. Facilitation may appear as singular moments in a classroom, and it may appear as classroom structures and norms that develop over months.

This is where effective facilitation synergizes with quality tasks: as students work through a particular task, teachers must make sure that the insights students are having are solidified into conceptual understanding. Of course, conceptual understanding is nearly impossible to draw from a low-quality, rote task. And even the best tasks won't elicit understanding without an adept facilitator guiding students into, through, and beyond the task.

I provide examples of effective facilitation through the classroom experiences of teachers who have demonstrated positive student outcomes. I also provide templates and guides to ensure that your facilitation rises to your own sky-high expectations. Effective facilitation—the long-term structures and the shorter, within-a-lesson facilitation moves—is concentrated in but not limited to Chapters 6 and 7.

FIGURE 1.5 Effective facilitation encompasses short- and long-term moves that help pave the way for mathematical thinking.

This is our pedagogy of secondary mathematics.

We will spend a lot of time in individual classrooms, departments, and whole schools that are tackling the hard work of enhancing their instruction and improving student outcomes by attending to these three elements. All three elements. All in synergy with one another. My work as a math instructional coach for a network of schools has afforded me the unique opportunity to visit exceptional teachers across the country, documenting their tasks, teaching moves, and academically safe learning environments. You'll experience dispatches from these effective classrooms in which we'll observe how teachers attend to all three elements that make up the ecosystem. You'll also experience times when a particular element isn't going so well, and we'll consider what can be done to diagnose and treat that particular element.

More than examples, though, you'll walk away with implementable next steps for your own classroom: guidelines for quality tasks, templates to help structure your next lesson, models of fostering social and emotional safety, and the like. And although I hope that your classroom becomes a thriving ecosystem of rich mathematical experiences, I also hope that it becomes a beacon at your school, your school in the district, your district in the state, so that others may learn and create an ecosystem of their own.

Most important, though, this book is about Damien—Damien and the discipline that will miss him so very much.

ACADEMIC SAFETY

Academic Safety

We are here

Effective
Facilitation

Quality
Tasks

eather is a researcher at the Cooperative Institute for Research in the Atmosphere, a partnership between the National Atmospheric and Oceanic Administration and the Colorado State University Department of Atmospheric Science. She works in satellite meteorology, using code to visualize and validate satellite measurements of atmospheric features such as clouds, water vapor, and carbon dioxide. She regularly uses two- and three-dimensional matrix algebra and incorporates atmospheric models that draw upon math topics such as differential equations, both partial and ordinary.

She's also a friend. She's telling me about her experience in school mathematics. "I thought I was no good at math," she starts. Initially I assume this is just Heather displaying her usual humility, considering she double majored in math and physics before going on to receive an advanced degree in atmospheric science. So, I inquire further, asking her why and when she could possibly have thought this.

"No, really," she says, "it started in middle school. In fifth grade I was in an enrichment class for math in a Montessori program. I was confident in my math abilities. Then I got to middle school." She lets out a big sigh. "We were working through some modules where you're supposed to learn and work at your own pace. At the end of the school year, about half of my peers went on to an accelerated math program at the school. I was placed in the nonaccelerated program: it turns out I didn't work fast enough to be placed in the accelerated program.

"I've always been relatively slow but thorough with my math. Even though I tended to do well on assignments, the message I received was that I wasn't good at it because I wasn't fast enough. I hated math because I didn't think I was good at it. I didn't think I was good at it because I wasn't fast enough at it."

Of all academic disciplines, math seems to be the one that cuts the deepest. Educational trauma can come from all subjects, but few seem to induce as much pain as math often does. Adults who survived their math experience in school are often quick to discuss how much they hated the subject and how much the subject hated them. Sometimes the trauma is so deep that they can describe individual moments of ultimate anxiety and humiliation.

Fortunately, this all-too-common tale has a happy epilogue in this instance. "But you majored in math," I point out helpfully.

"I went into college thinking I would major in Spanish because that's what I thought I was good at," Heather says. "Then, sophomore year, I had a math professor who turned it around for me. He was the first teacher to make me feel like working my butt off was what made me successful, rather than just knowing stuff and working quickly. He would work with me and praise my effort and tell me that's what makes for a successful mathematician. It wasn't about speed; it wasn't even necessarily about these seemingly disconnected rules of math. Rather, it was about effort and persistence."

I find Heather's story both heartening and dismaying. I'm heartened that she had a college professor who could help turn around her self-image as a mathematician. I appreciate the messages that he, a mathematician, communicated to her. I'm dismayed that it took so long for her to receive that message, that it bypassed her entire secondary-school math career.

The gap between Heather's ability and her self-regard resulted from a lack of academic safety in her math schooling.

Academic Safety

Academic safety consists of two levers:

1. creating an accurate representation of the discipline of mathematics, and

2. communicating to each student and all students—with words and actions—that they have unfettered access to the discipline of mathematics.

We will explore these levers in the next two chapters. In Chapter 2 we will examine the very discipline of math itself. We'll consider how math is typically represented in schools and how that representation often runs counter to the practice of math by mathematicians while closing off an otherwise open and creative discipline. In Chapter 3 we will unpack the baggage many adolescent students carry with math as a discipline, with an eye toward rebuilding their mathematical self-regard.

Math and the Mathematician

What Math Is . . . and Isn't

We math teachers are frustrated that it's become socially acceptable to self-identify as "not a math person." After all, one wouldn't say with pride, "I don't read" or "I'm not a reading person." It's important, though, to understand *why* math has become a four-letter word to so many students and former students. It stems in part from a misunderstanding of the discipline.

A few years ago, teachers at Ridgeland High School asked themselves a fundamental but rarely asked question: What makes a mathematician? They read books and articles written by mathematicians. They watched and discussed lectures by

Well, it takes time. I mean, there's so much history to it. When you're reading math, you're trying to relive the work of countless mathematicians. Travel through the development of a formula and you might be following centuries of work. With depth like that, it's not enough to just read. You have to become a mathematician yourself.

—Hiroshi Yuki, *Math Girls*

mathematicians they found online. They reflected on the apparent disconnect between the math they presented to students and the work they saw from mathematicians.

The Ridgeland teachers found that the types of tasks their curriculum provided bore little resemblance to the work of mathematicians in the field. Their textbooks presented math as a series of step-by-step procedures, applicable only to specific, arcane scenarios; the mathematics that the Ridgeland teachers learned about was creative, playful, useful, collaborative, *and* personal. They discovered that math is in many ways the exact *opposite* of what their textbooks and their facilitation presented.

After reflecting on artifacts of mathematicians, they decided they needed a new approach and a new message. They discussed what mathematicians actually *do* and what *dispositions* they demonstrate. Their notes from an early discussion in this process reveal their discoveries:

- Mathematicians persist through challenging problems.

- Mathematicians communicate their ideas as cleanly as possible.

- Mathematicians don't always get the answer.

- Mathematicians are creative.

- Mathematicians try several approaches to a problem.

- Mathematicians encourage each other.

- Mathematicians find beauty in their work.

- Mathematicians find meaning in their work.

With these actions and ways-of-being in mind, they now had a purpose to their math program. They oriented their tasks and facilitation to the work of math, rather than to the work of the district scope and sequence or textbook examples. They then began communicating behaviors emblematic of the work of mathematicians to their students. Teachers now had a vocabulary with which they discussed math and their students-as-mathematicians. We'll see how they operationalized the list above to promote academic safety in a systematic and routinized way in Chapter 3.

The teachers at Ridgeland offer a word of caution, however. Not only does the work of mathematicians differ from the work of math in school, but it *really* differs. Teachers who dive deep into authentic mathematical work find it difficult to square the work of mathematicians with the system of schooling and courses. Consider the briskness of a typical scope and sequence against the work of a mathematician. A mathematician may take years to solve a particular problem, such as Yitang Zhang, who toiled in relative obscurity for years before becoming the first mathematician to prove the *Bounded Gap Conjecture*, that there is a finite distance between consecutive prime numbers. Other math problems remain unsolved entirely, such as the *Moving Sofa* problem (Figure 2.1). Our task is to figure out how we can present the discipline of math accurately in a system that demands immediacy and achievement. Fortunately, these days we can go right to the source.

It's never been easier to access the work of mathematicians. You don't have to read a doctoral dissertation on string theory to see the work of modern mathematicians. Many mathematicians have written books in friendly, accessible language, such as Steven Strogatz's ode to abstract math "from one to infinity" in *The Joy of x* (2014), or Jordan Ellenberg's *How Not to Be Wrong*, in which he describes how "problems of politics, of medicine, of commerce, of theology—are shot through with mathematics" (2015, 3). You can hear the work of mathematicians on podcasts such as *Freakonomics* and episodes of NPR's *Invisibilia*. You can see the work of mathematicians via streaming TED Talks that provide yet another approachable, bite-sized avenue for mathematicians to present their work and their discipline. Any and all of these provide pleasurable, engaging, authentic mathematical work for us to consume, both to educate ourselves about this discipline and to share it with our students.

FIGURE 2.1 The *Moving Sofa* problem asks, "*What is the greatest area of a sofa that could be moved around a hallway corner?*"

Math Access for All

Defining the work of mathematicians had an unexpected yet pleasantly surprising result for students at Ridgeland High School. It *opened up* the discipline.

One of the teachers tells me, "Until we began researching, I'd have thought that the more we presented the work of mathematicians, the more *exclusive* it would become. It turns out it was just the opposite." As Ridgeland teachers continued presenting the work of mathematicians, they saw an increase in engagement.

"I never thought of math as something *I* could be good at," one student, Marquisse, tells me. "I just assumed it was for only certain types of students." The phrase *certain types of students* is deeply dismaying, because I know what he means. He means math is for students who are quick to understand, well behaved, and studious. Practically speaking, math is for someone who "gets good grades." After all, that's the only metric most students have about their ability as mathematicians. Fortunately, because of his experience at Ridgeland, Marquisse has a better understanding of how his unique talents map on to the attributes of a mathematician.

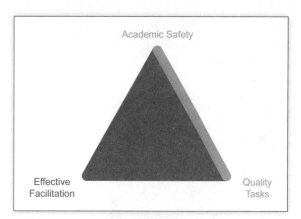

Academic Safety

Effective Facilitation   Quality Tasks

FIGURE 2.2 Here we see the interaction between academic safety and quality tasks.

"I'm a good communicator," he says. "I'm really good at explaining things. Growing up, I never got a chance to explain things. Or if I did explain things in math, it would just be demonstrating a division problem." Now Marquisse is explaining solutions to complex problems. "I'll have a diagram in there. I ask questions of the audience to make sure they understand."

Figure 2.2 shows the overlap between the accurate representation of math and the quality tasks that Ridgeland teachers present. Ridgeland teachers are providing Marquisse with challenging, complex tasks. These tasks amplify the mathematical practices students display in a way that rote tasks cannot. It is impossible to praise students for, say, showing creativity when they have been given a solution method that requires no creativity, just rule-following.

We can also see the overlap between facilitation and access. Teachers at Ridgeland regularly provide time and structures for groupwork, revision, and presentation to better reflect the work of mathematicians (Table 2.1).

Typical Ridgeland Agenda Before	Typical Ridgeland Agenda After
• Warm up and collect homework.	• Warm up and collect homework.
• Present the concept.	• Present a problem.
• Present three example problems and the step-by-step solution method.	• In groups, students work toward a solution to the problem.
• Hand out problem sheets for in-class work.	• With help, students discover the concept.
• Students work through the problems and turn in the sheet when they're finished. (Whatever isn't completed in class is homework.)	• Groups present their solutions.
	• Students discuss and debrief with the teacher.

TABLE 2.1

I don't want to present the story of Ridgeland High School's math department as an easy and linear progression. It took teachers years in fits and starts to reshape ideas about math and their students' ideas about themselves. They had to peel away years of inaccessibility and faulty messaging. Teachers had to acknowledge their own biases, which were as ingrained as students', and rebuild their understanding of the discipline. They then communicated this understanding directly to students through their words and actions. From the types of language they were using to the tasks they were assigning, they made a concerted effort to improve access and understanding. With that caveat—that it was a nonlinear process—here is the path they followed:

1. Understand the discipline of math.

2. Discuss and synthesize what makes a mathematician.

3. Present more authentic mathematical experiences for students.

4. Communicate to students the attributes of a mathematician.

5. Communicate to individual students what makes them *specifically* a mathematician.

The first two steps involved engaging in inquiry, research, and discussions as a staff. Appendix A and B contain a bank of potential artifacts (books, podcasts, videos, articles) to aid in that process. The last two steps are discussed more fully in the next chapter as we discuss academic status.

As for the middle step—presenting more authentic mathematical experiences for students—we must revisit our tasks and facilitation. What types of tasks are we giving? Do they communicate math as a place for creative types? Does our facilitation lend itself to mathematical exploration? The next section offers some guidelines toward designing experiences that do just that.

Reimagining the Discipline Through Mathematical Experiences

Part of orienting (or reorienting) students around their ability to do math at a high level and to *want* to do math at a high level involves reimagining the nature of the discipline. Among the reasons why students and adults display such an allergy toward math is a misunderstanding of the math itself. Students who self-identify as "not math people" may very much be "math people," but not in the way they've experienced math. To reorient students around the discipline of math itself, here are three suggestions.

1. Do Math *with* Students.

Any parent will tell you that the best way to teach kids how to read or develop a love for reading is to read with them. The same is true for physical education, enjoying the outdoors, or origami. But how much time do we reserve for doing math *with* students rather than *at* students?

As Leanne facilitates a lesson on geometric series, she takes the time to explore students' ideas. She's written a sequence of numbers on the board:

$$3, 6, 12, 24, \ldots$$

Leanne asks a specific student to identify the next number in the sequence, which she does: "Forty-eight."

"What about the number after that?" A few hands go up, some a few seconds later. Within ten seconds everyone has their hand up. "Kyle?" Kyle was one of the last to put his hand up.

"Ninety-six."

"Sandra, do you agree with Kyle?" Sandra agrees with Kyle.

"Great. Now." Leanne pauses for a moment, thinking. "What about the tenth number in this sequence? Take a minute by yourself and then take a minute with your group to find the tenth number in this sequence." Students scramble to identify the number. Once everyone confirms their answer, Leanne poses a question in a way that suggests that she wants to partake as well.

"I want to see if we can find the sum of all the numbers in this sequence up to the tenth number we just figured out." This provides quite the challenge. Students are constructing their understanding of how to calculate the sum of a geometric series. Leanne's along for the ride but having too much fun to stay out of the fray. As I'm watching Leanne explore these comments and questions, it strikes me: *they're doing math together*. Somewhere—probably in the students' textbooks—there's a formula for the sum of a geometric series. She's not giving it to them. Or maybe she doesn't recall it offhand (I certainly don't). Nor are students demanding it. They're figuring it out for themselves. Some students—with a partner or a group—make a table of values and manually calculate the first several sums of the series. Other students scribble values on scratch paper and test out various iterations of a formula they've concocted. Students are using some of the tools in their toolbox from earlier in the year. They're finding the difference, and the difference of the difference. During this time, Leanne floats to each group to check on their progress, ask probing questions, demand clearer articulation of their work, or give students values to check to see if their hypotheses hold. She asks groups that are struggling with getting going to start with a smaller case and build upward: What's the sum of the first three numbers, the first four numbers, the first five numbers, and so on? Is there a pattern we can pick out?

Thinking back to my own teaching career, nearly all of it involved me doing math *at* students. Or students doing math back *at* me. Rarely did we do math *together*. Leanne certainly is the expert in the room, and she's well prepared, well trained, and well versed in the topic at hand. But she's also learning and playing with ideas based on her students' comments and questions.

Leanne's lesson happened to be about geometric series, but I encourage you to consider other areas where you can do math with students: explore what happens when you connect the midpoints of a particular shape (Figure 2.3), inscribe a circle around an object and see if any interesting properties pop up, and—a personal favorite of mine—see if you and your students can discover why the heck raising a number to the zeroth power equals one (and not zero).

2. Do Creative Math.

"Every mathematician creates new things, some big, some small," says Jordan Ellenberg in *How Not to Be Wrong* (2015, 436). Sometimes the math itself can be creative. In Chapter 4 we'll see examples of creative tasks that draw upon students' creativity to co-develop mathematical understanding.

Theresa is an eighth-grade teacher in the giant metroplex of Dallas. She has her students create their own patterns for other students to solve in an activity she calls *Guess My Pattern*. After dissecting a few patterns and developing multiple representations of them (formula, graph, pictures), she has students create their own patterns. Students then swap and find multiple representations for one another's patterns. They're creating something new and unique and sharing it with one another.

Brett is a high school teacher in Columbia City, Indiana. He has students design a sample level for Raging Raptors, modeling quadratics for the birds' trajectories. He gives students the task of designing a level (Figure 2.4).

Each student creates a level along with an essay explaining the trajectory of the birds. The essays contain properly formatted and cited equations, including the

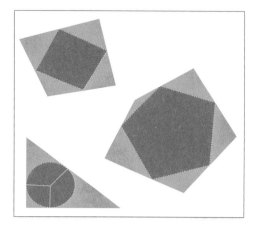

FIGURE 2.3 Play around with shapes. What happens when you connect the midpoints? What happens when you connect the midpoints of the midpoints?

Raging Raptors—Parabola

Design your own Raptors level.

Your assignment must include

- Colorful layout that clearly shows structures, slingshot, raptors, pigs, etc.
- Clearly shows flight path (different colors) for every raptors that hits every pig.
- Flight paths must be parabolas showing the vertex, axis of symmetry, and zeros.

Equations of each parabola showing all work to develop each equation.

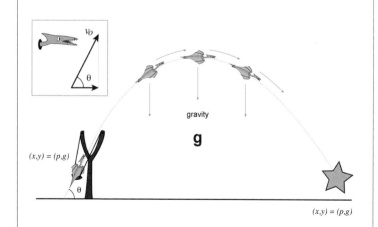

FIGURE 2.4 Prompt for Brett's Raging Raptors creative task

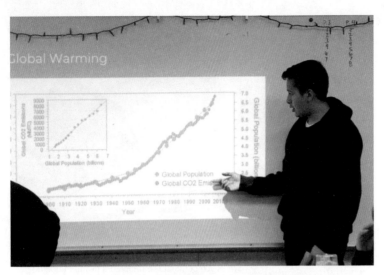

FIGURE 2.5 Students present their ideas and arguments on issues of choice through a mathematical lens.

quadratic formula to find the roots of the quadratics. Students use their creativity to design levels and use mathematics to walk through the levels with the reader.

Creative math also appears when students communicate a mathematical idea. "In order to explain we have to create something," Paul Lockhart tells us in *Measurement* (2014, 7). Communicating a solution path concisely is an act of creativity. Also, in-depth writing requires a certain imaginative flair. As Ellenberg puts it, "All mathematical writing is creative writing" (2015, 436). Students demonstrate their creativity by organizing and articulating a mathematical argument.

3. Do Useful Math.

Some students see math as too abstract and irrelevant to be of interest. Consider invigorating your classroom with math that is tangible or useful. In Chapter 4, we'll see how Christine from Seattle uses actual wheelchair ramps as an inroad to trigonometry.

At Bell Academy, in Detroit, Michigan, teachers reserve a capstone course for seniors for just such a math experience. Each student is tasked with designing a personal passion project using data and statistical analysis to investigate an issue of social justice they are care about. For example, one student was concerned about the stray dog population in Detroit. She designed a project that analyzed publicly available data about stray dogs. In a written portion of the project, the student provided analysis and visuals of the data. In a presentation, she used her analysis to convince community members of the need to spay and neuter their dogs. Students use mathematics in a real, tangible, community-oriented way (Figure 2.5).

Mathematics is such a rich discipline, we do a disservice when we portion it out in rote worksheets and practice problems. To be sure, one singular math activity is not going to reshape a student's vision of what mathematics is. It takes a sustained approach over the course of a year or several years to allow students to see the beauty, the utility, and the community that mathematics embodies. As French mathematician Cédric Villani puts it, "You have to balance. Every time I say something about the utility of mathematics, I will balance it with something about its beauty. And vice versa" (in Haran 2017).

Conclusion

To foster a generation of new mathematicians, we need to provide students with authentic mathematical experiences. The word *authenticity* often gets lumped in with the "useful" part of math tasks. I encourage you to think about the word *authentic* more broadly. Rather than link it solely to useful or "real-world" tasks (which are important experiences to provide!), consider the very work of math and mathematicians. You'll find, as Ridgeland teachers did, that authentic mathematical work opens the door for all students. Of course, once the door is open, we still must invite students in and clear the obstacles in the way. In the next chapter, we'll examine issues of academic safety that encourage or prevent students from walking through that door, including strategies that convey to individual students how they are mathematically brilliant.

REVIEW

- The first step to treating issues of access and safety is to consider the rich, exciting discipline of math itself.

- The work of mathematics and mathematicians often looks wildly different from how it's presented to students in school settings.

- Many articles, videos, and accessible books about math by mathematicians present the discipline accurately and with joy.

- Mathematics, contrary to what we typically think, is an open discipline, drawing on many dispositions.

- Provide mathematical experiences that help students reimagine the discipline of math:

  ▲ Do math with students.

  ▲ Do creative math.

  ▲ Do useful math.

- Communicate high mathematical expectations for all your students.

3

Math and Academic Safety

Erdős himself would appear, a short, frail man in a shapeless old suit, clutching two small suitcases that contained all of his worldly possessions. Stepping off the plane he would announce to the welcoming group of mathematicians, "My brain is open!"

—BRUCE SCHECTER,
*MY BRAIN IS OPEN:
THE MATHEMATICAL JOURNEYS
OF PAUL ERDŐS*

We were sitting around a tight array of desks in a sunlit room after school, debriefing the day's events. There were six of us, part of a small learning community of teachers. I was facilitating a conversation in which teachers could present a problem or dilemma.

"I'm really struggling with groupwork right now," John said. "I've done all I can to try to make my classroom an environment in which kids want to work together. For most of them, it's working. I'd say 90 percent of my students are excellent at working together and solving problems. But 10 percent of the kids sit back and refuse to do anything. They'll fold their arms and say they're not working with the others. I've tried everything to help them out and encourage them to rejoin the groups. At this point, they simply refuse to work with other students. They literally would *rather take a zero* than be an active group member." There was a hint of exasperation in his voice. John was a thoughtful teacher who no doubt wanted the best for his students.

Lorena shared her experience with the same group of students. "I know some of the students to whom John is referring," she said. "I had the toughest time working with them. I talked to a couple of them one day. They've been in the same district for years now. This cohort of students attended the same middle school and the same elementary school, for the most part. They told me they weren't participating in groupwork because over the years, they've learned not to. In middle school when they tried to fit in, the other group members would take over the project.

"A couple of them did admit that they were probably bad group members at the time, but once that stigma was attached to them, it became impossible to break out of it. Eventually the more productive students would complain if they were partnered up. It became an issue of 'Oh yeah? You don't think I'm a good student? Let me just show you how I'm not a good student.' They withdrew from groupwork and most academic work entirely."

John's dilemma—a problem of effective groupwork—reflected a breakdown of *academic safety and status*. The students to whom John was referring had no academic status in the classroom. They saw themselves as failed students. Their peers saw them as failed students. It didn't take much for these assessments—from themselves and from their classmates—to become calcified and eventually self-reinforcing. Academic stigma is particularly sticky. Consider the humiliation and defensiveness these students must have felt when their peers complained audibly about being grouped with them.

It was hard to know where the trouble had started for the students in question. It's possible that at some point in sixth grade they were behind their classmates in a particular slice of content, and that the gap widened during unstructured or unproductive groupwork. Maybe one of the students missed a week or two of school, or transferred in from another school, or had a difficult situation at home. Or maybe the group had a long-term substitute during a lengthy or crucial time. Perhaps none of these things happened and they just didn't like school. Regardless of the root cause, John wanted to invite them into groupwork.

The discussion of John's dilemma yielded no easy fixes, but it did uncover new understanding and better appreciation of what students experience. From that point forward, John engaged in empathetic conversations with students who weren't participating in groupwork. He became curious, rather than jumping directly to solutions or strategies for group management. He also worked to identify and publicize moments in which these students were displaying academic brilliance. The dilemma protocol the team used is in Appendix C.

John's story reveals just what a complex system students pass through. Too often we treat the symptom of troublesome issues rather than attending to the underlying social and emotional safety and the regard students have for themselves. An academically safe classroom honors the individual as a mathematician and welcomes him or her into the social ecosystem of math. In Chapter 2 we examined what it means to be a mathematician with the aspiration that all students see themselves as mathematicians. That is the foundation for academic safety; in this chapter, we build on that foundation.

Academic Safety: Each and Every Student

An academically safe classroom honors the individual student while leveraging social interactions to build up self-regard. Students are tragically insightful and aware of where they reside in the academic hierarchy—they have been conditioned to believe that their place within the hierarchy is determinative. They enter classrooms with preconceived ideas about their abilities as mathematicians and a corresponding willingness (or unwillingness) to engage with the teacher, their peers, and the content. An academically safe environment has to chip away at this exterior and soften the interior to ensure that every child believes he or she can succeed in mathematics.

We must better understand the complexities of academic status that go beyond our teacher training manual or curriculum maps. Issues of mindset, race, gender, identity, and social pressures affect how students learn in math (and all subjects). In this chapter, we'll dig deep to identify and understand such issues. We'll do this primarily because we care for students; achieving better outcomes is just a nice side benefit. Our journey toward academic safety will take us in a lot of different directions (Figure 3.1), illustrating the complexity of the system and our students (while giving you a preview of what's still to come in this chapter). Many elements influence a student's self-regard as a mathematician, and multiple players are responsible—in part or in whole—for these elements. Some factors are opportunities for us to act, and others are things to be aware of and curious about. Most are both. This work may take us to uncomfortable places. Ultimately, it's worth it. Our students are worth it.

We'll begin this journey with mindset.

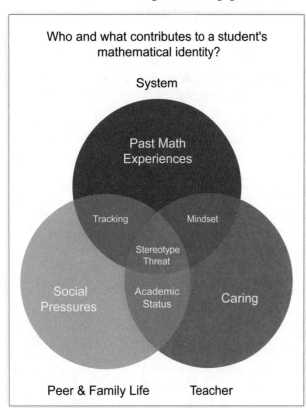

FIGURE 3.1 Multiple players are responsible for a student's sense of academic safety, which is made up of several elements.

Mindset

Sometimes I hear comments along the lines of "The first week of school is great because students are a blank slate." This is incorrect—think back to John's dilemma. His students had disengaged long before because they figured "What's the point?" Our students enter our classrooms with accumulated years of experiences and messages around math. By the time they are in middle school, students have already sorted themselves academically and believe that they are one of the smart kids or one of the not-so-smart kids. Students in such cases have what Carol Dweck refers to as a *fixed mindset* (2016). They believe that their math ability is unchangeable, so they tend to muddle through, hoping to get enough passing grades to move on to the next course. In these students' defense, it's understandable why they would have such a view. Student achievement and course placement is quite fixed. A student who enters a class with middling grades and achievement scores will often exit the class with middling grades and achievement scores. Year after year of this experience naturally leads them to believe that their abilities in mathematics are locked in place.

As understandable as this mindset is, we now have research studies suggesting the opposite: that a student's ability to learn math is fluid and expandable. The human brain can quickly acquire and retain new information (Abiola and Dhindsa 2011; Woollett and Maguire 2011). This is true generally and it is true for the learning of mathematics (Blackwell, Trzeniewski, and Dweck 2007). Dweck calls this attitude—that the brain can grow and that everyone has the capacity to do math at a high level—a *growth mindset*. One who has a growth mindset believes the following:

▲ By working hard, one will be able to achieve success.

▲ Mistakes are welcomed as opportunities to grow and learn.

▲ Challenges help one get better at a given task.

Students who have a growth mindset achieve higher scores on tests (Organization for Economic Co-operation and Development 2012). But even adult experts, such as teachers, can display fixed-mindset thinking, whether they know it or not. Take the example of the "two" musicians.

The "Two" Musicians

Tsay and Banaji (2011) conducted an experiment in which professional musicians listened to two excerpts of music. For the first excerpt the professional musicians were given a profile of the performer that suggested (via "weak clues") an innate, natural ability in musicianship. They were informed that the second musical excerpt was from a musician who had had to struggle and overcome a lot and had put in extra work to achieve this level of musicianship. When asked questions about "likelihood of future success" and "talent," the professional musicians rated the first performer more highly. In actuality, *the excerpts were from the exact same performance by the same musician*, and the profiles given had been taken from different aspects of the same musician's biography. Yet the professional musicians displayed a bias toward talent over effort.

Individual classrooms and whole schools have structures in place that reinforce this type of fixed mindset, despite the presence of individuals who believe otherwise. Our system of schooling has so entrenched itself as a promoter of fixed-mindset practices that it can seem daunting to swim against the stream. Nevertheless, we'll see how teachers and math departments are deploying strategies to combat fixed mindset and send messages of growth mindset—in students and in ourselves.

From Fixed to Growth Mindset: Practical Steps for Change

It can be a challenge to rethink practices that unintentionally reinforce a fixed mindset. In particular, the practices around *time*, *correctness*, and *grades* are rooted in fixed mindsets. Let's look at strategies to transform these historic practices to ones that prioritize academic safety and instill growth mindsets.

From Speed to Thoughtfulness

Adults and adolescents alike often wrongly associate speed with understanding. We all remember—and many of us felt the trauma of—"minute math" as elementary school pupils. But secondary classrooms and systems also emphasize speed in a destructive manner. For example, if a student needs additional time to work through a problem once the end-of-period bell rings, she's out of luck. Another class is outside the door, ready to file in. And she'd better get to her next class in time or else she'll be counted as tardy. She'll have to complete her work at home, where she'll likely face additional distractions and limited support.

Dina, from Samueli Academy in Santa Ana, California, makes "Speed is not important" the norm in her class and reinforces it with the way she plans her lessons, assessments, and curriculum. "My lessons don't have an expiration date," she tells me. "If we need to go over the same content the next day, that's what we'll do. If a student

FIGURE 3.2 Dina values thoughtfulness, effort, and demonstrations of knowledge over speed, correctness, and grades.

needs more time, they get more time. Sometimes I'll even grade them *only* on the problems they completed or the work they've shown."

"Does that encourage students to work slowly?" I wondered.

"I haven't had that problem. I've found that kids tend to work better and more deliberately when they know they're being graded only on what they've demonstrated. Students actually work *harder*."

Combating the need for speed:

- Review content from prior days' lessons.
- Grade only what students produce.
- Prioritize standards.
- Give students all the time they need for assessments.
- Establish "Speed is not important" as an explicit and lived-out norm.

From Correctness to Effort

Secondary classrooms often use correctness as the ultimate distinguisher for math understanding, even though we know—as Ridgeland teachers discovered in Chapter 2 —that "Mathematicians don't always get the answer." Even the teacher who awards "partial credit" when students attempt a solution may be indirectly valuing correctness over effort. I often gave a point for the correct solution and a point for an attempt. With the benefit of hindsight, I realize what I should have realized then: one out of two points is 50 percent. I can't say I'm truly honoring effort when a student will still receive a failing grade.

One strategy to push back against the supremacy of correctness is to allow for revisions for full credit. Rather than allowing students to retake an exam for, say, a maximum of 70 percent, just give them the whole grade they earned that second time around. And make the same allowance for all students.

Clearly, we want students to achieve correct and repeatable solutions on content for our class. Yet we must square this desire with the need to ensure that every student believes they can do well in math if they put in the effort. Dina goes so far as to take the issue of correctness off the table entirely: "I just give them the answers," she tells me.

"Come again?" I ask. Once again, my stubborn skepticism shines through.

"Sure. I just give them the answers. Here are the questions, here are the answers. Now, how do you get that answer?" Dina's ideas are so profound and so simple. "Their answers are naturally going to be correct because they're right there on the paper.

I'm more interested in how they get there." Dina's students typically try a problem on their own and check their answer. If it doesn't match up, they'll go back and see where they got it wrong.

"Since I've started giving them the answers, I've had students going back and trying to figure out where they went wrong. Before, I would hand back an assignment and it would say 'seven out of ten' and they'd just crumple it up and toss it, like, 'Well, I guess that's what I got.' Now students see it as a challenge." Using card sorts (Chapter 5) also naturally allows for a check for correction, since the answers are right there.

Combating the need for correctness:

- Allow for revision to proficiency.
- Allow for full credit on exam retakes.
- Facilitate peer-editing protocols before submitting a problem.
- Provide the answers and ask for the solutions.
- Celebrate alternative solution methods.

From Grades to Demonstrations of Knowledge

Numerical and letter grades are as much a part of our secondary system of instruction as attendance and bus routes. At the end of a grading period, students receive a numerical score (or a letter) that indicates their performance in that class. Not only does that grade reveal very *little* about what the student did or understands, but it also serves to reinforce preexisting notions of what "type" of math learner a student is: a good student or a not-so-good student. It's hard to break the cycle of fixed mindsets when every six weeks students receive yet another data point permanently affecting their GPA for their high school career. So long as colleges demand GPAs as a primary determiner of admittance, it's hard to stray from this ingrained system.

So how can we dampen the harmful effects of grades? Or even make grades work for students?

Dina starts off by telling me that she "allows" for revised work. "Sometimes, I *demand* it." She tells me she regularly returns work that was imprecise and has students revise it until they get a ten out of ten. "There are times when I demand that students give me 'advanced' work. I call these 'demand excellence' assignments. They know it'll take more time, and most students won't get 100 percent the first time through. It'll have maybe two or three challenging problems, and I take it only when it's 100 percent correct. The grade will remain 'incomplete' until we're both satisfied. By the end of the grading period, every student has a 100 percent on these assignments because I won't take less."

Some teachers grade for effort, or have the students assign themselves a grade for effort. With complex problems, Dina asks students to give themselves a score against a rubric (Figure 3.3) and explain why they gave themselves that score. "I find that students are much harsher on themselves than I am. They know when they've put in effort and they know when they haven't." Dina tells me she has to *raise* her students' self-assigned grades more often than not.

Through her norms and actions, Dina flips the message of grades from a diagnostic tool (yielding messages of fixed mindset) to a standard of excellence that everyone can achieve (yielding messages of growth mindset). We'll learn a lot more about general assessment practices in Chapter 10.

Agency: Develop Growth Mindset

1. Describe the effort or practice you have used for this current task and how it has affected your skills, work quality, or performance. How do you need to put in more effort for this project? In what ways is your effort sufficient?

2. Your reflection will be assessed using the following domains from the agency rubric. Explain next steps you might take to improve.

	Emerging	Developing	Proficient	Advanced
Build Confidence	Struggles to identify academic strengths, previous successes, or endurance gained from personal struggle to build confidence in academic success for a task, project, or class	Identifies an academic strength, previous success, or endurance gained through personal struggle, but does not use these skills to build confidence in success on a task, project, or class	Builds confidence to succeed (on a task, project, or class) by knowing and using academic strengths, previous success, or endurance gained through personal struggle	Consistently confident that success is possible (on a task, project, or class) by knowing and using academic strengths, previous successes, or endurance gained through personal struggle
Use Effort and Practice to Grow	Describes effort or practice in a limited way	Describes effort to practice but does not connect it to getting better at a skill, improved work quality, or performance	Understands how effort and practice relate to getting better at skills, improved work quality, or performance	Understands that effort and practice improve skills, quality, and performance and that the process takes patience and time

FIGURE 3.3 Rubric for student self-reflection

Combating the messaging around grades:

- Allow students to self-assess.
- Grade for effort.
- Use well-designed rubrics (Chapter 10).
- Provide time for students to reflect on growth.

Systemic Change: From Tracking to De-Tracking

FIGURE 3.4 Offering all students a high-quality math education is crucial for creating an academically safe learning space.

I'd like to tell you a bit more about Samueli Academy, the school where Dina teaches, because they have a remarkable story to tell around academic safety. We'll see a lot of Dina and her colleague Kala throughout this book. Dina, Kala, and their department do incredible work to build up students' mathematical identities. And they, with the support of their administration, were able to make a monumental shift at their school in which they eliminated the tracking of students to create a more equitable math environment.

Tracking—the practice of separating students into different academic tracks based on past performance or potential achievement—is a prime example of how noble intentions serve to reinforce issues of fixed mindset. Starting in elementary school, students are identified according to reading ability and math aptitude. There often is a soft movement toward ability grouping in early grades, and a movement toward a more rigid bifurcation of the student body in later grades. Even at fifth grade, such ability grouping "act[s] as a sorting event that sets youths on different developmental trajectories" (Fuligni, Eccles, and Barber 1995, 87). As students enter secondary school, the multiperiod day lends itself to ability grouping: honors and Pre-AP for the achievers, remedial classes for nonachievers, and "regular" classes for the mass of students in the middle.

Research about the effectiveness of tracking is mixed, setting aside the moral quandary for a moment. Offering accelerated math and enrichment courses can lead to high outcomes for high-achieving students (Stinnett 2013). It's clear, though, that the effects of tracking and classifying students according to teacher recommendations or standardized metrics result in worse outcomes for students who have been traditionally underserved (Beaton and O'Dwyer 2002; Oakes 2005).

Even the mechanism of student placement in tracking systems can be arbitrary and imprecise. Dina is describing the process by which students have historically been sorted for high school course placement. "Students take a test at the end of eighth grade and supposedly *that* told us where they ought to be placed: in Math

1, Honors Math 1, or Math 2. It was the only metric that would determine what classes their kids would be placed in. This was our system. This, despite the fact that one year the eighth graders at one of the middle schools had a long-term sub the *entire year*. Of course, they did worse on the test! So, because they essentially didn't have a teacher for a year, they're placed in a lower-level math class? How does that make sense?"

Dina is also quick to point out the inequities that arise along lines of race and socio-economic status. Noting that the class with the long-term sub was from the middle school with more students of color, she describes her unease with this de facto segregation. That is why Dina and her department made the decision to de-track, restructuring their math pathway such that *all* incoming freshmen would take Math 1, no ifs, ands, or buts. There would no longer be a separate class for "honors," nor would kids be accelerated along into Math 2. *Even*—and I find this truly remarkable—*for students who took algebra and geometry in middle school.*

"Wasn't there pushback from parents?" I wonder. My experience as a teacher and as a parent led me to think some parents would be upset that their kids could no longer be accelerated.

"That's why we began communicating early about this change," Dina says. "Our message to parents was that we were trying to create a productive learning environment for *all* kids. We told parents that every kid can achieve highly in math: their kid, others' kids. And that we want to create that environment. Ultimately it will help their kids too. We emphasized that even the kids who had been accelerated in the past had deficiencies when it came to, say, explaining their work or communicating their ideas or collaborating with other students. And those are all skills their students will need in college."

While the teachers were shifting to de-track, they were also intentionally making their classrooms inclusive, academically safe environments. "We have that conversation all the time now: that everyone is a mathematician and that everyone can be good at math. The kids in their group are valuable to their learning and thinking. The class-room is an ecosystem, and everyone is important to the learning process."

According to Dina, the students' academic output has improved as well. "At this point, every student in my class can and will present the solution to a problem. From the shiest kids to the most outgoing, they'll get up there and present for a full five to ten minutes. And students in the audience are quick to ask questions. Kids are much clearer about their explanations, *especially* the kids who would have been accelerated into Math 2 in past years.

"Also, the quality of the work has improved," Dina continues. "When I look at the growth in the quality of work I'm receiving on problems from September to March, across the board I'm seeing better explanations and, yes, more correct solutions!"

Samueli Academy still offers an "honors" program for kids (or, perhaps truthfully, for parents) who want it. Honors students are in class with the rest of the student body, but they are tasked with additional assignments and projects. The rubrics on which they are scored have additional demands.

It's important to note that Dina and her colleagues were all individually compelled by research as well as their own values to make this change at Samueli Academy. It was not a decree from administration or the district that led to the change being so positive. It was an organic decision from a united math department. In addition to the structural realignment of courses, they had to undertake new learning about how to create a welcoming and equitable classroom and attend to those things throughout the year. It's hard to imagine the change being so positive if it were a top-down decision with little support surrounding it.

Self-Worth and Stereotype Threat

It's impossible to discuss issues of academic safety and self-regard without mentioning the very real effects of race, gender, sexual identity, multilingualism, ethnicity, and socioeconomic class in the math classroom. Issues of identity are often unmentioned and unmentionable in professional settings. Living in a country with such a tortured history on these issues and all the discomfort that rides along with them has conditioned us to *not* talk about such topics. But if we are being honest about all the ingredients that go into a student's experience of math, we must recognize that identities play an outsized role in defining how students see themselves as mathematicians. Almost always unintentional, often unspoken, and invariably repeated throughout a student's career, messages and micro-messages around students' identities have an undeniable effect.

I'm talking to Cara about some of the discipline issues she's having in her classroom. She's having difficulty getting a few kids to engage. She's tried hard to make her instruction engaging. She continually conveys positive messages about students' abilities to achieve at high levels. And yet, she has a few students who simply won't participate or turn in work. As the conversation continues, she notes that many of them are students of color in a mostly white student body. This adds extra complexity to an already complex dilemma. Issues of groupwork, self-regard, and academic status comingle with issues of race and equity. Cara's students were suffering from *stereotype threat*.

Stereotype threat occurs when people are placed in a situation where they feel at risk of confirming a stereotype about their group(s) based on societal myths. In addition, when an individual experiences repeated discrimination or is the object of assumptions over a period of time, he or she begins to internalize these myths of math achievement and identity. Stereotype threat can metastasize and become a self-fulfilling prophecy, so teachers must understand it and be vigilant. It's important to remember that our students have multiple, intersecting identities, each worth understanding. Here, we'll focus particularly on race and gender.

Gendered Stereotype Threat

In 1999, Spencer, Steele, and Quinn published the results of a study that convincingly demonstrated the existence of stereotype threat according to gender. Math tests were administered to college students, and the results were divvied up by gender. In the control group the test was administered as any standardized test might be: instructions were given, a sample problem was identified, and participants took the test. In the experimental group, the test was administered similarly except participants were given the explicit message that men and women had been shown to perform equally on this particular test. The results showed that in the control group men outperformed women, but in the experimental group—where the students were explicitly told that this test yielded no differences in performance based on gender—women and men performed equally. The simple act of telling test takers that this test had no gender bias resulted in no gender bias.

Where does this self-evaluative threat come from? When does it start?

Frome and Eccles (1998) published a study demonstrating that parents often have gender-based perceptions of their own children's abilities in math, and that these perceptions track with their children's self-perceptions. When given a questionnaire asking parents to identify their own child's mathematical ability, parents rated boys higher than girls in math and girls higher than boys in English. Eccles, Jacobs, and Harold (1990) showed that parents' attitudes directly affected student performance as well as a student's desire to take additional future and more challenging math courses. There is undeniable and growing research that suggests that gendered stereotype threat in math is real, that it starts early and develops into a self-reinforcing feedback loop. And all of this can be exacerbated in a school setting.

Dina is telling me what she does to combat stereotype threat. "If I see patterns of behaviors that aren't serving groups fairly, I'll bring that up explicitly in class. For example, if it seems like only boys will answer questions out loud or are more forceful at getting my attention, that's an opportunity to talk about that issue."

She's not kidding either. We're in the middle of a class when she calls a quick time-out to discuss how she's heard only from boys in the first few minutes of a lesson. Right then and there, she calls it out and takes it head-on. I admire her courage, honestly.

Tackling thorny issues of gender bias often requires intentional, direct, and persistent messaging to specific students. Jaime is a teacher in Seattle who has had to train himself to be aware of gendered stereotype threat and actively work to help his girls overcome it. He found that he was spending significantly more time talking to boys in his classroom—both for instruction and reprimanding. Watching a video of himself facilitating, he noticed that groups of girls might go an entire class without being addressed. "Once I became aware of how girls were experiencing math differently, I knew I had to make changes. It was very convicting, though. I had to first accept that I was contributing to the inequity." Rather than wallow in defensiveness, Jaime began addressing his implicit bias by ensuring that he spent as much time checking in on the work of girls as boys. He wanted to make sure that each girl experienced the following daily:

▲ A nonacademic conversation, in order to build and rebuild their relationship

▲ Praise for a specific mathematical action, to build and rebuild equitable assignment of academic status

Initially, these goals required carrying around a clipboard and checklist to ensure he'd achieved his daily outcomes. Eventually it became second nature and he could put away the clipboard.

Other schools have designed math clubs specifically for girls. These clubs can offer a safe space for girls to talk math and be honest if they're having difficulty with a particular mathematical concept. Although a girl may be unwilling to ask questions in front of her peers in the classroom because of stereotype threat, she may be willing to engage with difficult concepts in a smaller, more private setting.

Racial Stereotype Threat

Stereotype threat also manifests harshly for students of color. Steele and Aronson (1995) conducted a study similar to that of Spencer, Steele, and Quinn's (1999) in which they tested the performance of black students based on messaging. Two groups were administered the same test. One group was told that the test was a diagnostic measure of intellectual ability. The other group was told that the test was merely given as a laboratory study in the psychological factors in problem solving. Black students performed significantly worse than their white counterparts in the "diagnostic" group, while they achieved equally in the "laboratory" group.

Negative attitudes about race are pervasive and begin early in life (Baron and Banaji 2006), earlier than the first day students enter your secondary classroom. In school, these negative racial attitudes correlate with data on how students of color are disciplined. Students of color, particularly African American students, are suspended at a higher rate, expelled at a higher rate, and referred to the principal's office at a higher rate than their white counterparts (Lewin 2012; Cody 2013; Lyfe 2012). The same attitudes that lead to imbalanced discipline practices cross over into instructional practice.

One silver lining these studies demonstrate is that the messages teachers communicate have the potential to affect performance in a positive manner. In both studies discussed here, the mere message of the nature of a test—that it was a laboratory study rather than a evaluative exam—was enough to nearly eliminate the gender and race gap in test performance. What else can we do to reduce the gaps in performance?

Issues of identity require difficult conversations and even more difficult self-examination. Who are you calling on over and over again? In the same way that Jaime watched himself unintentionally attending to more boys than girls, you may wish to keep track of how often and in what ways you're calling on students of color.

On a more macro level, which students are tracked toward or away from advanced math after your class and in your school? If there is a lack of diversity in your upper and advanced math courses, it's worth a difficult conversation with other members of your department. Consider being intentional about inviting students from underrepresented groups into STEM-related clubs and/or advanced math class.

Similarly, when you discuss famous mathematicians, who is being represented? Are your students aware of the work of nonwhite and female mathematicians? In Appendix B, you'll find short biographies to help you get started.

A teacher must examine symptoms of inequity with data and react accordingly. We can't just assume that we're good people and hope for the best. As Jo Boaler puts it, "[I]t may not be enough, as a math teacher, to treat students equally in the pursuit of equity" (2016, 107). It's not that Teacher A is racist or Teacher B is sexist, it's that racism and sexism are the resting state of our society. They are the norm, not the individual outliers. Addressing them requires explicit action, not passivity.

Some math departments I've worked with track who is being called on, and for what: whom is the teacher questioning, and who are the respondents? An observing teacher or instructional coach will make tallies and notes, tracking the conversations and then sharing the resulting data with the classroom teacher. These quick data dives and analyses result in classrooms in which students of color are treated more equitably.

Above all else, listen to the concerns of your students, and listen to what *isn't* being said, because issues of race, sexuality, gender identity, ethnicity, language, and socioeconomic status often go undiscussed and are left simmering beneath the surface. One way to create an environment of honesty and safety is to use restorative circles.

Restorative Circles

Although not a math-specific strategy per se, or one created specifically for identity, restorative circles can go a long way toward repairing the strained relationship students may have with mathematics.

In a restorative circle, seats are arranged in a circle, often around some sort of centerpiece made up of items of importance. In one classroom I observed, the centerpiece included pictures, meaningful mementos students had brought in, and other markers of individual identity. Typically, some sort of "talking object" is part of that centerpiece. Only the holder of that object may speak. A chime signals the start of the restorative circle. The facilitator—be it a teacher or student—begins by offering some sort of prompt to invite conversation. The first time around a circle, the prompts are low level, yet open ended and insightful. The intention is to get acquainted while opening up the conversation. Here are some examples:

▲ If you could meet anyone from history, who would it be?

▲ What animal do you feel like right now (and why)?

▲ If you could change one thing about your local community, what would it be?

The facilitator asks the prompt and hands the talking piece to a participant. Participants may choose not to answer the prompt and instead silently pass the talking piece.

The second (or third) time around, the prompts may become deeper:

▲ Have you ever felt foolish in front of your peers?

▲ Have you wanted to disengage from the class recently?

▲ What does it mean to be a friend?

These questions induce vulnerability and must be treated as such. You may wish to withhold the deeper questions until you think significant trust has accumulated through the acquaintance questions over the course of a few circles.

Lastly, the circle is closed with a closing prompt, such as the following:

▲ Give two words that describe your experience in today's circle.

▲ What's an attitude you want to have for yourself the rest of the day?

After the final question, the facilitator rings the bell, thereby closing the circle.

For restorative circles to work, teachers must make themselves as vulnerable as students, describing failures of their own and being honest about their state of being. This vulnerability works to repair the relationship between students and the system of education that has contributed to past inequities.

Restorative circles are part of a much broader, comprehensive approach to social and emotional learning and identity known as restorative practices or restorative justice. They're also something that can occur only in classrooms where there is ample trust among the students and teacher. Significant norming around restorative circles is essential. Although it's beyond the scope of this book to delve fully into restorative justice, I highly recommend further investigation to learn more about the motivation and research behind restorative circles. It is a time commitment, but teachers may use it in lieu of a more typical warm-up for the day once a week.

Recruitment of Teachers of Color

Another elephant in the room is the racial dynamic in most US classrooms. The teaching profession is racially homogeneous. About 80 percent of teachers in the United States are white (Goldring, Gray, and Bitterman 2013), compared with about half of the student body (US Department of Education 2016). Meanwhile, we know that students demonstrate higher achievement when they are instructed by a teacher of similar racial background (Grissom, Kern, and Rodriguez 2015; Dee 2005; Pitts 2005; Meier 1993; Weiher 2000). Students also show a positive preference toward teachers of color (Cherng and Halpin 2016). Therefore, the dearth of teachers of color needs to be addressed at a systemic level. This is another way to combat race-based stereotype threat: schools can provide students with a more diverse set of instructors, and society must encourage more students of color to pursue education as a career.

When Social Pressures Seep In

It's hard to overestimate just how much nonclassroom events affect the classroom for a secondary student. Alfredo, an eleventh grader, is a challenging student. He isn't great about turning in his work, particularly his homework. "Teachers don't understand how much other stuff I have going on," he says. One of his closest friends—his "cousin"—is staying on his couch. I don't inquire further about the reason. I suspect the story involves eviction—by either the parent or the bank. Alfredo's friend keeps him up late in the evening, imploring him to play another round of *Fallout*. "I *want* to do well in class, but it's just so hard." I detect an air of pleading in his voice. I've had countless conversations with teachers who have told me that specific students "just don't want to try" or something similarly dismissive. In truth, by and large, students want to do well in class, even in classes they don't particularly like.

One of the drawbacks to a system of secondary education that employs a multiperiod day according to subject matter is that teachers are given only a very small window into the social creature that is the adolescent student. It's possible for a secondary teacher to be ignorant of a student's social groups or how those groups affect classroom performance. We've seen the effect of academic status in terms of self-regard; social status is critical too.

Alfredo also works after school. Although not an explicitly social effect, his job is a physical distraction that manifests as an academic one. Alfredo works three afternoons and evenings a week to help support his family.

"When I'm falling asleep in class, it's not always because I'm bored. It's because I'm exhausted." If I didn't know Alfredo and saw him nodding off in class, I'd probably assume he's insubordinate or has a poor work ethic. In truth, he's the hardest-working individual in this room. Effective teachers know these things about their individual students. This gets us to caring.

Passive Caring Versus Active Caring

Briana is a tenth grader, talking about her middle school math experience. "I was invisible to the teacher," she begins. "I always got my work done. I never got in trouble. I would raise my hand to ask a question, but my teacher would never call on me. It got to the point where I would ask my friend to ask a question for me so I could get something answered." Briana is soft-spoken but clearly motivated. It's tragic but understandable how she would feel "invisible" to her teachers. In the hustle and bustle of a noisy middle school classroom, soft-spoken students get short shrift.

Recently an administrator I know took part in a "shadowing a student" challenge, in which the administrator identified a student and followed her around for an entire day. From the moment she got off at the city bus stop in front of the school until the moment she got back on it at the end of the day, the administrator followed the student around to each class, every passing period, even lunch. Debriefing the experience, the administrator was stunned by how little interaction with teachers the student had. Other than a greeting here or there, the student received few words from her instructors.

Again, it's quite understandable: a secondary teacher may have upward of 130 students enter and exit his or her classroom per day. It's a challenge to have meaningful conversations with *half* that number in a given day. Few secondary educators are explicitly uncaring. But many aren't *actively caring*. Active caring distinguishes the truly safe academic environments from classrooms that unintentionally further the status quo and reinforce access and achievement gaps.

Passive caring refers to nonspecific attitudes of care from teachers. Teachers are "welcoming" in the sense that they don't actively work to harm students, but they also don't do anything specific to care for students. The relationship is one sided or dependent: the student must care for the work of school before the teacher will demonstrate personal care or interest.

Active caring demands a two-way relationship independent of the student's academic dispositions. Students who don't demonstrate a preternatural appreciation for the subject receive the same level of personal and cultural care as those who do.

The question of passive versus active caring cuts deep. Most secondary teachers demonstrate passive caring. They love their subject and don't hate the company of students. Teachers have special relationships with a few students, typically those who demonstrate enthusiasm for the material or have naturally attractive personalities. The rest of the teacher's students don't experience active harm or trauma, but the state of the classroom serves to reinforce long-standing gaps in status. Students who like math or like schooling are elevated, whereas struggling students slide further behind in achievement and/or self-regard.

Fewer teachers demonstrate active caring, which represents a disruption of social and academic norms. Teachers actively work to demonstrate specific caring for individuals as individuals. In Chapter 1 we saw how Leanne greets each student at the door, shaking his or her hand and welcoming them into the classroom after a brief interpersonal interaction. She does this every day, with every student. She asks about their lives, how their cousin is doing, or how a certain test in another subject area went. That's one of many ways Leanne demonstrates caring for her students throughout the day. Table 3.1 describes additional distinctions between passive and active caring.

Passive Caring	Active Caring
Teacher greets students at the door.	Teacher inquires about students' well-being at the door.
Teacher has positive relationships with good students.	Teacher has positive relationships with each student.
Teacher knows each student's name.	Teacher knows each student's passions.
Teacher knows which social groups students hang out with.	Teacher knows which social groups students struggle with.
Teacher invites all students to participate.	Teacher encourages each student to participate.
Teacher allows retakes on exams.	Teacher allows retakes and reaches out to specific students and encourages them to retake an exam.
Teacher offers general praise.	Teacher offers authentic praise specific to each student.
Teacher cares about how the student is doing in math.	Teacher cares about how the student is doing in all subjects.
Teacher asks how a student is doing generally.	Teacher asks how something specific, such as work, is going.

TABLE 3.1

It's no coincidence that Leanne also holds each of her students accountable and to a higher standard than they're used to. She's built up social capital with her students over the course of the school year and is therefore able to push them when they're not meeting her standards. When she wants a kid to retake a test because he didn't score high enough for her liking, he comes in at lunch or after school and does it. When a student fails to turn in a homework assignment, she holds her feet to the fire to get it turned in.

Happily, Briana doesn't feel invisible anymore. She's telling me about her teachers now. She says her teachers know her—I mean *really* know her: that she's passionate about dance, that she takes the city bus to get to school, that she waits tables on the weekend at her aunt's restaurant, and so on. In this environment and with these relationships, Briana is flourishing.

Academic Status: Defining and Assigning

Now that we've established a demonstrable practice of active caring for our students, it's time to build them up as mathematicians. We do this through assigning *academic status*. Ilana Horn, a professor and researcher at Vanderbilt University and author of *Strength in Numbers*, offers the following definition of status: "Status is the perception of students' academic capability and social desirability" (2012, 21).

The factors that affect one's learning and understanding of math stem from social- and self-perception. Issues of academic status are a social creation, rather than a truly academic one. Dembo and McAuliffe (1987) show that a lack of *perceived* academic ability is a predictor of participation, whether it's relevant to the task at hand or not. If students believe they are poor math students, or if *they believe that their peers believe* they are poor math students, they are likely to fulfill those low expectations. That's why teachers at Ridgeland High School treat issues of status head-on.

Assigning Academic Status

In the previous chapter, we learned how Ridgeland teachers undertook a process of inquiry about the discipline of math. They discovered that math—according to mathematicians—differs from how it appears in school textbooks. As teachers learned about the discipline, they provided their students with increasingly authentic mathematical experiences.

Now we'll learn how Ridgeland teachers "assigned academic status"—publicly and thoughtfully ascribing mathematical brilliance—to their students. This practice may be considered part of facilitation, so we find ourselves at the intersection between effective facilitation and academic safety (Figure 3.5).

The Ridgeland process of assigning academic status starts at their department meetings. Teachers at Ridgeland meet regularly as a staff to discuss problems of practice, design tasks, and attend to how their students feel about themselves as mathematicians. They'll tell you that the last of those goals is the most important.

Teachers have a list of class rosters printed out and affixed neatly to clipboards—all their class rosters, in fact. For the entire hour they have together, the teachers run down the list of each class roster and ask the group, "How is this kid smart in math?" Ridgeland is just shy of 900 students; teachers know most of the students in their academy. For each student, two or three teachers chime in with responses such as "Jeremiah is incredibly

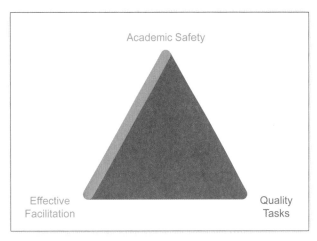

FIGURE 3.5 Here is an example of a connection between academic safety and effective facilitation.

persistent," "Carlie is quite creative," "Jesse is quick to argue," "He's also good at giving constructive feedback," and so on.

The teachers take dedicated notes based on their peers' input. Throughout the next two weeks, they hold on to those clipboards during class and make a concerted effort to praise each and every one of their students for a mathematical skill or "smartness." Within two weeks (though most complete the exercise within one) every single student of theirs has been praised by his or her teacher for a mathematical skill.

I ask one of the teachers, Kate, about some of the parameters of this exercise. "We want to make it clear that we're not just saying 'good job' for some generic thing a student has done," she told me. "The praise needs to be specific and mathematical in nature. We're not just giving kudos for pretty drawings. We're rebuilding these students' understanding of math and their understanding of themselves as mathematicians."

According to the staff norms, the praise must be

▲ public,

▲ specific,

▲ mathematical, and

▲ true.

To be an "acceptable" offering of praise, an assignment of academic status, it must meet all four of these criteria.

The practice of assigning status is near and dear to the Ridgeland staff. It's something they talk about often and that they credit with their continued improvement in student achievement over the past half-dozen years or so.

Recall that the math team at Ridgeland spent significant time unpacking what it means to be a mathematician, which informed their practice of assigning academic status in mathematics. After a decade or so of red pen marks on exams, students have received the message that math is about finding the right number after using the right formula. Ridgeland teachers have developed an alternative vision for their students to internalize—a clear manifesto about what it means to be smart in mathematics. One way they transmit this vision is by recognizing students when they exhibit behaviors that are authentic to mathematics.

When I'm in a math classroom at Ridgeland High School, I can hear the voices of the math teachers from the staff meeting through the mouths of students while they're working. They have taken on the same language that their teachers have spent their entire secondary career explicitly using with them:

"That's a really good estimate."

"I don't want to give up quite yet before we ask the teacher."

"Is there another way we could approach this?"

Once the Ridgeland teachers have completed their status-assigning assignment, they print off a new class roster and start again, making sure to let every student whose name is on that clipboard know, again, that he or she is a budding mathematician.

Conclusion

When I'm asked what an academically safe classroom looks like, my response is to answer by describing what an academically safe classroom *sounds* like. Who is doing the talking, and to whom? What is he or she saying? Answer those two questions and you'll have an insight into the culture of the classroom. I know I'm in an academically safe classroom when I see each student speak mathematically without the teacher prompting. The most academically safe classrooms are ones in which students are quick to ask questions of other students and are as quick to listen. Groups work equitably. The teacher engages in one-on-one or small-group conversations with students. Students from different backgrounds work together productively. They continue to work productively when the teacher is elsewhere in the room.

Despite being invisible in any mass-produced curriculum, academic safety is no less important than tasks or facilitation. In fact, it's the most permanent of all three. Adults may not be able to recall specific content or lessons, but they will sure be able to tell you if they disliked math as a child. The root causes of this dislike can stem from one (or several) causes: mindset, stereotype threat, social pressures, tracking, and/or an inaccurate representation of the discipline itself. Teachers have an obligation to communicate to students that they are mathematically smart and that they are welcome at the table. A kind word or other demonstration of authentic caring goes a long way.

As I was writing this chapter, I discussed it with a teacher. I was describing how crucial it is to understand where students are coming from, academically and personally. At one point in the conversation the teacher helpfully offered, "Maybe you should just write 'Give a crap' over and over again." We laughed because it was funny and true. That should be the biggest takeaway from this chapter: to give a crap. Students—particularly adolescents—are such a joy, with all their quirks, their humor, their ups and downs. Let them know it. And let them know that their unique talents are uniquely suited for math.

REVIEW

- Academic safety involves the self-regard of students as mathematicians and contains many, many layers.

- Students must believe that hard work is useful to their learning and must be rewarded by their teacher.

- Many classroom practices can be reimagined to present students a growth mindset view of math, including the following:

  - ▲ From an emphasis on speed to an emphasis on thoughtfulness
  - ▲ From an emphasis on correctness to an emphasis on effort
  - ▲ From an emphasis on grades to an emphasis on demonstration of knowledge

- Tracking students into particular mathematical pathways can lead to issues of equity and access.

- Stereotype threat (race and gender based) is invisible, real, and treatable. It must be addressed in the classroom.

- Adolescents have countless pressures on them, and it's important to understand where they're coming from.

- There's a difference between passively caring for all students and actively caring for *each* student.

- Assigning academic status is a key part of rebuilding a student's mathematical self-worth.

QUALITY TASKS

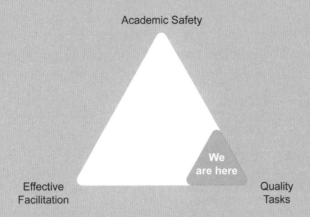

Academic Safety

Effective
Facilitation

Quality
Tasks

We
are here

J essica is a teacher in a small community in Indiana. She and I had the opportunity to design units as part of a grant intended to enhance student outcomes in literacy in all content areas. She chose to design a unit around equations of parallel, perpendicular, and intersecting lines. Her idea, being a football fan in a community rife with football fans, was to have students design football plays on a Cartesian coordinate plane. But she didn't stop at the design of the contrived scenario.

She invited the coach of the high school football team to talk to her algebra class. His message to them was that he needed to expand the playbook, and he wanted Jessica's math class to help him out. Different plays had different requirements: some plays required two receivers to run parallel with each other, another required the receivers to run perpendicular routes. To make the conversation more lasting, the coach even left the class with a letter of request.

To the students of Ms. Brees's algebra class,

I know that you have such great pride in our football team. Now I'd like your help in making it better. I'm calling on you to help me expand my playbook to include additional running routes for our wide receivers.

Please design football plays for each of the following wide-receiver routes:

- a crossing route in which the two receivers cross in perpendicular paths

- a route in which two receivers run parallel

- a route in which they cross at a nonperpendicular angle

I'd like your newly designed plays on my coach's desk by 0900 this Friday. Go, Bulldogs!

Coach T

Students began working on the coach's request. Most students could recall what *parallel* and *perpendicular* meant, and those who couldn't were quickly reminded by their peers. They also generally understood how to create equations from lines on a coordinate plane. That was enough to get started on their playbooks.

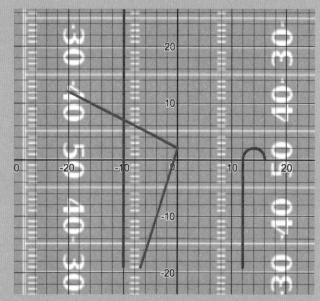

FIGURE B.1 Example of a football play with wide-receiver routes.

As students were creating plays and wide-receiver routes of all sorts, Jessica checked their work to ensure that they had created parallel and perpendicular lines. Once they had successfully created plays with the requested wide-receiver routes, she had the groups draw their plays on giant grid paper, accompanied by the equations that mapped onto the lines created by the wide-receiver routes (Figure B.1).

Each group took time examining other groups' plays. Jessica instructed them to pay careful attention to the equations and to jot down anything peculiar, interesting, or noteworthy they noticed about the plays they designed.

When students analyzed a variety of solutions to the same constraints, they could identify patterns. For example, students noticed that when the receivers ran parallel routes, the slopes of the lines were identical. When the wide receivers made a perpendicular cross, the slopes of the lines were the opposite reciprocal of one another (for instance, $\frac{4}{3}$ and $-\frac{3}{4}$). From that experience, students connected the parallel and perpendicular equations they were creating on their coordinate planes and the similarities and unique differences in slopes.

Once students noticed these patterns, Jessica raised additional, related questions: *Was this always true? Why would this be so? Why would perpendicular lines necessitate that the slopes be opposite reciprocals of each other?* Students posed a few questions too: *The negative slope thing seems kind of random, doesn't it? Or does it? And what about equations with undefined slopes?* The exploration yielded as many interesting questions as it did answers!

The task was immediately engaging to students, helpfully co-facilitated by the football coach. Even students who didn't particularly care for football were hooked by having the coach as a guest speaker. Jessica's own football fandom didn't hurt: authentic teacher excitement can be contagious.

The task also allowed creative access: students chose their own running routes for their receivers. In fact, the task didn't just allow for creativity; it relied on it. It was through looking for patterns across the variety of plays drawn up that the sense making occurred. Students made conjectures about parallel and perpendicular lines and tested those conjectures with one another's examples.

Students spent the rest of that day refining their plays and making their solutions clear: they were to submit a formal written version to the coach by the end of the following day. At one point in the lesson, Jessica had students move around in stations to talk through their equations with other students. Students eventually submitted a written proposal of their plays to the football coach, complete with equations denoting the running routes of the receivers, and what made them parallel or perpendicular.

This task was followed by a few short-answer assessment items. The first item asked the students to analyze a football play, and the others asked questions in different contexts that required the same or similar math concepts (Figure B.2). Could students apply their conjectures about parallel and perpendicular lines to other scenarios or in other abstract situations? Could they make additional conjectures or stretch their thinking with some additional complex problems? We were getting into some pretty exciting, rich territory.

A task is the action item provided by the teacher for students to perform. It's a catchall term for a wide variety of prompts. A task could be a sprawling project, or it could be a series of questions on a worksheet. A task could be a game or a problem. It's what the students are doing at any given time. As much as possible, we want students to be working on tasks that are of high quality.

But what makes a high-quality task? How does a teacher with limited time, resources, and curricular wiggle room incorporate tasks that pave the way for our entire ecosystem of learning mathematics? Over the next two chapters, we'll explore what makes a task high quality. In Chapter 4, we'll dig deep into five hallmarks of high-quality tasks: what high-quality tasks do. In Chapter 5, we'll see ten models of high-quality tasks and learn how to find, adapt, and develop our own.

3. Sam sold 25 tickets to the one act play. He has $57 in his envelope, but can't remember how many $3 adult and how many $2 student tickets he sold. Use a system to find out.
   Variables: _____and _____

   Equation #1: _____

   Equation #2: _____

4. The winning entry at a cake baking contest was an Italian Cream Cake. The perimeter of the rectangular cake was 46 inches. The length was 4 less than twice the width. Find the length and width.
   Variables: _____and _____

   Equation #1: _____

   Equation #2: _____

FIGURE B.2 Follow up questions of Jessica's football task.

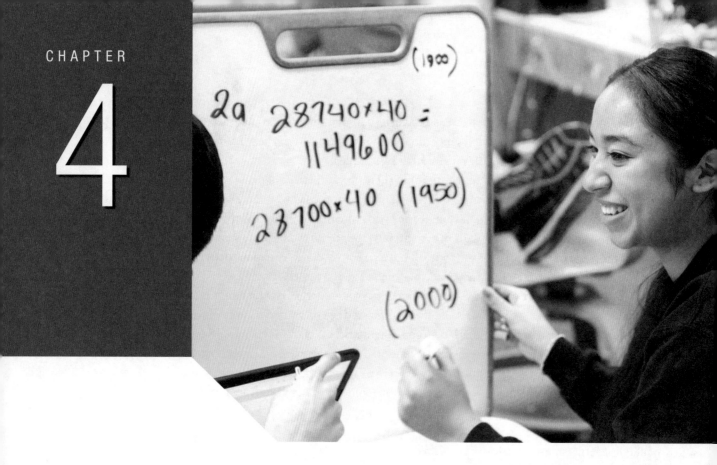

CHAPTER

4

Defining Quality Tasks

It is as though I feel my way through the darkness, find a switch to light up the room, and come to appreciate how perfectly organized and beautiful that room really is. I look around and understand the role of each piece of the problem I stumbled over in my wanderings searching for that switch.

– HEE OH

The tasks teachers provide are the most concrete aspect of our three-legged pedagogy. On any given day, the task is one of the first things a student experiences in a math class. Besides some initial socializing and perhaps being welcomed at the door, students are often greeted with a warm-up, a mathematical task.

A quality task enhances the other elements in our ecosystem. A quality task will open up conversations around academic safety (as we have seen in Chapters 2 and 3). It also allows for effective facilitation in a way that a low-quality task cannot, as we'll see once we start defining what makes for a high-quality task. We're looking for tasks that *enable* effective facilitation and *yield* an academically safe environment with rich mathematical content, as Jessica's did. To that end, here are five design elements common to high-quality tasks. They do the following:

▲ Spark curiosity and foster engagement

▲ Yield creativity and lead to new ideas

▲ Promote access for all students in the classroom

▲ Require and convey deep, crucial mathematical content

▲ Connect and extend content

Although it's not realistic to expect that every task will adhere to all five elements, that is our goal. Let's look at each trait individually in more detail, recognizing that they naturally interrelate and overlap.

1. Quality Tasks Spark Curiosity and Foster Engagement

Brett—also in Indiana, but not at the same school as Jessica—told me, "I know a task has landed well if I immediately get genuine questions or if students begin working on it before I tell them to. That happens with some of the problems I pose. Not all of them, but some. I make sure to take note of it. I wish I had a working theory of which tasks promote curiosity."

We know curiosity is an important driver in a student's understanding of a topic and is instrumental in his or her willingness to engage deeply in a task (Day 1982). What sparks that curiosity is tougher to predict. How do we know what's interesting? What will engender curiosity? Although it's difficult to predict with complete accuracy how much curiosity a task will generate, we do have some guideposts for engagement offered by research and modern practices.

Guidepost for Engagement 1: Consider Your Own Curiosity.

The quickest check on whether a task may spark curiosity in students is whether it sparks curiosity in you, the teacher. Typically, if teachers find the task interesting, their students will, too. Janice—a ninth grader—offers, "It's fun when I see my teacher excited about the task. Like, it's not just something they *have* to teach, but it's something that they actually *want* to teach. I can tell." Sometimes teachers can get so caught up in trying to identify their students' interests that they neglect their own time for mathematical engagement. Students can tell when their teacher is or isn't excited about a topic, and it's contagious either way.

Guidepost for Engagement 2: Elicit Student Questions.

Missy, a teacher in Texas, is playing a video of two men running across a baseball field in some sort of footrace. The video pauses before the completion of the race and the following appears on the screen: *What's the first question that pops into your head?* (This is a facilitation move that we'll examine more in future chapters.)

Initially, the near-universal response is *Who wins the race?* or something along those lines. Eventually we get to more pointed questions such as *Who is running faster?* or *Are they running at a constant rate?* All these questions are coming from students, and Missy is recording them. For some questions, she has quick answers; others she puts on hold for students to answer for themselves. There's nothing particularly fancy about the video editing other than a pause and fade-out before the race ends, but leaving the questions to the students imparts agency and status, and students respond.

Missy uses one of the quickest and most effective methods I've seen to boost engagement. The teacher poses a scenario—be it a picture or an audio clip or a video or a paragraph—steps back, and asks students to generate questions. Co-developing questions with students about a puzzling scenario is a routine that has been gaining in popularity with the advent of modern curricula. Dan Meyer is the chief academic officer at Desmos, a company that produces math activities, among other things. He developed and maintains a website that allows users to upload pictures or videos and subsequent users to ask questions based on these artifacts. The website is called 101 Questions (101qs.com) and is a precursor to the *Three-Act Math* task model that appears in Chapter 5.

Guidepost for Engagement 3: Keep Information or Know-How Just Out of Reach.

Loewenstein (1994) discusses the "knowledge gap" in a task as one potential predictor of engagement. That is, to complete a task or solve a problem, how much information or know-how does a student need to acquire? Lowenstein posits that curiosity is more likely to be stirred when the knowledge gap is small than when it is large. When the needed information is *just out of reach*, as in Missy's footrace scenario, students are more likely to be curious. Conversely, when there is a large knowledge gap—significantly more know-how or information is needed—students are less likely to be curious and more likely to feel overwhelmed (Figure 4.1).

I find this observation unavoidably true for both real-world and abstract scenarios. As soon as a teacher gives a convoluted task, almost all hands go up as students ask for additional information or hand-holding. An overly large gap between the posing of the problem and the solution results in folded arms and other body language that

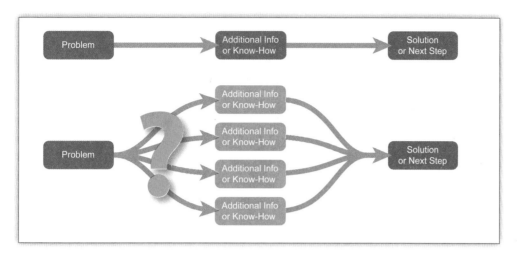

FIGURE 4.1 Students are more likely to engage with a task if the needed information or know-how is imminently attainable.

conveys disengagement. On the other hand, problems that keep the information or know-how closely attainable result in momentum that keeps students "falling forward" through a problem.

Loewenstein also posits that someone else's knowledge or insight is a harbinger for curiosity (1994). Understanding that someone else—be it a peer, a teacher, or an expert from outside the classroom—has the requisite information or know-how can be enough to stir curiosity. Unfortunately, this often manifests itself in the secondary classroom as students eliciting steps or formulas from the teacher, a habit that is reinforced when teachers immediately (and sometimes without prompting) explain how to solve a problem before allowing actual problem solving (more on that in Chapter 9). Instead, consider a task that offers the teacher (or better yet, peers or experts from outside the classroom) as a resource, rather than the sole arbiter of know-how.

Guidepost for Engagement 4: Solicit Predictions.

Predictions are catalysts for curiosity. Related to the just-out-of-reach knowledge gap phenomenon, if students forecast the outcome of a scenario, develop a hypothesis, or make an educated guess about the result, they are more likely to engage with the task at hand. They are now invested intellectually. Some teachers explicitly solicit an estimation or a response of "too high/too low/best guess at a solution" before any problem solving occurs (see "Estimation," Chapter 5). You'll notice how we're straddling the line between the task and facilitation here (Figure 4.2).

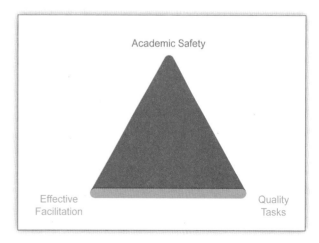

FIGURE 4.2 Soliciting predictions is an example of a connection between quality tasks and effective facilitation.

Guidepost for Engagement 5: Break Expectations.

Another initiator of curiosity is when a student's expectations are broken—that is, when a result does not align with what was expected. Science teachers and magicians know this well. They design experiments and performances that are specifically intended to surprise. The difference is that the science teacher goes on to help students understand the phenomenon, whereas the magician leaves *How did you do that?* to a wanting imagination. In math, we expose students to a scenario where their predictions don't match the solution, and then we encourage them to figure out what's going on.

FIGURE 4.3 Dina breaks expectations by using previous content that doesn't work for the given scenario. In this case, she's demonstrating that a linear model doesn't work for a scenario displaying exponential growth.

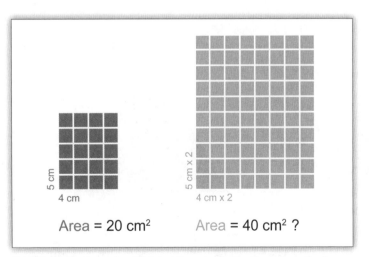

FIGURE 4.4 Students often think that if you double the dimensions of a shape, you double the area.

Dina's tenth-grade class is working through a problem on the population growth of California. Students calculate the change in population between 1850 and 1860 and create a linear model to predict the population of California going forward (Figure 4.3). They work diligently, using their skills as linear modelers to create a function that predicts population as a function of the year. Eventually, Dina asks students to make a prediction of the current population of California according to their linear models, which start in the 1800s. As you might expect, predictions are *way off*. The linear models predict a population of somewhere around 6 million, which might be less than the number of cars on Highway 5 at any given moment. Rather, the actual population of present-day California is around *40 million*. The math must be wrong! We must investigate what happened there. At this point Dina discusses the concept of exponential growth and why it's a more appropriate model for the scenario. Now that the students' expectations have been sufficiently broken, they are primed and ready for new material.

In my geometry class I had students predict and then calculate the effect of scaling the dimensions on the area or volume of a two- or three-dimensional object, respectively (Figure 4.4).

The students' expectations were that if you, say, doubled the length of a radius of a circle, you'd double the area. Or if you scaled a prism by a factor of three, you'd end up tripling the volume. These near-universal expectations are quickly shattered upon manual calculation. When one doubles the lengths of a two-dimensional object, the area is quadrupled; when one triples the lengths of a prism, the volume is increased twenty-seven-fold. Once students were steeped in this dissonance, we were able to discuss what was really going on and why this happens, as well as when it doesn't happen.

These curiosity and engagement guideposts are instructive; they are certainly not exhaustive. But if you're able to stick to a few of them, you'll be more likely to spark curiosity and engagement.

2. Quality Tasks Yield Creativity and Lead to New Ideas

Mathematics is often seen as an uncreative discipline, particularly as children advance in school age. Even at young ages mathematical creativity and idea building can be stifled. Everything already has a predetermined vocabulary word: *point, line, plane, acute triangle, regular hexagon.* The rules seem etched in stone with little to no room for new ideas.

I recently invited teachers to have their classes opt in to an informal, nonscientific survey for secondary math teachers to gauge math attitudes. About a dozen teachers volunteered, and I received 350 student responses. The survey contained the question *Agree or Disagree with the following statement: "Math is about using the right formula."* Sixty percent of students agreed, and only 11 percent disagreed with that statement (Figure 4.5).

These responses fly in the face of the work of mathematicians, who thrive on creativity, rule-breaking, and elegance. Mathematician G. H. Hardy, in his treatise *A Mathematician's Apology*, wrote, "A mathematician, like a painter or a poet, is a maker of patterns. . . . The mathematician's patterns, like the painter's or the poet's, must be beautiful; the ideas like the colours or the words, must fit together in a harmonious way. Beauty is the first test" (2004–1940, 14). Paul Lockhart, in his 2009 essay *A Mathematician's Lament*, says, "Math is not about following directions, it's about making new directions" (6). The protagonist in Hiroshi Yuki's

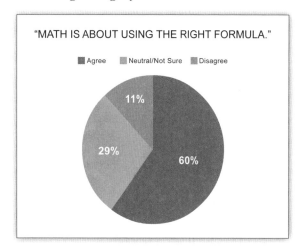

FIGURE 4.5 In a survey of 350 students, only 11 percent of students disagreed with the statement "Math is about using the right formula." Sixty percent agreed.

Math Girls tells us, "Math isn't about dredging up half-remembered formulas. It's about making new discoveries" (2011, 7).

How can we incorporate tasks that encourage creativity, beauty, and idea making?

Mathematical creativity can appear in a variety of ways. One such way happens when an activity is primarily student generated. (Here I use the word *activity* in the sense of actual student *actions*, not as typical educator-speak of activity as an assignment.)

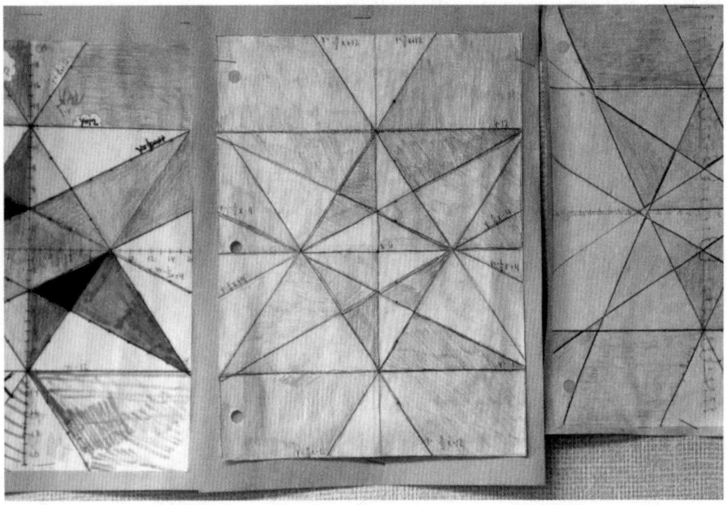

FIGURE 4.6 Ray's design using lines reflected over the *x*- and *y*-axes led to discoveries about properties of slopes.

Ray is showing off his creation. The class's prompt was to generate a design using linear functions so that it reflects over the *x*- and *y*-axes. There wasn't much more instruction than that, other than to be as precise as possible. After playing around with pencil-drawn lines on a grid paper, Ray came up with a pattern he quite liked (Figure 4.6). His teacher prompts the class to determine the functions that generated these lines. Some students chose to use a separate piece of paper to identify their questions. Ray chose to mark them right there in his design.

Ray's teacher asks the class, "What do you notice about the lines you drew and the equations you made?" Students make connections about the relationships among lines reflected over the two axes:

- ▲ Their slopes are always reciprocals of each other when reflected over the *x*-axis.

- ▲ Their slopes are always opposites of each other when reflected over the *y*-axis.

- ▲ Lines reflected over the *y*-axis always have the same *y*-intercept.

- ▲ The reflection of horizontal lines are just "*y* equals the opposite number," as in, $y = 12$ and $y = -12$.

Quite a bit of sense making and discourse can occur around student-generated lines, shapes, and numbers. A creative task can be as simple as asking students to create a few things and then facilitating some discussion about what patterns they see.

Another path toward creativity can involve a singular solution but encourage a variety of unique, creative, or elegant solution methods. Nicolas and Mirah are working through a problem on similar triangles (Figure 4.7). They are given the lengths of three sides of one triangle and of one side of the other. Nicolas points out that the side of the larger triangle that corresponds with the known side of the smaller, similar triangle is larger by a scale of 1.5, or $\frac{6}{4}$. Therefore, to find the missing sides, he multiplies each side of the smaller triangle by 1.5 to come up with the remaining side lengths. Mirah solves it differently. She sets up a proportion for the corresponding sides to solve for the missing length, x. Both methods yield the same solution, yet there is allowance for creativity in how they arrived at that solution (Figure 4.8).

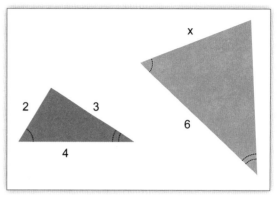

FIGURE 4.7 Similar triangles for which students are asked to find the missing side length.

A task may yield creativity in a multitude of ways, ranging from the discovery of a new idea, to the use of quadratics to design a stained-glass window, to two students using differing methods to come up with the same solution to a problem. Lockhart puts a fine point on it: "If you deny students the opportunity to engage in this activity—to pose their own problems, make their own conjectures and discoveries, to be wrong, to be creatively frustrated, to have an inspiration, and to cobble together their own explanations and proofs—you deny them mathematics itself" (2009, 5). So take a look at the tasks you are implementing: Is there a way to infuse student choice or creativity? Could students generate their own pictures

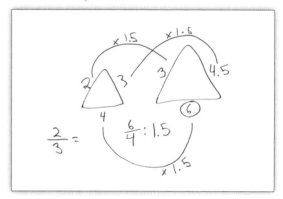

FIGURE 4.8 Nicolas and Mirah work on the similar-triangles problem.

and then deduce mathematical identities from those pictures? Are there multiple, novel ways to approach and solve a problem? Look for places and content clusters in which creativity might be a potential boon for student understanding and engagement.

3. Quality Tasks Promote Access for All Students in the Classroom

Although all these descriptors for quality tasks are desirable, this one is a requirement: all students must be able to access every task. Take particular note of the word *access*. It's not essential for all students to already have all the tools in their toolbox to *complete* a particular task, but they ought to be able to understand the problem and identify with it, ideally with a potential launching point. Students need a conceptual understanding of what the problem is asking or the scenario in which the task occurs.

Without that attribute, a task becomes inaccessible for the student, which implies the math is inaccessible, which leads to disengagement and disinterest.

An accessible task is understood by each and every student in the classroom. A task that *promotes* access is understood and immediately engaging to students. Teachers mention how frustrating it is when students hand in answers that make no sense: the speed of a car is moving faster than the speed of light, the mass of an object is heavier than the earth, or the student has dutifully copied the number in his or her calculator to the tenth decimal place (or whatever the calculator will yield). These are often indicators that a student didn't understand the problem from the outset (or had no interest in doing so).

This is *not* to say that quality tasks must be unchallenging. That's a crucial distinction to make at this point: an accessible task is not the same as an easy task. In fact, often the opposite is true: challenging and clear tasks are more accessible than unchallenging tasks. Ilana Horn argues that by "starting with challenging problems, teachers send the message that all students can engage with difficult content especially when they have each other as resources . . . starting with the easy stuff contributes to inequitable teaching" (2012, 39).

Desmos is a graphing calculator company that produces, and invites teachers to produce, math activities. Among their recommendations, they suggest that teachers "create activities that are easy to start and difficult to finish" (Desmos 2015). Tasks that are easy to start promote access. Tasks that are difficult to finish will maintain it.

Consider the following tasks:

Biology	Cone and Cylinder Volumes
Suppose a microorganism is shaped like a cylinder and grows by increasing its length, l, and not its radius, r. The surface area S (in square micrometers) and the volume V (in cubic micrometers) of the microorganism can be modeled by $$S = 2\pi r^2 + 2\pi r^2 \text{ and } V = \pi r^2 l.$$ a. Write an equation that models the ratio y of the surface area of the microorganism to its volume. b. Suppose the microorganism has a radius of 50 micrometers. Incorporate this information into the model from part (a). c. Describe how the ratio changes as the length of the microorganism increases.	A cone is twice as tall as a cylinder of the same radius. What is the ratio of their volumes?

TABLE 4.1

The task on the left may not be accessible to all students. To be more precise, it may not be *accessed* by students. Even if the task is technically accessible, it's not particularly inviting, which results in a lack of accessibility. On first glance, one might assume that the task on the left is the more "challenging" task. It has more words, several steps, and intimidating-looking formulas. However, it's a relatively unchallenging task, assuming one understands how to input numbers into a formula and subsequently into a calculator.

In contrast, the task on the right has fewer words, has no intimidating formulas or symbols, and isn't affixed in a real-world context. But students will be able to access it, provided they have some understanding about what a cylinder and cone are (and if they don't, that can be remedied with a drawing and discussion). It also is the more challenging task. Although inviting, it facilitates predictions and conjectures that will result in more permanent learning.

Attributes of an Inaccessible Task	Attributes of an Accessible Task
Overlong	Concise
Draws heavily on technical language	Language is friendly and inviting
Includes a formula	Solicits students to recall prior knowledge
Includes prescribed, rote steps	Can be started multiple ways
Solely text based	Includes or invites visuals

TABLE 4.2

Brett attempts to suss out the level of access by asking students to restate (or state) the problem. "In your own words, what is this problem about? What is it asking you to do?" he asks as part of his instructions, before asking for any calculations. He has students compare each other's unique responses to this prompt. When students are in agreement, they proceed with the task. When students are uncalibrated in their idea of what the prompt is asking, Brett can help clarify before moving on. This ensures understanding of the problem itself, while co-developing the question with students.

Issues of access are particularly acute when dealing with special student populations, such as students with special needs or English language learners (ELL). We will address issues pertaining to students with special needs and ELL students throughout the book. Even the most accessible task will require some prep work or modification to ensure access for each and every student.

4. Quality Tasks Require and Convey Deep, Crucial Mathematical Content

In addition to increasing access, engagement, and creativity, well-designed tasks are built around crucial content understanding. Stand-alone brainteasers, puzzles, and problems-of-the-week are excellent ways to increase engagement and rebuild self-esteem in math, but they may not draw on or connect to content that is required for achievement in that particular class. Given that classrooms reside in a system that provides external standards, we need to employ tasks that engage with those content standards so that students can build on those standards in future grades.

It's also not enough for a task to require a small bit of crucial content knowledge that is quickly forgotten once the task is complete. Many administrators are heartened when they see a matrix of standards on the wall with a checked box indicating that content has been taught or "covered." But covering a standard can mean wildly different things, depending on the task provided. For example, consider a problem that requires understanding of ratio and proportion in the context of track and field:

> Arthur runs for four miles. Rick runs two-fifths of the distance that Arthur runs. How far did Rick run?

This is a more-or-less typical problem one might see in a seventh-grade textbook. To solve it, a student might set up and solve a proportion, even using a nifty trick such as cross multiplying.

$$\frac{x}{4} = \frac{2}{5}$$

$$4 \times 2 = 5x$$

This solution may yield the correct answer, but there is little real wrestling with the content or allowance of permanent learning. A student who doesn't know how to solve it initially might learn a technique to solve it that day and quickly forget it, or not be able to use it in a different context, or not be able to use it with a different arrangement of words. For example, if a student learns how to set up a proportion and cross multiply solely for the task above, how confident are we that he or she could accurately solve the following, slightly altered problem?

> *Arthur runs four miles* farther *than Rick. Rick runs two-fifths of the distance that Arthur runs. How far did Rick run?*

To solve this particular problem, a student may set up their proportion thusly:

$$\frac{x}{x+4} = \frac{2}{5}$$

If a student had only a surface-level understanding of cross multiplying or setting up a proportion, however, he or she might set up and solve it exactly as he or she would the previous problem: $\frac{x}{4} = \frac{2}{5}$. We learn little about students' thinking from the first version of this problem. We learn a little more from the second.

A quality task ought to pave the way for the content to be used on a deep level, potentially from multiple angles, so it sticks. Consider the following task, which draws upon both a similar context and the same content standards as our Rick-Arthur problem.

From the Illustrative Mathematics website

Track and Field

Angel and Jayden were at track practice. The track is $\frac{2}{5}$ kilometers around.

Angela ran 1 lap in 2 minutes.

Jayden ran 3 laps in 5 minutes.

Who is running faster? Explain your reasoning.

This task enables students to engage with the concept of ratio and proportion on a deep level. They will have to identify both runners' speeds based on varying intervals (one lap in two minutes versus three laps in five). A student may choose to organize his or her information in a table (Figure 4.9).

Angela

Lap	Minutes
1	2
2	4
3	6

Jayden

Lap	Minutes
1	1.667
2	3.33
3	5

FIGURE 4.9 Students may organize their information in a table.

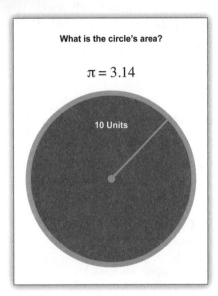

FIGURE 4.10 A rather rote problem about the area of a circle

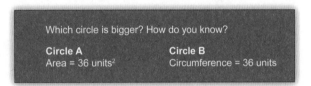

FIGURE 4.11 A slightly more complex problem compares the sizes of two circles given different dimensions.

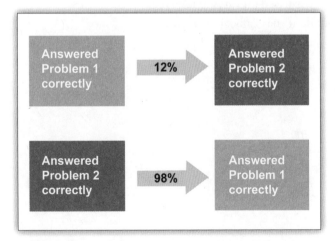

FIGURE 4.12 Answering Problem 1 correctly was uncorrelated with answering Problem 2 correctly. But answering Problem 2 correctly almost certainly resulted in answering Problem 1 correctly.

Two tasks that ostensibly "cover" the same concept can yield drastic differences in student understanding. Robert Kaplinsky is a math instructional specialist in California who has researched students' depth of understanding based on various tasks. For example, he gave 396 seventh graders the task shown in Figure 4.10, asking for the area of a circle given the radius (Kaplinsky 2014).

He found that 79 percent of students were able to answer this problem correctly (in this case "correct" meant the correct answer with a sufficient explanation). Were that the end of it, we might walk away with the assumption that 79 percent of students understand the standard about the radius and area of a circle. However, Robert then gave the same students the problem shown in Figure 4.11. Despite the fact that this task is from the same standard, only 12 percent of students answered this problem correctly with explanation. Robert found that there was little correlation between getting the first problem right and getting the second problem right. But there was a high correlation between getting the second problem right and getting the first problem right. Of the students who were able to answer the *second* problem correctly, 98 percent answered the first problem correctly (Figure 4.12).

When one looks in a textbook or at worksheets, one sees problems much more like the first of the two that Robert assigned. A student may receive an assignment consisting of several of the first type of rote problem—let's call them "surface-level problems," since they only scratch the surface of the content—and perhaps a few of the second type—the "deeper problems." In such a scenario, a teacher may see that a student answered a majority of the problems correctly and assume incorrectly that the student is well steeped in the standard (Figure 4.13). Consider examining the level of content students are engaging with before assuming that a standard has been "covered."

FIGURE 4.13 Assessments with mostly surface-level problems may yield a "false positive" about a student's understanding of a concept.

I encourage you to take stock of the types of tasks students receive in your class. Could a student potentially hide behind a surface level of understanding about a topic? Are there opportunities to highlight misunderstandings of the concept? Are they complex enough to draw distinctions between what students know and what may need to be taught? Are your tasks aligned to the standards in a deep way that portends future success? Although working on a deep mathematical task is satisfying in and of itself, aligning it to standards crucial for students' continued success ensures that our system of math supports students. In Chapter 5, we'll see how we can adapt problems to increase the cognitive demand while opening up access to the problem. In Chapter 8, we'll see a "scoring guide" we can use to assess task quality overall.

5. Quality Tasks Connect and Extend Content

Selecting and aligning tasks that build deep content knowledge is necessary but not sufficient. Students are also well served by tasks that connect and extend to other standards or mathematical disciplines. Sometimes we are reluctant to employ tasks that don't fit neatly into our specific content area. If we are addressing a concept, our thinking goes, then the task should fit neatly and *wholly* within that concept. Any task that includes content from previous units has already been "covered," and any task that includes content from future units is deemed "too advanced." This is unfortunate, because much of the value in mathematics is learning how mathematical ideas connect to one another. Students often see math as a series of disconnected rules and steps to follow. Most curricula reinforce this belief by dividing content distinctly and cauterizing the edges along chapter breaks. This is reinforced by our typical high school progression of math, separating algebra from geometry, trigonometry from probability. It's as if these subjects do not occupy the same universe. Even in "integrated math" courses, the content is typically broken up into isolated bits of knowledge instead of presented as a connected discipline.

Instead, we want to present a universe of mathematics that is interconnected and logical, rather than arbitrary. Employing tasks that connect and extend content helps communicate that message. Tasks that connect content also allow us to revisit crucial content. We often complain that students tend to purge mathematical knowledge the moment it is no longer useful, say, after a unit test. If we continue to use the essential mathematical content for weeks and months after the specific unit, however, students have reason to remember it.

Lastly, such tasks are naturally more complex and challenging than tasks that don't connect to other topics. As an example, consider the following task from Illustrative Mathematics (Figure 4.14).

This problem requires the application of multiple standards from algebra. It draws upon standards of both quadratic and linear equations, perpendicular slopes, and a conceptual understanding of systems of equations. It reinforces perpendicularity while aspiring to hone what an equation truly means (should one attempt to solve it using equations). In short, if students can demonstrate mastery on this problem, I'd be convinced that they are well versed in a whole host of mathematical content areas.

Tasks that involve the coordinate plane are ripe for supplying connected content. Many concepts from geometry can be overlaid with a grid to gain a whole new perspective on a task. Consider the different versions of similar tasks, only employing a coordinate grid, in Figures 4.15–4.18.

TASK

The figure shows graphs of a linear and a quadratic function.

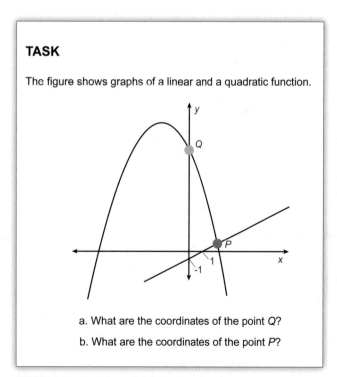

a. What are the coordinates of the point Q?

b. What are the coordinates of the point P?

FIGURE 4.14 A task from Illustrative Mathematics connects systems of equations with quadratics.

Find the area of this parallelogram. Explain how you know.

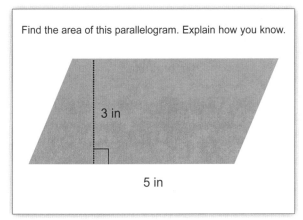

FIGURE 4.15A A problem about the area of a parallelogram

Find the area of this parallelogram. Explain how you know.

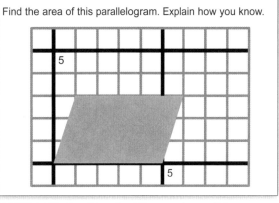

FIGURE 4.15B A problem about the area of a parallelogram mapped onto a Cartesian coordinate plane

Draw the next shape in this sequence.

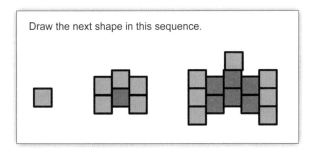

FIGURE 4.16A A pattern problem

If each block is a unit square, what will (X_4Y_4) be?

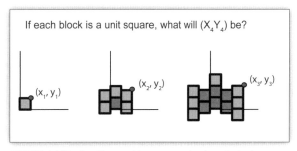

FIGURE 4.16B A pattern problem mapped onto a Cartesian coordinate plane

Draw a rotation of this shape of 90 degree counterclockwise rotation around point R.

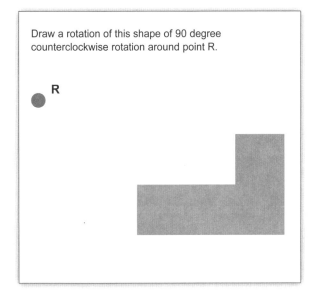

FIGURE 4.17A A rotation problem

Where would point R have to be to achieve the following transformation?

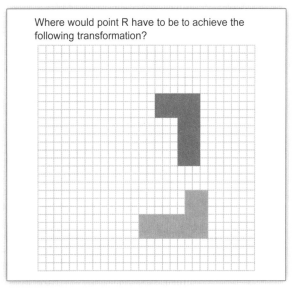

FIGURE 4.17B A rotation problem mapped onto a Cartesian coordinate plane

Prove that $3(x - 5) + (x - 2)^2 = x^2 - x - 11$.

FIGURE 4.18A A problem about proving an equation

Prove that $3(x - 5) + (x - 2)^2 = x^2 - 11$
using a coordinate plane.

FIGURE 4.18B A problem about proving an equation mapped onto a Cartesian coordinate plane

Each of these tasks connect algebra to geometry and/or visuals, allowing students to use visual methods toward solutions as well as algebraic ones.

We often overestimate what students know about prior content and underestimate what they can do with content yet to be taught. It is important to periodically use tasks that go beyond the current topic in the scope and sequence and to connect it with other content.

Moving Beyond the False Choice of Real-World Versus Abstract Math

One trope that math teachers grapple with is the alleged dichotomy between "real-world" and abstract tasks.

Curriculum designers often attempt to tailor their mathematics to supposed student interest. Kids like sports? Let's be sure to model the trajectory of a field goal with a parabola. Kids are into movies? We can design a task involving box-office profits. To be sure, these attempts can sometimes work and work well, like they did in Jessica's football problem. Janice—a ninth-grade student—is describing what she'd like to do more of in math class. "I like it best when we're doing something that is real world. That way I can visualize and understand it better. I get lost when it's all numbers and letters and I don't have anything I can connect it to." Teachers of math in elementary school have long understood the value of turning math into something concrete and attainable: counting the number of pencils, dividing the amount of candy among classmates, and so forth. Secondary teachers often find real value in linking a standard to a context with which students are familiar: modeling projectiles with a parabola or the rotation of a Ferris wheel to model periodic equations.

But then there's Ty, also a ninth grader: "I prefer when we're doing things that seem like puzzles or number games. I guess I like *pure* mathematics, as long as it's interesting." Apparently sometimes purely abstract puzzles, or even the pure content, can be engaging for students.

We seem to be at an impasse, but we're not. Although it sounds like Janice and Ty are in disagreement, the common theme I hear is that they're looking for tasks that are *interesting*. As much as Ty enjoys abstract puzzles and Janice prefers real-world tasks, each admits that there are boring versions of both. Too, this seemingly at-odds take on mathematics as a discipline is an accurate representation of the inherent tension that mathematicians experience. In a 2017 interview with *Numberphile*, French mathematician Cédric Villani discussed that tension:

> There has to be some useful and some useless. Sometimes the useful becomes useless, sometimes the useless will become useful. There has to be room for all kinds of mathematicians and it's a big illusion to think that there is a real recipe. . . . You know you have to allow some uncertainty in the system. If you try to predict, you lose the most interesting parts. (Haran 2017)

When teachers plant a flag in either camp (real-world or abstract), they end up harming both. Real-world tasks can be unengaging; abstract problems teachers are interested in may not be interesting to students. It's not feasible or preferable to orient one's entire curriculum in either realm. Instead, as we draw upon the best from both realms, we can identify the tasks that adhere to as many of our hallmarks for quality as possible. Let's get beyond the false choice of real-world versus abstract and acknowledge we need both to represent authentic mathematical work. In Chapter 8, we'll see a quick scoring guide that will help us identify quality tasks, and in Appendix D is a quick checklist to check for quality.

In this next chapter, we will examine models of quality tasks that have been developed by teachers, as well as identify how to design, find, and adapt tasks for your classroom.

REVIEW

- Quality tasks set other parts of our pedagogy in motion.

- Quality tasks spark curiosity and foster engagement. To assess and refine engagement, look to these design principles:

  - Consider your own curiosity.

  - Elicit student-generated questions.

  - Require just-out-of-reach information or know-how.

  - Solicit predictions.

  - Break expectations.

- Quality tasks yield creativity.

  - Tasks with creative components better represent the discipline of math and the work of mathematicians.

  - Student-generated artifacts can be aggregated and synthesized to elucidate mathematical truths.

- Quality tasks promote access from all students in the classroom.

  - Accessibility is essential to communicating that all students are capable mathematicians.

- Accessible tasks are clear and understood by each and every student in the classroom.

- Accessible tasks are challenging.

- Accessible tasks are particularly necessary for special populations of students.

- Quality tasks require and convey deep, crucial mathematical content.

  - Tasks are well aligned to content standards.

  - Tasks require a deep, conceptual understanding of the content.

- Quality tasks connect and extend content.

  - Employ tasks that communicate and demonstrate the connectedness of math.

- Debates over real-world versus abstract tasks are a red herring. Students ought to be provided with both, assuming they're of high quality.

Task Models and Designing, Finding, and Adapting Tasks

How many slams in an old
screen door?
    Depends how loud you shut it.
How many slices of bread?
    Depends how thin you cut it.

—Shel Silverstein,
"How Many, How Much"

Now that we know hallmarks of quality tasks, it's time to see
some concrete examples. In this chapter, we'll explore a taxon-
omy of tasks, categorized by the way the tasks are structured
rather than the content they include. Although it's difficult to
pin down a task's type into a rigid category—much in the way
that it's difficult to pin down a single specific content standard
required for a particular task—consider this an attempt to clarify
and illuminate the ever-growing phyla of tasks that are designed
by teachers every day.

Models of Quality Tasks: Ten Essential Task Types

Here are ten types of tasks, some of which are deeply involved, others that can be implemented with minimal preparation. Some of the tasks discussed here take multiple class periods, some are single lessons, and others are mini-lessons that take about fifteen minutes. Some of the tasks are barely tasks at all: they're more accurately referred to as routines, perhaps. These shorter tasks do not require too much prep work, nor do they take up too much class time, but they can still achieve high levels of discourse and cognition. As teachers transition toward more dynamic classrooms, I often recommend these shorter activities to begin laying the groundwork for students to develop their own sense of agency over their learning. For veteran teachers, they make excellent warm-ups to get the day's math talk jump-started.

We'll start with the shorter routines and work our way up to tasks that constitute the entirety of a lesson and potentially several days of class time. Subsequent chapters will address how to select tasks with intentionality and build coherent lessons around them, with an eye toward a yearlong curriculum map. For now, consider these our Ten Essential Task Types. Although they're not intended to be the entirety of a curriculum, they do offer a menu of options to allow for deep understanding across the mathematics curriculum.

Number Talks

In a Number Talk, or Math Talk, students are given an arithmetic or visual counting problem that they work out mentally before sharing their solution method with a partner or the class. The teacher then facilitates the mathematical conversation so students notice similarities, differences, and connections among responses.

Number Talks are often thought of as an elementary school routine. Recently, however, I've seen middle school and high school teachers use Number Talks with great success. *Making Number Talks Matter: Developing Mathematical Practices and Deepening Understanding, Grades 4–10*, by Cathy Humphreys and Ruth Parker, is an excellent resource for secondary teachers looking to add Number Talks into their practice (2015). Let's look at an example Number Talk, from Theresa's Integrated Math 9 class.

It's near the beginning of the class period. The bell just rang and students are getting situated. Theresa displays the following prompt on the screen at the front of the class:

What's 60 percent of 40?

Theresa sets a timer on her phone for two minutes and asks students to calculate the solution silently and mentally. During this time, the entire class is silent, yet fully engaged. Students squint, scratch their chins, and sometimes trace imaginary numbers in the air with their fingers while they do mental math.

I see this everywhere I go: students are silent and intensely focused during mental math. Perhaps the novelty makes it inherently interesting. Maybe having two minutes of academic silence is a nice respite from the stressors of an adolescent's day. Whatever the reason, the mental math portion of a Number Talk offers high cognitive demand for students, and they meet it.

After the two minutes, Theresa asks for student solutions and—just as important—how they got them.

One student responds, "I know that 10 percent of forty is four. So 60 percent has to be four times six. So it's twenty-four."

Theresa translates the student's verbal response into mathematical notation on the whiteboard at the front of the class:

$$(10\% \times 40) = 4$$

$$60\% = 10\% \times 6$$

$$4 \times 6 = 24$$

Another student offers his take on the problem: "I also got twenty-four. Fifty percent of forty is twenty. And you need an extra 10 percent, which is a fifth of the way from 50 percent to 100 percent. So a fifth of twenty is four. Twenty plus four is twenty-four." I could see Theresa working it out in her head as she was transcribing this response on the board. She makes an audible "huh" as she nods and tells the class that she hadn't thought of that method before. Theresa solicits a couple more solution methods, illustrating the connections between the methods, before thanking each student.

After the lesson, I ask Theresa what value she finds in doing arithmetic Number Talks with her class of algebra students.

"There are a couple of things I value about it. First, there's the direct math. Even in a class of algebra students, let's be honest: they're not too keen on mental math or arithmetic. There's actually value in having students practice arithmetic in a way that's not just a list of remediation problems.

"The other thing that I like about it is that it helps us practice talking about math generally. Although it's tough to draw a direct line, I certainly find a through-line between the Number Talks we have regularly and the conversation that occurs while students are working on a more complex problem or in groups. We're building those muscles—not only the mathematical knowledge muscles, but the ones that allow students to communicate ideas with one another."

Number Talks also work well with visual patterns. Different students see the progression of a pattern differently. I was in a classroom recently where the teacher provided the following pattern (Figure 5.1).

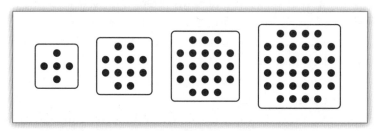

FIGURE 5.1 Pattern for an image-based Number Talk

The teacher asked her students (1) how the pattern was growing, and (2) how they *saw* it growing. One student saw the pattern as an inside box that was growing by one "length and width" dot, plus four additional sides (Figure 5.2).

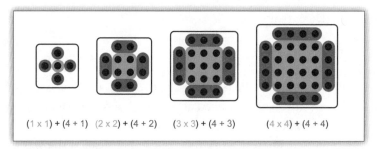

(1 x 1) + (4 + 1)   (2 x 2) + (4 + 2)   (3 x 3) + (4 + 3)   (4 x 4) + (4 + 4)

FIGURE 5.2 Some mathematicians saw the pattern growing according to an inside square and sides.

Another student saw it as outside boxes with their corners sliced off (Figure 5.3).

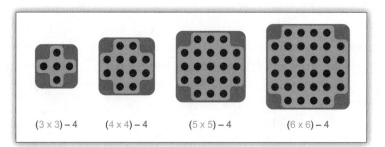

(3 x 3) – 4   (4 x 4) – 4   (5 x 5) – 4   (6 x 6) – 4

FIGURE 5.3 Other mathematicians saw the pattern as a larger square with the corners missing.

Yet another student saw it as columns growing by count and by size, with smaller columns on the edges. Students were not only sharing how they saw the pattern changing but yearning to see how their classmates saw it. Eventually, the conversation turned to algebraic expressions. And wouldn't you know it: regardless of how students saw the pattern growing, their expressions were equivalent, even if they didn't look like it at first. The expression from the first student looked like this:

$$n^2 + 4n$$

whereas the expression from the second student looked like this:

$$(n + 2)^2 = 4$$

With a bit of algebraic manipulation, students were delighted to find that the expressions were equivalent. And sure enough, they began to test one another's ways of seeing and associated expressions. Better yet, the whole thing felt organic. The teacher posed the task, and the students jumped on the various ways of seeing.

Number Talks have a way of doing that.

Fawn Nguyen has compiled hundreds of visual patterns that you may wish to draw from at www.visualpatterns.org.

Estimation

A few times a week, Brett begins his class by showing a picture on the screen in the front of his room. On this particular day, he's displaying a picture of a large jar of cheese balls (Figure 5.4). "How many cheese balls are in this container?" he asks. His students begin conferring, making silent counting gestures with their hands, and squinting to get a better look. "Once you have a best estimate, I'd like you to also tell me an answer that you know for sure is too low and another that is too high." Students have a piece of paper in front of them with space for those three potential estimations: a best estimate, a "too low," and a "too high." After a minute of chatter, counting, and squinting, students jot down those three numbers.

FIGURE 5.4 Estimation task: How many cheese balls are in the container? (From Estimation180.com)

At this point, Brett asks for some best estimates and starts writing them on the board. He does the same with the "too lows" and the "too highs." Soon enough, Brett reveals the true number—629 cheese balls—and his students make note of it in their math journals. I glance into students' journals and see rows of previous estimation activities, along with columns for their best estimate, the actual number, and the percent by which they were off. One student shares with me, "I was way off today, but you can see that I think I'm getting better with time, more or less."

Brett pulled the image of cheese balls from a website created and maintained by digital learning coach Andrew Stadel: Estimation180.com. Andrew has done yeoman's work of capturing and organizing more than 200 images and videos that incorporate estimation to help students build number sense. These images and videos are wide in their scope, involving the estimation of volume, distance, population, time, and so on. Andrew has also created a student handout to aid the discussion, which you can find on his website.

Brett uses estimation activities in his class often, for multiple reasons: "For one, it warms up kids' brains, gets them ready for the day's lesson. But it's also great to build their number sense. Since I started using estimation regularly as part of our warm-ups—and sometimes even as the central point of our lessons—I've seen students check their answer to see if it makes sense. And I've seen students slowing down to think about what a reasonable solution might be *before* they start working on the problem."

Estimation tasks can take as little as five minutes to prepare and five to ten minutes to facilitate. With every one of us having a camera on us at all times via our phones, everything we see has the potential to be part of our estimation curriculum: the height of a building downtown, the wingspan of a plane, the number of people at a baseball game. In Chapter 4 we learned that having students estimate before problem solving increased engagement (Lowenstein 1994). Incorporating daily estimation yields engagement and boosts number sense while honoring students' agency over their mathematical ideas.

Always/Sometimes/Never

In this type of task, students are asked to classify a statement as "always true," "sometimes true," or "never true." Theresa likes to provide these statements on small strips of paper so students can organize them into columns on a chart.

Always	Sometimes	Never

Although eventually the statements are intended to be mathematical in nature, Theresa likes to start off the activity with some more familiar statements.

It is cold in the winter.

Bigger cars use more gas.

Dogs are bigger than cats.

The earth orbits around the sun.

Theresa soon adds statements that are more explicitly mathematical:

A circle with a bigger radius will have a bigger area.

A rectangle with a larger perimeter will have a larger area.

The sum of the interior angles of a quadrilateral is 360 degrees.

As I watch students work through this activity, I'm struck by a couple of things. First, students are quick to grab a sheet of scratch paper and begin drawing shapes to test their hypotheses. Although examples and counterexamples are not specifically called or asked for, students in Theresa's class are quick to begin the process of drawing shapes that adhere to or refute the statement.

The other thing that is remarkable is how much content is visited in the span of perhaps twenty-five to thirty minutes. In this short period of time students have discussed topics from nearly the entire year of geometry.

What's more, Theresa has even managed to sneak a few additional statements in:

$2x$ is greater than $x + 2$.

$y + 3$ is less than $y + 5$.

Prime numbers are always odd.

Despite this being a geometry class, students are reviewing and discussing topics from algebra and even discrete mathematics.

Always/Sometimes/Never has a unique structure that invites access. At the very least, and perhaps also at the very most, a student can toss a statement into one of the categories and start testing it out. Without realizing it at first, students will be mimicking the work of a mathematician: making conjectures and testing hypotheses. You can design Always/Sometimes/Never by searching through your textbook's mathematical postulates and theorems. There are also several statements from multiple different content areas in the Task Libraries at the back of this book.

Which One Doesn't Belong?

In this routine, teachers post or project a group of four objects, numbers, or elements (Figure 5.5). Students are asked to identify the one that doesn't belong with the others, and why. Students are then able to flex their mathematical vocabulary and develop (and break) definitions on their own.

At first, students may look around for the "right answer." As they keep looking, they'll find that every answer is the right answer! As Christopher Danielson, author of *Which One Doesn't Belong? A Teacher's Guide*, put it, "All choices are correct, which shifts the focus to justification. *Which One Doesn't Belong?* isn't about guessing the right answer; it's about expressing mathematical relationships precisely in order to communicate with others" (2016, 3). In Malcolm Swan's 2005 seminal work *Improving Learning in Mathematics: Challenges and Strategies*, he refers to a similar activity called *Odd One Out*.

Theresa facilitates a Which One Doesn't Belong? that shows four different nonlinear functions (Figure 5.6). "Take thirty silent seconds and think about which one you think doesn't belong, and why." After this think time, Theresa continues: "Now turn and talk to your neighbor about which one you chose, and why." Students begin to discuss their choices and rationales, and then naturally move into figuring out at least one reason for every item not to belong. Theresa probably couldn't have prevented them from doing so if she'd tried. In my experience, this shift happens spontaneously with every Which One Doesn't Belong? task: the teacher asks students to find one item that doesn't belong, but students invariably and with great vigor discuss why *all* of them might not belong.

Theresa then proceeds with a class discussion about why each item could be the odd one out. She

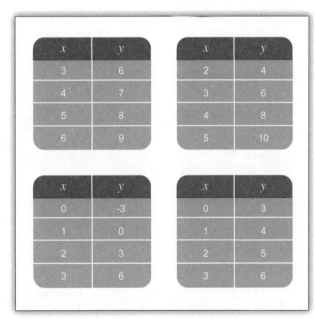

FIGURE 5.5 Which one doesn't belong, and why?

is careful to make sure to get two or three responses for each item:

"I think the bottom left one doesn't belong because it comes to a point."

"I think the top left one doesn't belong because it doesn't cross the *x*-axis at all." A student nearby reminds the class that this means the quadratic doesn't have any—what's that called again?—ah yes, *roots*.

"I think the top right one doesn't belong because it's on the right of the graph."

"I think the bottom right one doesn't belong because it's pointing down."

"I think the top right one doesn't belong because it's the only one entirely within the quadrant."

This final comment leads into an interesting discussion about whether that curve does indeed remain in the quadrant, or if it will eventually cross the *y*-axis.

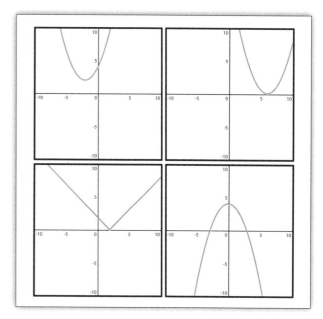

FIGURE 5.6 A Which One Doesn't Belong? task involving various nonlinear functions

Theresa honors each answer, regardless of the level of apparent sophistication in the reasoning. With almost all responses, she probes for precise descriptions. If a student proclaims, "The graph goes down," she is quick to pull that apart with students: "Say more about what it means for a graph to 'go down,'" eventually getting to the crucial concept of slope and where it shows up in an equation.

By engaging in this exercise, students have demonstrated agency in their choice, received academic status via a valued answer, and reinforced crucial vocabulary and concepts. You can design your own or find more, and more about them, in *Which One Doesn't Belong?* (Danielson 2016) and at WODB.ca. There are also some sample secondary-focused Which One Doesn't Belong? tasks in the Task Library in this book.

Polygraph or Guess Who?

One effective mathematical game that produces creativity and discourse is based on the classic children's game *Guess Who?* In the original version, one participant—the picker—chooses a mystery person among many different faces, and the other participant—the guesser—attempts to identify that person based on a series of yes-or-no questions. For example, *Does your mystery person have facial hair? Is your mystery person wearing a hat?* Guessers ask yes-no questions until they can identify the mystery person with certainty. Math teachers have adapted this game for mathematical content, starting with shapes.

Students attempt to identify a mystery shape by asking a series of yes-or-no questions: *Does your shape have right angles? Does your shape have pairs of parallel lines?* and so

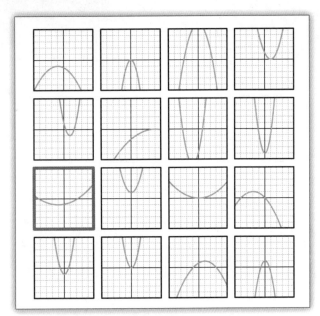

FIGURE 5.7 Students choose one artifact out of several in *Polygraph*. Partners ask yes-or-no questions to decipher which one it is.

forth. The activity can be extended to a multitude of mathematical concepts, including linear equations.

Desmos has codified this game into a series of online activities they dub *Polygraph*. In this version, the picker selects one shape or function out of sixteen options that are randomly arranged on the screen (Figure 5.7). The guesser asks yes-no questions, eliminating possibilities as he or she gathers information, until he or she can accurately identify the picker's mathematical object. Then students switch roles and play again. Desmos has developed free *Polygraph* activities for multiple grade and content levels and has an easy-to-use interface that allows teachers to develop their own sets quickly.

The game is particularly interesting and effective when students have yet to learn formal, mathematical vocabulary. For example, Patrick and Reese are playing a version of *Guess Who?* in which the mathematical "objects" are quadratic equations. Patrick asks if Reese's mystery shape "looks like a U." Later in the game, after they've switched roles, Reese asks Patrick if his quadratic crosses the x-axis twice.

After a few rounds, Leanne is debriefing the game with the class. She identifies a few of the descriptors she overheard students use as she floated around, listening in on conversations and taking notes. She identifies Patrick's question about "looking like a U," and talks about the features that make for a parabola that opens upward. She takes Reese's question about "crossing the x-axis" as an opportunity to discuss roots. In the barest sense, she is delivering a vocabulary lesson, but rather than providing the rote, by-the-book definitions, she is using her students' intuitions and their own informal, everyday words to craft meaningful descriptions of these mathematical concepts.

Card Sorts and Dominoes

Card sorts also encourage discourse. Using physical items such as cards or cutouts, these activities draw upon tactile as well as collaborative learning.

One common activity is to match like objects or models, such as multiple representations of algebraic expressions: equations, data tables, and graphs. Similarly, one could have students match real-world scenarios with graphs that model the given scenarios (Figure 5.8). Students are given a set of these paper cutouts and prompted to match them according to the like representation.

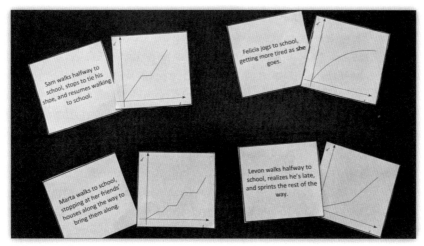

FIGURE 5.8 Card sorts prompt students to match like items. In this instance, students match functions to descriptive scenarios.

Another take on card sorts and matching is the "domino" approach. In this case, the cutouts are carefully structured so that they form a series of linking objects that circles back on itself (Figure 5.9).

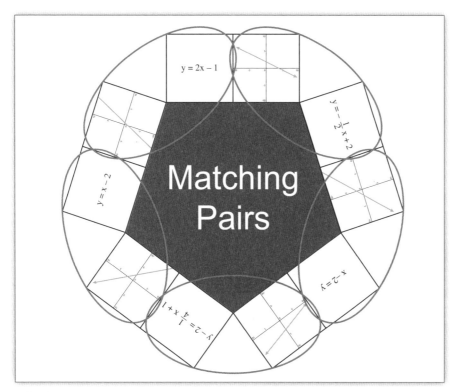

FIGURE 5.9 Dominoes are a variation on card sorts. In these tasks, the like items are on opposite ends of different cards. The object is to link the like items until they form a complete loop.

Although developing dominoes takes a little more intentionality than random jumbling, this approach includes an *in situ* check for student understanding. That is, should the set not link back onto itself, there must be a correctable error in the domino set somewhere. Students will recognize when they're off without teacher intervention.

Admittedly, there's little cognitive difference between a tactile matching activity and a matching exercise on a worksheet. However, in a card sort, the emphasis rests on the conversation among students rather than the conversation between the student and the worksheet. Because students can arrange and rearrange shapes or cards on the table, they naturally refine and test ideas, and talk about them. In this way, card sorts can reinforce our message that errors are welcome learning opportunities. Later in this chapter, we will see how to adapt low-level, preexisting tasks into more meaningful learning experiences in socially safe classrooms. Moving from a matching exercise on a worksheet to a card sort is one such quick adaptation.

One minor drawback of sorting activities is that they require prep from the teacher, whether it's cutting out the objects or organizing them into baggies or envelopes so that each student group has the proper number and type of objects. As a parent, I take advantage of my children's cutting and sorting skills. Before my kids were old enough to cut and sort, I often had a student office aide whom I could ask to perform such routine work. To help streamline the process of creating card sorts, there is a template for matching and domino card sorts in the Task Libraries.

Would You Rather . . .

Would You Rather . . . (WYR) tasks are problems posed such that students must use mathematics to make a decision. For example, see Figure 5.10.

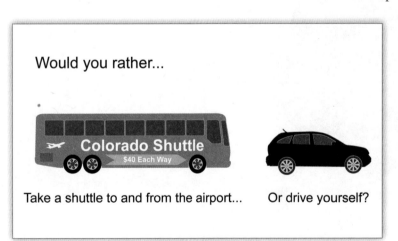

Would you rather...

Colorado Shuttle
$40 Each Way

Take a shuttle to and from the airport...   Or drive yourself?

FIGURE 5.10 In this *Would You Rather . . .* problem, students must use math to determine whether they would like to take a shuttle to the airport or drive and pay for parking.

I'm chatting with a student who likes these tasks. I ask, "What is it about the *Would You Rather . . .* tasks that make them compelling?"

"It really makes the problem about *you*, the student," she said. "You get to make the choice. You have the final say. It's not about 'Billy' or 'Jimmy' or 'Farmer Joe.' It's something I can take ownership of. And it lets me argue. I like to argue."

Something a little subtler is going on as well. I'm watching Theresa's students receive a WYR, and I notice they begin deconstructing the two choices right away. When they look at them side by side, students are able to identify variables such as time, distance, velocity, mass, or cost—even if the units are different—more easily than when they work on a stand-alone problem. Something about comparing two choices helps students come up with equations or diagrams to model the choices. It also feels quite natural for them to make an initial guess at which of the two scenarios is better.

Steve Leinwand (2015) suggests that "'construct viable arguments and critique the reasoning of others' (Standard for Mathematical Practice #3) may be the nine most important words in the entire Common Core." *Would You Rather . . .* tasks specialize in this practice standard. If you're looking to increase mathematical argumentation in your math classes, you can find plenty of WYR prompts at http://www.wyrmath. com/, a free website for teachers hosted by John Stevens, co-author of *The Classroom Chef* and an educational technology coach in California.

Three-Act Math

One lesson format that is gaining traction is that of the *Three-Act Math* task. Developed and defined by Dan Meyer (2011) and built upon by countless educators since, a *Three-Act Math* task is a math problem with a narrative structure. Like in a movie or play, the first act establishes the scenario and creates a narrative conflict or tension. The second act builds the story by establishing crucial elements to the "plot." The third and final act resolves the conflict by showing the resolution to the scenario (Figure 5.11).

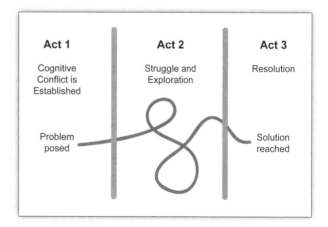

FIGURE 5.11 Three acts of a mathematical task: conflict, struggle and exploration, and resolution.

In the opening chapter of this book, we saw how Leanne used this format to generate curiosity and elicit genuine need-to-knows from her students. The initial "act"—two students heading toward Jack in the Box from different starting points and at different speeds—initiated the cognitive conflict. In the second act, students worked toward a solution, often through multiple approaches, sometimes with Leanne intervening at crucial moments. In the third act, students came to a solution and presented their methods, demonstrating which student arrived at the destination first, and why.

Three-Act Math tasks align well with our triad of elements of math instruction. In fact, the *Three-Act* framework may help us understand it. Consider how this framework can develop an environment of social and emotional safety. In a good act 1, all students are engaged and can access the task via questions, estimations, or need-to-knows. In act 2, students may work together in groups or pairs so that they may all contribute using their particular mathematical strengths. The teacher can provide as-needed instruction or workshops (Chapter 7). In act 3, students share their solution methods, which the teacher and peers may celebrate by pointing out their particular mathematical brilliance.

Act 1 of a *Three-Act* task could be nearly anything: a clip from a movie, a picture, a statement of fact. Anything that draws mathematical interest has the potential to be an opening act. Peter is a teacher in Napa, California, who took a clip from the slapstick comedy *Hot Rod* in which the daredevil protagonist attempts to jump his motorcycle over several dozen school buses. As the tension in the scene rises—will he make it or not?—Peter pauses the video and asks his students to begin developing the question and identifying additional information they may need to deduce the solution. In act 2, he has students pause the video at various moments to plot the daredevil's flight path. After students develop a mathe-

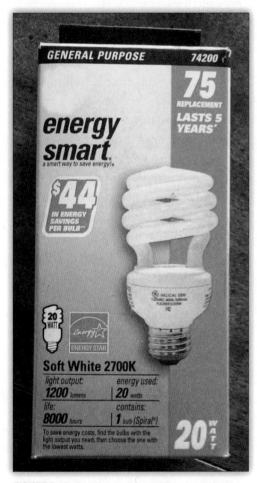

matical model (in this case, creating a quadratic function based on three points on a coordinate place) and share their methods (Chapter 7), Peter plays act 3, the conclusion of the clip. The daredevil indeed makes it to the other side . . . but with a sidesplitting crash typical of Andy Samberg farcical comedies. The lesson plan for this task—Hot Rod Quadratics—is in Appendix G.

Problem-Based Learning

Brett is teaching a lesson on how to solve a system of equations, although the word *lesson* doesn't feel entirely appropriate. He begins the class by showing students a picture of the box of an energy-efficient light bulb (Figure 5.12).

He asks students what they notice about the box. He makes sure to note every response on the board, no matter how seemingly significant or insignificant. He writes one particular

FIGURE 5.12 Brett begins his problem-based lesson by asking students to examine the claims on an energy-efficient light bulb.

response—one about the claim of forty-four dollars' worth of energy savings over the life span of the light bulb—a little off to the side. After gathering a few more "noticings" he launches students into the problem. He posts the following and asks them to read it:

> This is a picture of an energy-efficient, 20-watt light bulb. It produces the same amount of light as a 75-watt incandescent bulb. So it should save us money in the long run, right? But unfortunately, it costs a lot more: $12.00 compared with its incandescent cousin at about $1.00.

At this point, he asks what questions students have about this scenario. The two questions that crop up are

1. *How long before we start saving money with the energy-efficient light bulb?*

2. *Will it* really *generate forty-four dollars' worth of savings?*

These are the problems Brett's students will now solve. He elicits a bit more information—enough to ensure students can get started on the problem. He makes sure that every group of students knows what to do for their immediate next step: create a model of energy costs yielded by (1) this energy-efficient light bulb, and (2) "its incandescent cousin."

Students begin creating the model using the information they've accumulated. The two concerns for each light bulb are

1. the initial cost of the light bulb, and

2. the ongoing energy usage and associated cost used by each light bulb.

At this point in the year in Brett's algebra class, his students can create equations when given a scenario. Once they do, they begin graphing the two equations on graph paper: one for the energy-efficient light bulb and one for the cheaper but energy-hogging light bulb. The students are humming along through the problem until this point. They've created their models. They've graphed their equations. But now they need to identify when the energy-efficient light bulb becomes the more cost-effective option: when exactly do the two lines intersect (Figure 5.13)? Several students have their hands raised with that very question: *How do we figure out where these lines meet?*

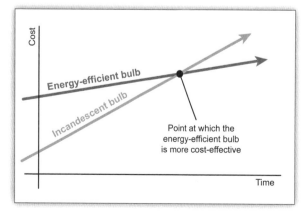

FIGURE 5.13 The light bulb task necessitates knowing how to find the solution of a system of equations.

At this point Brett calls a "problem time-out" and gives the students a lesson on how to find the intersection of two lines by solving a system of equations. More specifically, he demonstrates how to find the solution of a system of equations via substitution. He provides the vocabulary for what they're doing (*system of equations, coordinate solution*), works an example system-of-equations problem, has students do a couple of examples, and then turns them back to the energy-efficiency problem for completion.

The instructional part of the day's activities was similar to a more-or-less typical lesson. Brett introduced the topic, did some examples, and had students do a couple of examples. What was different was that students had a real *need* for this instruction—I'd even go so far as to say a *desire* for the instruction (Harel 2013). Students also had some context for why they were learning and using this technique. They were learning how to solve a system of equations, not because it happened to be assigned that day in a particular section of the book, but because it was necessary to solve the problem at hand.

Problem-based learning is a lesson model in which students are given a problem *before* the instruction on the germane content occurs. For example, in Brett's *Energy Efficiency* problem above, we see students solving an initial portion of the problem: they are able to identify key variables and construct a graph with two equations. What students haven't learned yet is how to find the intersection of those two lines. The new content learning in this case (identifying the solution to this system of equations) is necessitated by the task at hand.

In most classrooms and in most lessons, teachers give the solution method before providing a sufficient need or desire for the method. Typically, a lesson in a secondary classroom starts with a lesson on how to do X—say, find the distance between two points on a coordinate planc. In the lesson, the teacher may begin with a plenary discussion or a few probing questions, but the how-to portion of the lesson tends to come quickly and toward the beginning. The instruction is then followed by some practice problems.

Problem-based learning flips this sequence around (Figure 5.14): the problem is launched first, followed by student work time. When students come to a part of the problem they can't solve with their current know-how, they ask, *How do we do X in order to solve the problem?* Students ask for instruction, which teachers provide.

Research suggests that students retain content better when given the opportunity to struggle with a task before the teacher demonstrates methods by which to find a solution (Schwartz and Bransford 1998). When students grapple with the

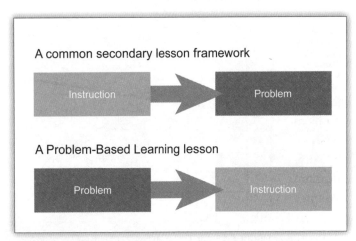

FIGURE 5.14 Problem-based lessons put the problem first and then incorporate the content.

problem first, they get engaged, generate ideas, and develop a need for new mathematical ideas (Harel 2013). Students can affix their understanding of the lesson to a concrete problem, rather than seeing it as just another set of rules and steps to follow for seemingly no reason.

Problem-based learning, and problem solving in general, is given additional treatment in subsequent chapters because it aligns particularly well with all the elements in our ecosystem.

Project-Based Learning

Similar to problem-based learning, project-based learning ties the content learning to a real-world context by providing the challenge that makes the math content necessary. The key differences between the two are the length of time required and the level of authenticity.

Christine is a geometry teacher at Ridgeland High School. As she is kicking off her unit on trigonometry identities, she provides students with the following letter:

Dear Ridgeland Students,

As you know, our school buildings were reconstructed and remodeled five years ago. As the principal of Ridgeland High School, I strive to ensure that our school buildings are healthy, safe, and secure physical environments for learning. The administrative team does this by continuously creating effective learning spaces and improving the function of our school.

As I plan for retirement, I hope to ensure that all students can access the wonderful opportunities our school provides. In my effort to improve our space and make it functional for all students, I am conducting research into the wheelchair accessibility at Ridgeland. And I need your help!

In pairs, please research any legislation with which we may need to comply when supporting disabled students. Based on your research, then determine if our school's wheelchair ramps are appropriate and compliant. Please individually prepare a formal report organizing your findings for review by Ms. Christine and our administrative team. Your work will help us inform how we use our funds to best maintain and further update the Ridgeland High School buildings.

Sincerely,
Principal Donna, Ridgeland High School

Christine instructs her students as follows:

1. First, just read through the letter start to finish.

2. Read the letter again, highlighting any information that might be useful. Underline any information or words that you have a question about.

3. Share with your neighbor what you highlighted and underlined.

After this process, Christine brings the discussion to the entire class. Soon enough, she and the class have generated lists of information students know about the project, what students need to know or research to determine the final outcome, and some next steps (Table 5.1).

Know	Need to Know
Principal Donna wants us to see if our school ramps are compliant with regulations.	What are the regulations that make ramps compliant? What regulations are there?
	What are the measurements of our schools' ramps?
We have to prepare a formal report.	How do we know if the ramps are compliant with regulations?
	What do we need to include in our formal report?
We are working in pairs.	

Next Steps
• Research: What makes wheelchair ramps compliant?
• Measure: our school wheelchair ramps—take pictures!

TABLE 5.1

Christine lets students get to work based on the next steps they've identified. Some students jump onto the nearest laptop and begin researching what makes a wheelchair ramp compliant with local and federal regulations, while others begin inspecting the wheelchair ramps around the school to determine the steepness.

The researchers quickly discover that, according to the Americans with Disabilities Act (ADA), wheelchair ramps need to have a steepness of no more than $\frac{1}{12}$. Meanwhile, the rest of the students are using rulers and tape measures to determine the height and hypotenuse of the wheelchair ramps at the school.

Once this information has been collected, Christine has students revisit the Know/Need-to-Know list they made earlier (Table 5.2).

Need to Know

What are the regulations that make ramps compliant? What regulations are there?

A: A slope less than $\frac{1}{12}$.

What are the measurements of our schools' ramps?

Ramp 1: Measurements

Ramp 2: Measurements

How do we know if the ramps are compliant with regulations?

What do we need to include in our formal report?

TABLE 5.2

After some conversation, it becomes clear that to solve the problem, students need to be able to derive unknown angles of a right triangle, given any two side lengths (Figure 5.15).

At this point, Christine leads the entire class in a lesson on inverse trigonometry: how to use inverse sine, inverse cosine, and inverse tangent to find an unknown angle, given any two sides of a right triangle. She has students solve a few practice problems before reminding

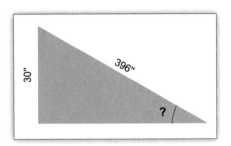

FIGURE 5.15 Student diagram of the school's wheelchair ramps

them of their project and report. Armed with the knowledge of inverse trigonometry, students are now ready to tackle the rest of the project and determine whether the wheelchair ramps at their school are ADA compliant.

Project-based learning is at its best when it imparts real-world and meaningful value to the mathematical work students are undertaking. One of Christine's students said, "I have never, *never* used math like that before. It's really the first time I've used math *in* the real world, except for, like, counting change."

I've seen students analyze survey data to make changes in their school and community. In one classroom, students worked with a horticulturalist to plan and build a sustainable garden, using geometric techniques along the way. In another, students used coordinate geometry and traffic maps to plan a light rail system for a city, which was then proposed to a city planner. Through these experiences, students are learning crucial content knowledge while feeling a sense of self-worth about their work.

One of the challenges of project-based learning is that, in addition to the project students are undertaking, they must engage deeply with mathematical content daily. Teachers sometimes report that it can be difficult to plan a project that takes, say, two weeks of class time and ensure that all mathematical standards are met while students are designing presentations and such. Still, the benefits of a unit of math instruction that ascribes agency and influence to math students make the once- or twice-a-year experience potentially valuable and long lasting.

Task Types and Quality Hallmarks

Although the ten models of tasks we've just explored don't make up an exhaustive list, they do include the task types I see regularly in effective math classes. As you develop in your practice, you'll build your own repertoire of task types and specific tasks that suit you and push your students' understanding.

These ten task types align with various hallmarks of quality tasks, shown in Table 5.3. Consider this table a road map showing what each task type is capable of.

	Initiate curiosity and foster engagement	Yield creativity and lead to new ideas	Promote access for all students in the classroom	Require and convey deep, crucial mathematical content	Connect and extend content
Three-Act Math	▲		▲	▲	▲
Project-Based Learning	▲	▲	▲	▲	▲
Problem-Based Learning	▲	▲	▲	▲	▲
Would You Rather . . .	▲		▲	▲	▲
Polygraph or Guess Who?	▲	▲	▲		
Card Sorts and Dominoes	▲		▲		▲
Which One Doesn't Belong?	▲	▲	▲		
Estimation	▲		▲		
Number Talks		▲	▲		▲
Always/Sometimes/Never		▲	▲	▲	▲

TABLE 5.3

Now that we have a sense of what quality tasks *are* and what task models are available to us, we can set about the difficult work of designing tasks. Let's explore the choices at our disposal: creating, finding, or adapting tasks.

Creating a Task

There are two approaches when it comes to creating a task from scratch: a teacher can start with either the standard or the scenario.

Starting with the Standard

Starting with the standard involves examining the crucial mathematical content for which we're designing the task. Throughout this chapter, we've examined several task types, which gives us a menu of options for creating tasks of our own. Especially given how strapped we are for time, working from models makes task creation easier and much more efficient than starting from scratch.

For this reason, I've included a section in the Task Libraries (pages 300-301) that shows which tasks align particularly well with specific Common Core content clusters and Standards of Mathematical Practice. Please consider it a starting point rather than the final say: complex tasks can address multiple content areas and most or all of the practice standards. When you and your colleagues sit down to design a task to meet a specific content or practice standard, use this table to get going, but add to it as you work. Personalizing your chart will help you find the task formats that are the most natural fit for your current mathematical and pedagogical goals.

Starting with the Scenario

Once you've experienced complex tasks and the richness they can bring into a math classroom, you'll start to develop a math-task radar of sorts. "I'm always on the lookout for something that could be a math problem," Brett begins. "It could be something in the news, an ad from a magazine, a picture I take with my phone while I'm out and about. And I think, 'That's an interesting math problem.'"

Recently, I was in Boulder, Colorado, with my family. We came across a monument dedicated to the Big Thompson Flood of 1976, showing how high floodwaters rose. In addition, it had markers for a 50-year flood, 100-year flood, and 500-year flood. That is, every 50 years we could expect a flood whose floodwaters reach so high, every 100 years, every 500 years, and so on. The marker for the Big Thompson Flood exceeded the 500-year marker by several feet, suggesting it was more catastrophic than we could expect every half millennium (Figure 5.16).

I got to wondering, "How rare was the Big Thompson Flood based on this monument? Was this a 1,000-year flood? A 10,000-year flood? Do floodwater projections rise linearly or exponentially?" Thankfully, my phone had enough charge for me to start snapping photographic evidence, along with the only unit of measurement I had on me at the time: my son (Figure 5.17).

Our little family excursion to the river than runs through the town of Boulder yielded an unexpected problem-based math—and weather—lesson. As mobile devices garner more memory and better picture and video quality, it's possible to be in task-collection mode at all times, a blessing and a curse, perhaps.

FIGURE 5.16 Monument for the Big Thompson Flood. Note the markers for the various years.

FIGURE 5.17 The only unit of measurement I had on me: my four-foot, five-inch son.

Recognizing an interesting mathematical scenario is nearly impossible to plan for, yet it is a learned skill that can improve over time. Just as bird-watchers grow more aware of the avian life in their community, so too can math teachers become more attuned to the interesting math that they experience in their daily lives.

Finding a Task

There's great news and rough news when it comes to finding quality math tasks in the twenty-first century. The good news is that there have never been more math tasks freely available online. The bad news is that there have never been more math tasks freely available online. Even teachers who are fastidious about keeping up with the latest research journals and going online to collect resources find it difficult to keep up with the ever-growing litany of tasks and lessons. Teachers new to the profession or new to the idea of going online to find a lesson or mathematical task get overwhelmed quickly. Not only are there countless resources from teachers, curriculum designers, nonprofits, and math advocates, but there is no way to gauge them for quality. Teachers have to develop discerning taste.

So how does one find the "good stuff"? "I think of it as concentric circles," Theresa tells me. "You start with a few resources that you really like. For me it was Dan Meyer's *Three-Act* tasks, *Illustrative Mathematics*, and NCTM's *Illuminations*. I would always start in those three places. Eventually one of those resources would link to something else. Like, NCTM's *Illuminations* linked to a blog from [Southern California teacher] Fawn Nguyen and her Hotel Snap task. I was like, 'Well, this is awesome,' so I subscribed to Fawn's blog. Then I'd see her point out someone else to follow. And so on. Now I have my go-to resources that I can count on, and they're usually really good."

Many of the task models you've seen in this chapter have a freely available online repository for tasks of that type. For instance, you can find many libraries of teachers' own *Three-Act* tasks. There are websites specifically devoted to image-based *Number Talks*. *Which One Doesn't Belong?* has two companion websites. And it's always growing. Chances are that by the time you read this, there will be an additional cache of a task type that wasn't included in this book. The potential is tremendous: never before have teachers in New Mexico been able to collaborate and share lesson ideas with teachers in Massachusetts so easily. Teachers are no longer bound to their state-provided, state-mandated textbooks to find quality tasks.

Understanding that attempting to publish an up-to-date list of online repositories of quality tasks is quixotic, I've flagged a few of my favorite resources and websites in Table 5.4, knowing full well it is both incomplete and will be out of date by the time you finish this sentence.

Task Type	Where to Find
Number Talks	ntimages.weebly.com www.mathtalks.net/
Estimation	Estimation180.com
Always/Sometimes/Never	Your textbook (specifically identities and conjectures) map.mathshell.org
Which One Doesn't Belong?	WODB.ca
Polygraph or Guess Who?	teacher.desmos.com/polygraph
Card Sorts and Dominoes	map.mathshell.org Problem sets (from, say, your textbook)
Would You Rather . . .	wyrmath.com
Three-Act Math	Dan Meyer: http://blog.mrmeyer.com/category/3acts/ Dane Ehlert: https://whenmathhappens.com/3-act-math/ Graham Fletcher: https://gfletchy.com/3-act-lessons/
Problem-Based Learning	Robert Kaplinsky: robertkaplinsky.com Open Middle: openmiddle.com Geoff Krall: emergentmath.com Julie Reubach: https://ispeakmath.org Fawn Nguyen: http://fawnnguyen.com
Project-Based Learning	Buck Institute for Education: bie.org New Tech Network: www.newtechnetwork.org

TABLE 5.4

Adapting Existing Tasks

It can be difficult and time consuming to design tasks from scratch. It's rare for the inspiration to hit teachers when they have the time and space to fully develop it. It can also be difficult to know ahead of time whether the task focuses on the crucial mathematical content you wish to teach.

For these reasons, using the tasks provided by a textbook or curriculum resource can be a good starting point. Although many of the tasks presented in a textbook might be rote or low level, many offer kernels that can be developed into richer tasks. These adaptations can make for quick work, if you have a repertoire of strategies that boost engagement and cognitive demand:

▲ Start with the answer.

▲ Remove the steps and sub-problems.

▲ Make the problem one of optimization.

▲ Choose your own problem.

▲ Blur or withhold critical information.

▲ Move from application problems to authentic experiences.

Start with the Answer

Consider a standard problem in which students are asked to find the area of a trapezoid (Figure 5.18).

The task, as it appears here, is rote and formulaic. It doesn't naturally allow or call for student ingenuity. After all, the area of a trapezoid can be found by plugging given values into the following formula:

$$A = \frac{(b_1 + b_2)\,h}{2}$$

Jessica adapts this task. She provides the following task instead:

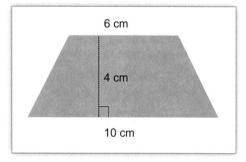

FIGURE 5.18 A rote problem about finding the area of a trapezoid: students are given the dimensions and asked to find the area.

> Draw and give the dimensions of two trapezoids that have an area of 48 cm².

Students begin discussing the task immediately, mostly by throwing out examples for guessing and checking (Figure 5.19).

In this class, students have seen the formula for the area of a trapezoid before; even those who

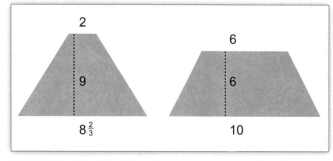

FIGURE 5.19 Potential solutions to our reworked trapezoid problem

don't remember it are able to identify the rote formula, mounted on the wall. They start drawing lengths and widths to make proper trapezoids.

After most groups have completed the task, again mostly via guess-and-check, Jessica asks them to do it again. "Okay, now give me two *more* trapezoids with an area of forty-eight square centimeters." After some initial groaning, students get back at it. However, soon students begin to realize that you can make additional forty-eight-square-centimeter trapezoids by adjusting each of the bases by a centimeter up and down (Figure 5.20).

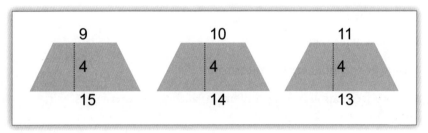

FIGURE 5.20 Additional solutions to our reworked trapezoid problem

Jessica identifies one group that used this technique of moving the bases one unit farther apart and has them draw and label their trapezoids on the board. She asks of the other groups, "What do you notice about what this group did?"

"They changed each side by one," a student says.

"Say more about that. What do you mean 'changed by one'?"

"I mean, they took one side and made it higher by one unit; they took the other side and made it one centimeter less."

"So then how did they calculate it to ensure that it wound up being forty-eight square centimeters? Preston?"

Preston says, "They added each length, divided by two, and multiplied by the height."

Exuberant, Jessica nearly jumps onto a desk: "Say that first part again!"

Preston looks puzzled. "Add each length and divide by two?"

"What do we call that: adding two numbers and then dividing by two?" Jessica looks excited, presumably because she knows her students are about to realize something important.

A child in the back raises his hand. "You're taking the average of the sides," he offers.

"Right! And where does that show up in the formula?" From here, students begin making that "aha" sound and pointing out that the part in the formula where you divide the whole thing by two is actually an artifact of taking the *average* of the sides before multiplying by the height.

"Miss, this is just like the formula for a rectangle!"

At this point, Jessica illustrates that yes, indeed: the area of a trapezoid is a generalized version of the area of a rectangle. Or rather, the area for a rectangle is a specific application of the area of a trapezoid, where the average of the sides of a rectangle is the actual length of the sides of a rectangle (Figure 5.21). Similarly, the area of a triangle can be considered a specific application of the area of a trapezoid. The students feel like they discovered something important, because they have.

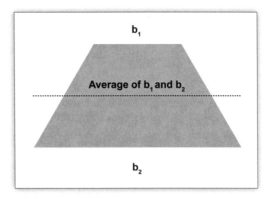

FIGURE 5.21 Students discover that the area of a trapezoid is the average of the base lengths times the height. It's actually quite similar to the area of a rectangle, they find.

Jessica's task is essentially the reverse of a rote, find-the-area task. By starting with the area and providing multiple examples of trapezoids with that area, Jessica's students were able to play around with the shapes on paper and eventually arrive at a discovery, one that will yield a deeper understanding of the formula, and of area formulas in general.

Starting with the answer and working backward is an effective way of transforming a rote, predictable task into one that reveals crucial content and develops conceptual understanding. Consider the difference between these two tasks:

Find the roots of this equation: $f(x) = x^2 + x - 12$	Write two equations that have the roots of $x = 3$ and $x = {}^{-}4$.

The first task yields an answer via rote and uncritical application of, say, the quadratic formula. The second task may take a little extra time but could spark a deep discussion about the meaning of *roots* and the structure of a quadratic. As students generate some of the infinite possibilities, they will apply and practice their creativity while receiving the message that mathematics is a creative discipline.

Remove the Steps and Sub-Problems

Many complex tasks in textbooks leave a trail of bread crumbs ushering the student from one small problem to another. A nonroutine task becomes a series of tiny routine tasks.

Jessica is walking me through a task she adapted from a preexisting problem. "I came across a problem about the sinking of the *Titanic*. I liked it because it included some real-world data and had some really good questions that work well for the probability and statistics standard I was trying to teach. However, I didn't care for the smaller rote questions—it had six or seven sub-questions. Although they were helpful, they kind of got in the way of the conceptual understanding I was trying to build, not to mention my own students' ingenuity."

To Jessica and to her students, the important and interesting question revolved around the survival rates of the various classes of passengers. So, she got right to the point and provided them as her opening salvo, rather than saving them for the end (Figure 5.22). She deleted the sub-steps, but she didn't lose those smaller questions in the process. To answer the question *What class of passengers had the best chances of surviving the sinking of the* Titanic? one must perform the calculations in the sub-steps of the original problem (i.e., *If one of the surviving passengers is randomly selected, what is the probability this passenger was in third class?*).

"I also suspect there's something about the cleanliness of a shorter, more to-the-point prompt," she continues. "The original problem has a lot of 'do this, then this'–type instructions. I hope the one I created is more engaging. There's also a lot more room on the paper for student work."

Surviving the *Titanic*

On April 15, 1912, the *Titanic* struck an iceberg and rapidly sank, with only 710 of her 2,204 passengers and crew surviving. Data on survival of passengers are summarized in the table below.

	Survived	Did Not Survive	Total
First-class passengers	202	123	325
Second-class passengers	118	167	285
Third-class passengers	178	528	706
Total passengers	498	818	1316

What class of passengers had the best chances of surviving the sinking of the *Titanic*? Who had the worst? Support your answer using two methods and showing all relevant work. Then explain what your answer means and the process you used to get there mathematically.

FIGURE 5.22 Jessica's version of the Titanic problem

Jessica will warn you not to discard those small questions entirely. Here is a different problem she adapted using a similar technique. The original problem from her curriculum also uses a real-world scenario, this time about the deforestation of the Amazon rain forest. As before, she removes the sub-questions and gets right to the point: *Given the deforestation tendencies, create a model showing the amount of Amazon rain forest left.*

As students are proceeding through the problem, Jessica floats around the room, examining their progress. As students get stuck, she gives them "hint cards," which are slips of paper containing the sub-questions from the original problem (Figure 5.23).

Some of the students require hints, others don't. Because Jessica removes them from the original problem and has them at the ready, her students have the opportunity to build models on their own, with support as needed, rather than being marched through the modeling by the problem's rote sub-steps.

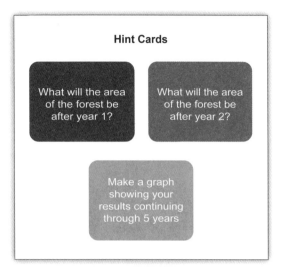

FIGURE 5.23 Hint cards taken directly from the sub-steps of the original problem

Make the Problem One of Optimization

One quick check for task quality—and one potential adaptation—is to include concrete optimization or maximization words such as *most, least, highest, lowest, closest, shortest, longest, fastest, slowest,* and so on. Try to avoid squishy qualifiers such as *best.* Using concrete qualifiers helps facilitate multiple attempts at a problem and sense making.

Similarly, consider tasks that offer a comparison of two or more artifacts. Questions such as *Which is faster? Which traveled farther?* or *Who gets there first?* result in students creating multiple models, enhancing understanding. Giving students two or more things to compare yields concrete understanding of the math at hand.

Choose Your Own Problem

In perhaps the single quickest modification of a rote task, David Coffey, a mathematics education professor at Grand Valley State University, offers a homework hack. He adds two sentences at the beginning and end of a mediocre homework assignment (eighteen computational problems about dividing fractions):

1. Select six of these computations to complete and explain why you selected the ones you did.

2. What would be the last six computations you would choose, and why?

By adding these two instructions, he ascribes agency to his students while inviting them to think conceptually about what makes particular problems "easy" and "hard."

David writes, "I found reading their rationale behind their selections much more interesting than simply checking their answers" (Coffey 2014).

Tim, a teacher in Australia, shared a related *Choose Your Own Problem*. Tim selected four "genres" of problems from his curriculum that cover the same content topic. There was one problem for each of the following genres:

▲ Culture

▲ Politics

▲ Sports

▲ Environmental Science

Each problem had similar content, but they were posed in different contexts. Each student selected the problem they wanted to solve, for whatever reason. They were then asked to solve the problem and share it with those who had selected a different problem. This adaptation allows students to

▲ have agency over their problem solving via problem choice;

▲ see their partners' problems, allowing them to see the content in another context; and

▲ communicate the important information contained in their problem with their peers.

Blur or Withhold Crucial Information

One way to generate curiosity as well as make learning visible is to take a picture and blur crucial information that would yield the answer. Photo apps such as Skitch can blur objects in a matter of seconds.

For example, Figure 5.24 shows two more-or-less cylindrical soda cans of different sizes. The larger soda contains 140 calories. The smaller can has a corresponding calorie count, but it is blurred out, which provides a natural inroad to curiosity.

Students will solve this caloric conundrum by establishing a relationship between the volume of soda and the calorie count. However, the information you give depends on which content you wish to emphasize. In Figure 5.24, you'll see the fluid ounces listed on the cans, which would fit right into a lesson on ratio and proportional reasoning. If you wanted students to find the volume of the cylinders, you could give the dimensions of the soda cans instead (Figure 5.25). Then students may once again set up and solve a proportional relationship.

FIGURE 5.24 In this problem, the number of calories on the smaller, similar soda can has ben "blanked out."

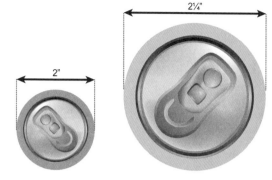

FIGURE 5.25 Dimensions of the larger and smaller similar, cylindrical soda cans

Move from Application Problems to Authentic Experiences

Sometimes a textbook word problem obfuscates the capacity to do great things with the information within the problem. I came across a problem in a book of performance assessments. The problem asked students to create a model of exponential population growth of Texas desert bighorn sheep, given a few data points.

I quite liked the scenario the task presented: linking exponential growth and decay to the population reduction and repopulation of a species. I did some digging into the issue, and Texas desert bighorn sheep had indeed been hunted to near extinction, leading officials to cease issuing hunting licenses for them. Even better, at the time I was teaching this topic, there was a debate about whether the state of Texas ought to reissue hunting licenses for them.

Because this was an actual issue in my state, I thought it might be worth going beyond posing the problem and take the chance to explore something a bit bigger. I e-mailed the editor of *Texas Parks and Wildlife* magazine to see if he would be willing to be a part of this task I was developing. I sketched out the letter in Figure 5.26 and asked if he would send it in his name. He said yes.

Having the editor of the magazine send the letter to my students immediately and palpably amped up their engagement. The editor also agreed to help me assess the final products, which he did. With a bit of Googling, I was able to turn a word problem into a two-week exploration of exponential growth and decay and argumentative writing.

One of the best and worst resources a teacher has at his or her disposal is the section in every unit titled "Application Problems." In that section, some kind soul

Desert Bighorn Sheep

To the students of New Tech High:

Throughout the ecological history of Texas, the plight of the desert bighorn sheep has been publicized and, we think, partially solved. However, we need you to evaluate whether or not the species population has become robust enough to allow its hunting again.

Among the many species that have been endangered at one time or another is the desert bighorn sheep. The desert bighorn sheep is important to preserve because it is sensitive to human-induced problems in the environment and is a good indicator of land health.

We have data on the desert bighorn going back to the 1800s. We noticed that the population had significantly dwindled almost to the point of extinction in 1950. The cause looked lost for the desert bighorn.

Efforts to Repopulate the Species

Efforts to reintroduce desert bighorn sheep in Texas began around 1957. By 1993, there were about 400 desert bighorn sheep roaming free or in captivity.

Issuing of Hunting Licenses

Authorities are beginning to issue licenses to hunt desert bighorns in Texas (see article here). It is your task to write an article examining the data from desert bighorns in Texas and decide whether or not it is safe again to issue hunting licenses without the threat of extinction of the desert bighorn.

Sincerely,
Texas Parks and Wildlife

FIGURE 5.26 Launch of a real-world project based on the Texas desert bighorn sheep task

has done the grunt work of establishing a context or need for the content of that very section. Although the problems as they appear are often dry, they sometimes contain a kernel of real-worldliness that we can expand upon.

Synergy with Safety and Facilitation

High-functioning classrooms are places where students tackle high-quality, challenging tasks. It's important to note, though, that tasks are only one-third of our ecosystem, and that the quality of the task is interconnected with teacher facilitation and the academic safety in the classroom. A student who feels academically unsafe may be unwilling to engage in a challenging task, regardless of the quality. A high-quality task is not a Crock-Pot where you can "set it and forget it." Far from it, a quality task requires the delicate touch of a teacher to make sure it communicates the mathematical messages we want it to.

I've seen the same task facilitated in two different classrooms by two different teachers. It's fascinating how different the experiences can be for students. In one classroom, students will take on a challenging task and work toward a solution, whereas in another, students will disengage from the problem-solving process entirely. In one classroom, students will work together in groups and ask one another questions to hone their thinking. In others, students will simply wait for the teacher to spoon-feed them the method of solution (because they know that eventually the teacher will). We are holding the task constant while adjusting the levers of the other two elements of our pedagogy: facilitation and academic safety. Each of these elements is individually important, but they are all intertwined. Even a vetted task that meets several of our hallmarks of a high-quality task carries no guarantee of effective implementation.

This ought to be reassuring to professional math educators: we are still needed! Despite attempts by curriculum designers to "teacher-proof" resources and automate instruction, teachers and the environments they create remain crucial to how a student experiences mathematics. Effective teachers don't just pose a curriculum task and get out of the way. They modify and improve tasks, they ensure that the tasks are meaningful, and they change course based on student need. They provide pathways to make sure that every single student understands the task at hand and can be successful at tackling it.

FIGURE 5.27 A quality task will open up other parts of our pedagogy.

It is also true that the quality of a task directly affects the facilitation and the academic safety of the classroom. A task that fails at several of our quality hallmarks leaves no room for effective facilitation and can communicate messages around academic safety that are in direct conflict with our goals. In Chapter 8, we will see a full treatment of how to ensure that you are attending to all three elements.

Conclusion

Incorporating complex, nonroutine tasks is difficult. Insipid, rote tasks can placate a classroom in a way that encourages additional insipid, rote tasks. Given the choice between a messy, challenging task and a rote, formulaic one, students will often choose the path of least resistance. Teachers can be lured into believing that students are understanding the math better when they have explicit steps to follow and are solving problems that hew closely to those algorithmic steps. Jo Boaler put it this way in 2009:

> *Students do think that they "get it" when methods are shown to them on the board and they repeat them lots of times, but there is a huge difference between seeing something that appears to make sense and understanding it well enough to use it a few weeks or days later or in different situations. (48)*

To be blunt, rote tasks are a drug for both teacher and student. With every passing lesson where students are rewarded for demonstrating low-level thinking and understanding, it becomes more challenging to wean them off rote tasks. Making matters worse is an obsession with standardized test scores and coverage of standards, which contribute to the cycle of low-level tasks. I've seen the cycle countless times. It goes like this:

1. Students exhibit low performance on standardized assessment.

2. Teacher decides to use complex tasks to enhance rigor.

3. Students struggle with complex tasks: the task feels aimless or students are highly reticent when it comes to tackling the task.

4. The teacher follows up the seemingly failed experiment with more rote instruction.

5. The rote instruction is seemingly well received.

6. Students exhibit low performance on standardized assessment.

Introducing complex tasks into a system that has encouraged rote thinking requires intentionality and persistence. It's crucial to consider which tasks are introduced first to maximize engagement and student success. Consider starting with the shorter or smaller tasks. I've seen teachers who are initially reluctant to consume an entire class period or two with *Three-Act Math* or problem-based learning get started by implementing a shorter task—such as Which One Doesn't Belong? or a Math Talk—in the form of a warm-up. Buoyed by their initial, incremental successes, these teachers are soon ready to tackle some of the larger tasks.

Most of all, employing quality tasks requires attendance to the other parts of our triad: effective facilitation and academic safety. This is precisely why an ineffective math classroom can't be fixed solely by using better tasks. Quality tasks are one element of a dynamic ecosystem, not a silver bullet, despite what curriculum developers tell you. As you review the task models and the tasks themselves provided here and in the appendix, consider how they open the door toward academic safety, which we discussed in the prior section. In the next section, we'll turn toward effective facilitation, which will allow us to see how we can marry all these elements into a three-part harmony.

REVIEW

- You were provided with ten models of quality tasks:

  - Number Talks

  - Estimation

  - Always/Sometimes/Never

  - Which One Doesn't Belong?

  - Polygraph or Guess Who?

  - Card Sorts and Dominoes

  - Would You Rather . . .

  - Three-Act Math

  - Problem-Based Learning (PrBL)

  - Project-Based Learning (PBL)

- To develop a task, you may wish to create a new task, find a task online, or adapt an existing task.

- To create a new task, you may choose to start with the standard or start with the scenario.

  - Use the camera in your mobile device as a scenario capturer.

- On finding a task, there have never been more freely available resources via the Internet (this is both a boon and a potential hindrance).

- Adapting existing tasks may be the most efficient way to design quality tasks while staying true to your standards. There are several ways to adapt existing tasks:

  - Start with the answer.

  - Remove the steps and sub-problems.

  - Make the problem one of optimization.

  - Choose your own problem.

  - Blur critical information.

  - Move from application problems to authentic experiences.

- Providing all students with quality tasks is essential to promoting academic safety while creating the path for effective facilitation.

EFFECTIVE
FACILITATION

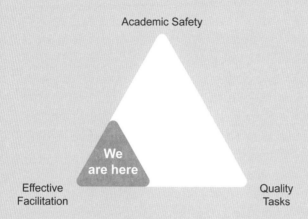

Students in Sarah's tenth-grade geometry class are working through a review packet for an upcoming test. They're grouped in desk clusters of either three or four and are solving problems together as best they can. The students are working diligently through the problems. After eavesdropping on various groups, however, I notice some repeated phrases coming from the mouths of students that feel—for lack of a better word—*artificial*.

"Can you justify that?"

"Does that align with our initial estimate?"

"Tell me how you know that."

I'm used to hearing teachers utter these phrases, but not students. The students themselves aren't settling for just the answer in the same way a teacher wouldn't.

I sit down at one of the desk clusters with only three students and ask them about their conversations. Initially, they're confused by my question. Clumsily, I ask, "Just a second ago, you asked, 'Does that align with our initial estimate?' Forgive me, but that's not a typical sentence that a high school student casually tosses out. Where does this kind of questioning come from?"

"Oh, that?" one of the group-mates begins. "We always talk like that in math class. Pretty much since the beginning of the year. We used to have these little cards with these questions on them." She pulls out her notebook and opens it to a clear plastic page with nine slots for cards. Anyone who collected baseball cards (or in my daughter's case, Pokémon cards) while growing up knows these plastic containers. Each sleeve has a card in it, each with a different question. Sure enough, this is what I see:

Does that align with our initial estimate?

"[Sarah] gave us these—one a week at the beginning of the year, I think. She had us practice using them each week and then gave us another one. Then we would practice that one, and then we'd get another one the next week and so on."

Sarah and I are talking after class. She's describing this process. "We always want students to ask questions of each other and probe for deeper thinking, but a lot of the time no one's *taught* them how or what to say. It's hard enough for teachers to come up with probing questions on the spot; it's incredibly challenging for a shy adolescent to do it. So, we used these as a kind of 'starter questions' set. I rolled them out one per week and challenged students to find an opportunity to ask that particular question that day. If a student doesn't get an opportunity to ask that question in class, that is their homework for the day: to ask that question at some point."

"Do you ever feel like it's over-scripted?" I ask.

"It probably feels that way at first," Sarah says. "In fact, it felt incredibly artificial when they had only one or two questions in their toolbox. But after a while, after they'd practiced it, I was able to relax a little bit. Eventually it became more and more natural, if still scripted. And eventually, we have what you see and hear occurring organically."

Here's what Sarah did. Before the school year started, she brainstormed with colleagues: *What are nine question that I want students to have in their toolbox as we're working throughout the year? If I could teach them nine questions, what would they be?* Once she had her nine questions established, she purchased the nine-pocket sheets in bulk for her students. The first day of every week she had students add an index card to one of the pockets, and that was their "question of the week."

She had students look for opportunities to ask that question of a peer through-out the week. After a student had asked that question successfully three times in that week, Sarah checked it off. If a student didn't ask that question in class three times in a week, they had to ask that same question outside of class and tell Sarah about it the following week.

INDEX CARD QUESTIONS

WEEK 1: Can you justify that?

WEEK 2: What assumptions are we making?

WEEK 3: Does that align with our initial estimate?

WEEK 4: Is there a different way we could do this?

WEEK 5: Tell me how you know that.

WEEK 6: Did we consider everything?

WEEK 7: What other problem does this look like?

WEEK 8: How confident do you feel in your answer?

WEEK 9: Did you communicate the math clearly?

I found it remarkable that Sarah was assigning students a grade based on their asking of a question rather than providing an answer. I ask one of the students about this: "Did that feel odd? Like, you had to ask a question in order to get a positive grade, even if you didn't necessarily feel like asking a question?"

"At first, yeah," she replies. "At first it was like 'Okay, I have to make sure I ask this question in class or I'll have to ask it for homework or something.' It was weird. It was like I was reading from a script. But after a while it became easier. And now it's at the point where I honestly didn't even realize that was one of these questions until you pointed it out. I guess it's just a part of our vocabulary."

In many secondary math classrooms, it's rare for students to ask questions. When you observe a classroom and map who is asking the questions, you'll find that almost all of them come from the teacher. Some classrooms have a handful of eager students who ask questions of the teacher, but rarely are all (or even most) students engaged in this process. Even more rare is the classroom where students consistently ask one another questions.

Many secondary math classrooms have posters on the wall begging students to "ASK QUESTIONS!" But at no point is that a skill that is explicitly taught. The result is another year where the only one asking questions is the teacher, and the poster ages another year. Implicit modeling of question asking isn't enough; teachers must teach this skill.

This concept of "starter" questions or items that are initially scripted is a consistent feature in math classrooms where students take ownership of deeper questioning. What's exciting, though, is that eventually students go "off script." Once peer-to-peer questions have become the norm in a classroom, students develop a questioning mindset and begin to ask questions more organically.

Effective Facilitation

Facilitation refers to the teacher actions that result in student understanding of the task, concept, and other outcomes. Facilitation spans a wide variety of actions, both grandiose and granular. Facilitation includes the norms teachers establish and the way teachers demonstrate example problems. It includes the routines teachers teach and the protocols for problem solving.

We need to consider two time frames when thinking about effective facilitation like Sarah's: (1) the in-the-moment, day-to-day facilitation moves, and (2) the long-term classroom norms and behaviors that are established over time. Both are crucial to creating an environment that is mathematically successful and safe. It is worth separating these two time frames out for analysis, even as we acknowledge the interplay between them.

Consider a periodic function—a sine wave, for instance. The short-term facilitation moves might be seen as the amplitude of the function: the highs and lows of in-the-moment facilitation. The long-term facilitation is the vertical shift, or the midline of the function. It's the routines, norms, and structures that anchor the classroom. Although they are separate parts of the periodic function, they are linked (Figure C.1).

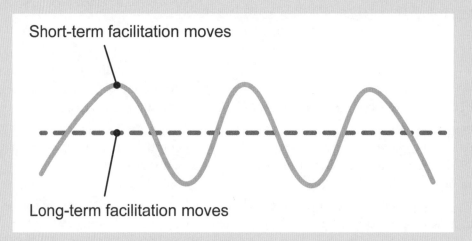

FIGURE C.1 Short-form facilitation moves are anchored to the long-term facilitation of the class, and both are important to the day-to-day well-being of the class.

Sarah's question-teaching activity demonstrates the interplay between the long-term and short-term facilitation of her classroom. In the long term, she's establishing the norm of asking questions. In the short term, she's provided the scaffolding necessary to realize her vision of students asking critical questions of one another.

Examples of short-term facilitation moves	Examples of long-term facilitation moves
• Asking a question to prompt for deeper explanation or sense making • Presenting new information in an engaging or exciting manner • Using a visual to enhance understanding of a concept • Using a protocol to enhance student contributions and discussion • Employing appropriate wait time before responding to a student query	• Establishing routines for retrieving supplies • Setting the expectation that students begin the warm-up without prompting from the teacher • Establishing well-understood group norms and roles • Teaching students to ask questions and share ideas with minimal prompting

TABLE C.1 This table gives a few examples of short-and long-term facilitation moves.

You can also conceive of these two time frames as the interplay between individual tasks and lessons and the long-term resting state of the classroom environment. Individual lessons feed into the long-term expectations and routines of the classroom. The expectations and routines will affect each individual lesson or task. And despite the slow-moving nature of long-term facilitation moves, they must be tended to on a regular basis. While planning a lesson, it is just as crucial to identify the long-term norms or routines you're focusing on as it is to identify which short-term probing questions you'll emphasize. These investments pay off with time and repeated iterations. Only after repeated practice, amplification, and debriefs will students engage in the high-quality, self-starting, group work we desire.

In the next two chapters, we will unpack long- and short-term facilitation moves. In Chapter 6, we will look at how to establish norms, structures, and routines that will enable a smooth learning experience for students. In Chapter 7, we will spend time within individual lessons and moments within lessons to make sure we're meeting the needs of our students.

6

Brains GROW AND CHANGE

MISTAKES ARE POWERFUL

BELIEVE IN YOURSELF

SPEED IS NOT IMPORTANT

Norms, Structures, and Routines

And this is why I like times
tables, because they make sure
I don't get lost in time.

—MARK HADDON,
*THE CURIOUS INCIDENT
OF THE DOG IN THE NIGHT-TIME*

Students are diligently working through a few pattern problems in Kate's algebra lab class. The physical space is a bit awkward. The layout of the room is oblong, as if at some point in the old building's past this may have been two separate classrooms and the wall was knocked out. Each group consists of four students around a large work desk, three for groups that have an absent member. In the center of each desk rests a green folder. I find one of those groups with only three students present, toward the back of the class, and grab the extra seat as Kate starts the lesson. She works an example problem representing a tiling pattern four ways: a picture, a data table, an equation, and a graph (Figure 6.1).

After working through the example problem, Kate directs students to the green folders in the middle of their desks. Inside are some practice pattern problems, similar to the ones Kate just worked through but with increasing complexity. As students get started on the assignment in their groups, Kate grabs a clipboard and some paper and begins circulating around the room. At this point, I shift my attention from Kate to the students at my table.

Almost immediately, all students begin working through the problems, and begin working on the problems *together*. In most classrooms, when teachers tell students to work together, students end up working individually while physically seated in groups. One student will blast on ahead while another puts his head down to take a nap. One "group" member will race to the finish to turn the assignment in, whereas another student at the same table—an alleged group member—will raise her hand, asking for help from the teacher.

In Kate's classroom, students are indeed working as a group. As I survey the landscape, I notice that every group is exhibiting similar collaborative behavior. Although I can't be at every group and listen in on every conversation, I see every student exhibiting the physical signs of working collaboratively on the problem: nodding as group members explain their thinking, turning their papers around to demonstrate how they came up with the solution. All this is occurring while Kate is gathering a clipboard and some other materials at the opposite end of this oblong classroom. I turn my attention back to the group I'm stationed with and listen more intently.

"Look, it's going up by three tiles each time."

"That means the slope of the graph has to be three."

"But where does it start?"

"It starts at four." A pause. "Wait, would it start at four or one?" At this point, students begin debating what the *y*-intercept should be. Should the *y*-intercept be where the first shape is, or lower than that?

"The *y*-intercept is going to be three less than the first shape because the first shape is going to be at *x* equals one."

Another pause. "I don't understand. Can you explain that to me?"

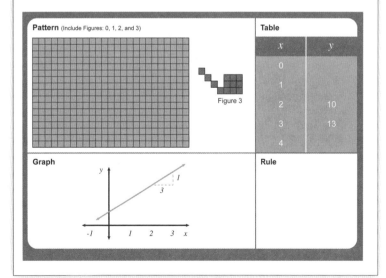

FIGURE 6.1 Tasks and instructions for pattern problems

Another student gets some scratch paper out. "This is shape *one*." He draws the first shape in the pattern. "And we know it's the first shape in the pattern. But the *y*-intercept is going to be where the *zero* shape is. Does that make sense?" The confused student is starting to display the looks and sounds of someone beginning to understand.

"Yeahhhh . . . I think I get it. So the actual *zero* shape would look something like this." He draws the zeroth shape. "And *that* would be the *y*-intercept. So, the *y*-intercept is at one."

After a brief confirmation from our group-mates, they finish out the problem.

After a few minutes, I hear from one of our group members, "All right, is everyone done with that one? Okay, we can move on." Throughout the rest of the work time, I hear similar interactions multiple times: a check among all group members, and then a confirmation that they may move on. The result is that every group member is working at roughly the same pace, and each group member is actively solving each problem.

This is an expectation in the classroom: that each group member is working on the same problem at the same time. One time, I hear a student preventing another student from moving forward: "Don't move on just yet."

I ask my group to explain the purpose of making sure everyone is working on the same problem at the same time. "It's a way to make sure that everyone is able to learn from one another," a student named Rory says. "If someone just blazes through and someone doesn't understand it, they may not be able to help." The students in Kate's classroom have bought in to the idea that they are smarter together than they are apart.

I'm wondering how this norm was established and the buy-in accomplished when I look up to the front of the room where I see Kate (who I'd almost forgotten was in the classroom) documenting group behaviors. Using a document camera, Kate has partitioned off eight rectangles for the eight work groups in the room (Figure 6.2). In each cell, she records the specific group behaviors that are commendable (with a +) and the ones that need to be changed (with a Δ).

She has recorded specific things students have said, from mathematical conjectures and questions such

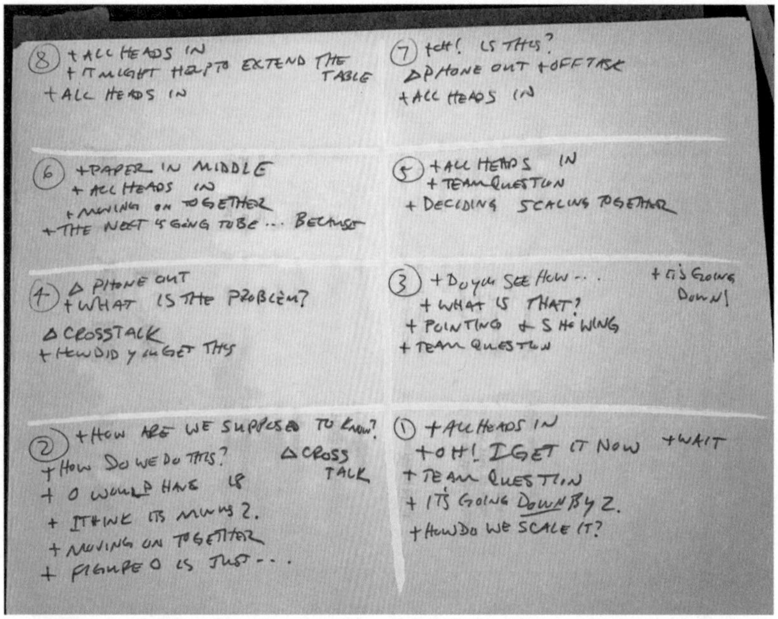

FIGURE 6.2 While students work in groups, Kate monitors their actions and behaviors. She marks the pluses and deltas for the groups, indicating successes and areas for improvement.

as *How did you get this?* and *It might help to extend the table* to the more colloquial, triumphant yawp of *It's going down!* (*it* being the assigned problem). Kate has also recorded physical behavior, such as *all heads in* and *paper in middle*. Some of the Δ behaviors include *phone out* and *crosstalk*. It's worth noting that there are about five +s for every Δ.

These behaviors aren't happenstance. The students are demonstrating previously established, discussed, and practiced norms. Kate and the class have a set of established ways of working that requires continual upkeep. Many classrooms I've seen have norms on the wall, but rarely are they practiced, reflected on, debriefed, made public, and even graded. "We can lose points if we don't adhere to the norms," Rory tells me. "We can make them up though," he adds. Students receive a grade on the assignment as well as a grade on how well they worked together. That grade is always accompanied by a debrief.

Kate is *not* merely recording behavior the way one might use a punitive behavior chart. She's recording behaviors that exemplify the norms they've established. One of the norms is that everyone will work on the same problem at the same time during groupwork. Other norms include, "Make sure every voice is heard" and "Make sure everyone is recording the group's ideas on their own paper," among others.

At this point in the year—early October—the students understand the norms of the classroom well. They can explain the reasoning behind them and what they look and sound like. This is because of Kate's diligence in facilitating groupwork on this day and every day.

Norms

Every classroom has norms. Norms are the typical ways of working in a setting. Whether the norms are stated or unstated, explicit or implicit, they exist. In effective classrooms, norms are clear and explicitly taught and reflected upon. In classrooms where norms aren't established and taught, norms still appear, just not the ones a teacher might prefer. And even classrooms with an expected set of norms need to have them addressed, redressed, taught, and retaught, or they will be superseded by unwelcome norms. When I ask teachers, "What are the norms in the classroom?" many point to a placard on the wall that lists expectations for ways of working. When I ask, "If you didn't have that poster, what would you *think* the norms of this classroom are?" I get a much different answer, if I get one at all. A teacher will often take a few seconds to gaze across the classroom and name the behavior taking place.

Norms differ from rules. Rules define what students are allowed to do or not to do. Norms describe the resting state of the classroom. You can veer from a norm. And if that veering isn't corrected, it can result in a new, unintended norm.

I've seen norms look wildly different in different classrooms. I've seen norms that are broadly aspirational, such as "We work together." I've seen norms that are more specific to routines, such as "Get your supplies out as soon as you walk in the door." The latter might straddle the line between a norm and a rule, but sure enough, students came in, got seated, and immediately retrieved their supplies for the day. Perhaps we can classify it as an *expectation*. Even if it began as a rule, the demonstrated behavior indicates it was now a way of working for the class.

The team at Ridgeland has an established set of norms under four categories: *Trust*, *Respect*, *Responsibility*, and *Relationships*. *Trust* comes with the explicit expectations to "Understand that there are many ways to be smart," "Be honest," and "Believe in the ability to grow." *Respect* means students are expected to "Treat one another with kindness" and "Honor the work of one another." Under *Responsibility* are the expectations to "Share your knowledge," "Contribute to groupwork," and "Be prepared to learn and participate." In the *Relationships* category, students are expected to "Believe in each other," "Communicate so that you are able to be heard," and "Know the strength of your peers."

> "In effective classrooms, norms are clear and explicitly taught and reflected upon. In classrooms where norms aren't established and taught, norms still appear, just not the ones a teacher might prefer."

These norms are made explicit on the wall via four posters, but that's not where I see the norms coming to life. Rather, they are lived out through the students and in their conversations. When I ask a student about their norms, he recites back to me their norms of *Trust*, *Respect*, *Responsibility*, and *Relationships* almost involuntarily. No, the student doesn't have the individual expectations under each category memorized, but he is able to articulate each category and more or less how it plays out in the classroom.

I've been in classrooms where students and teachers develop the norms together. That's a wonderful practice for empowering students. But to be clear, that's not what this was, in Kate's room. These were teacher-established norms that the kids had taken on themselves. How did it get to be this way? Kate treated teaching the norms in the same manner she teaches content: establishing the norms, teaching the norms, and constantly reflecting on the norms. And—as we'll see—teachers establish, teach, and encourage reflection on norms in a myriad of different ways.

Establishing Desired Norms

Effective teachers establish norms throughout the first week of school. Most of the time—and we'll get to the exceptions in just a moment—they decide on norms before the school year. In Appendix E, you'll find a menu of potential sample norms. Theresa has her students process the norms via short discussions: one norm for each day of the first week of school. She asks students, "What does this norm mean to you?" and "How do we know when we're achieving this norm?" and "How will we know when the norm is broken?" She allows students to understand and take some ownership of the norms she's established.

Some teachers go so far as to have students generate the norms. Although this can be cumbersome—each class having a different set of norms is one technical challenge this approach offers—it does allow true ownership. It also helps the teacher understand exactly what students want out of their math class for the year.

Teaching the Norms

In classrooms where there is an absence of desired norms, most of the time it isn't because the teacher hasn't thought about what norms he or she would like to establish in the class. It is because the hoped-for norms weren't explicitly taught, practiced, or reflected upon. We want students to know innately what good groupwork looks like, or what it means to "be positive."

Kate has demystified the expected norms at Ridgeland through explicit models and examples. Under each category of *Trust*, *Respect*, *Responsibility*, and *Relationships*, she has articulated what the desired demonstrated behaviors are. They're posted on the wall, and they're discussed regularly as a class. Each expectation is accompanied by examples of "What this sounds like . . . ," "What you say . . . ," and "What this looks like. . . ."

"At the beginning of the year, students answered some questions that fell into each category of Trust, Respect, Responsibility, and Relationships," Kate informs me. "Then I gathered their responses and highlighted them on the poster."

I've often heard that you can't expect that which you don't teach. That's usually said in the context of test giving. It's rarely applied to norms and ways of working. But students often need just as much support in social interactions and keeping work equitable as they do in, say, factoring a quadratic.

"We spend a *lot* of time at the beginning of the year teaching these seemingly inherent things," Kate tells me. "We're kind of teaching the kids *how to talk*. It sounds bad, like we're training them. But really, we're just trying to give them the tools to be able to have a mathematical dialogue. And they've never had that before."

Kate makes an interesting observation about the difference between her younger students and her seniors. "Freshmen slip out of the established structures the moment you let them. For seniors, especially my calculus students, I'm definitely more lax, but I also notice their insecurities about being right or wrong flare when things get hard. They need structures to push them to talk more. They do the work; they just need nudges to dig into making sense of it together sometimes. I like doing things with them that push for some pair conversations because some of those students are old enough and savvy enough with rule-following and groupwork to hide within the structures if you're not too careful."

Reflecting On and Debriefing Norms

Establishing norms and teaching norms are crucial to the long-term state of being in a classroom. It is their continued maintenance, however, that determines whether classes will function well throughout the school year. Kate uses two principal strategies for ongoing norm maintenance: she capitalizes on unplanned moments when she sees the norms in action, and she sets aside regular, planned time for students to revisit and reflect on norms.

Kate makes sure to amplify when norms are being exemplified, often using the same descriptors that she used to teach them. When a student, a group of students, or an entire class demonstrates one of these norms, she is quick to publicize it. Sometimes she'll make a note of it herself; other times, she'll ask the classroom to pause and reflect on which norm they feel like they're attending to well at that moment.

In addition to finding times throughout a class to amplify and publicize expected norms and ways of working, Kate makes sure to build in time for this explicit reflection and debrief on norms. For example, one day at the end of class, Kate is wrapping up the lesson. She has already recapped the hoped-for mathematical sense making, and there are about three or four minutes left in class. She posts a dual prompt on the screen: "What norm did you exhibit well today? Which norm would you like to focus on tomorrow?" She asks students to turn and talk to their neighbor and have a quick discussion about those two questions. After about a minute, she asks a few students to share which norms they thought the class exhibited well that day, and why. She then asks what norms her students saw from their peers, which results in students publicly praising other students for adhering to the desired norms of the classroom. Not only does this prompt reinforce Kate's desired expectations for the classroom, but it also allows students to award value to one another and assign status to their peers. Personally, it reminds me a bit of "passing the peace" in church.

Sometimes reflecting on norms can lead to establishing new norms. Dina is just finishing an overview of the day's agenda when she asks students to reflect on the five established norms they have for their class. She then asks, "Are there any norms you'd like to add?"

A student raises her hand and says, "We were discussing in our group the importance of recognizing our strengths. Can we make that a norm?"

"Say more about what you mean," Dina replies.

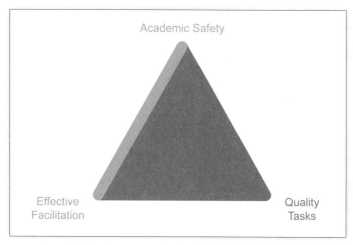

FIGURE 6.3 Norms that communicate positive ways of working connect effective facilitation and academic safety.

"We all have strengths and weaknesses, and we want to be more aware of those throughout the class." I'm listening to an incredibly self-aware group of adolescents.

"That sounds great," Dina offers. "Let's make that into a new norm for our class. Help me out: how can I phrase this as a new norm?" The class and Dina wordsmith this nascent norm until they land on the following: *Celebrate each other's mathematical strengths. Help each other out in areas where we are struggling.*

We are now again straddling the line between effective facilitation and academic safety, which we explored in Chapters 2 and 3 (Figure 6.3). In addition to making for a smooth-running classroom, well-established and well-functioning norms open up the potential for a welcoming social environment. Students are much more likely to value one another if the classroom norms intentionally hone the dynamic of social safety. Students are more likely to assign self-worth if the norms are conducive to the celebration of mathematical ideas.

Norms are particularly needed and powerful when facilitating groupwork. Once the norms of effective groupwork have been established, we can turn toward its facilitation.

Groupwork: Teaching, Establishing, and Maintaining Equitable Groups

Many teachers and schools aspire to make productive groupwork part of the classroom. It's important to consider why groupwork is valuable to math class. Groupwork can contribute to students' understanding of content because communicating their ideas to others makes their learning "more permanent" (Dale 1969; Prince 2004).

FIGURE 6.4 To use groupwork productively, teachers must teach and maintain norms and ways of working throughout the year.

Secondary teachers who consider it their job to help young adults grow into socially minded citizens argue that groupwork teaches empathy. Kate says, "I believe in the social benefits of groupwork when students are carefully led through the process. . . . Norms that require students to give and receive critical feedback from one another result in students who aren't afraid of criticism and welcome it as a way to grow." Missy, a teacher in Texas, adds that when it's done well, groupwork can "create a safe space for shy kids to participate" in a way they wouldn't in a totally individual or whole-class setting. If we're being utilitarian, we might suggest that working with others across social groups is an essential skill for the twenty-first-century employee.

In her indispensable book *Designing Groupwork*, Elizabeth Cohen succinctly encapsulates the benefits of groupwork, concluding it is "a superior technique for conceptual learning, for creative problem solving, and for increasing oral language proficiency. Socially, it will improve intergroup relationships by increasing trust and friendliness" (1994, 6). As we focus on academic safety in secondary math classrooms, we can also use groupwork to communicate that all students have something important to contribute in math.

Any and all of these arguments for groupwork are compelling, so feel free to pick your favorite.

Groupwork can . . .

- promote individual understanding;

- communicate that all students are capable mathematicians;

- encourage communication and empathy;

- create an atmosphere where mathematical discourse is the norm;

- allow for more complex math problems to be solved, drawing upon individual strengths; and

- teach collaboration and interpersonal skills.

The benefits of groupwork may be clear, but the actual practice of groupwork is challenging. Unproductive or inequitable groupwork can result in poor outcomes for a lesson. Missy—who consistently employs groupwork in her classroom—admits as such: "Groupwork can range from being a positive experience for all where students are learning, teaching, arguing, discovering, and ultimately growing, or not great because one person is doing all the work and others are what I call 'math mooching'" (Missy is loaded with these colloquialisms). Therein lies much of the understandable resistance against groupwork: it's a risk.

A lesson that incorporates significant groupwork has genuine risk for mathematical understanding: groups may not work well together, individuals within the group might miss crucial mathematical content, and the work may be inequitable. But groupwork has a high ceiling to which we must aspire. Whether it's reinforcing the culture of the classroom, increasing students' abilities to communicate mathematical ideas, allowing multiple minds to solve complex problems, or imparting social status, quality groupwork's benefits far outweigh the risks.

So how do we achieve quality groupwork?

Teaching Groupwork

Missy has a few words of advice for us: "Facilitate [groupwork] so all participants have a voice and use their voice. Groupwork *cannot* be something where teachers throw some kids together, give them a task, and then hang out and wait for results."

One underlying reason for poor groupwork is that we rarely teach students how to work in groups. We expect students to work together without any more guidance than, "Work with your group." Adults have difficulty working on a group task, so we need to be sure to scaffold and provide practice and structures for adolescents. Without preparation for groupwork, students will revert to unfocused or unproductive group dynamics (Webb, Ender, and Lewis 1986). In such instances, mathematical content is obfuscated by the low level of student-to-student interaction. How do we teach groupwork when our training has taught us only to teach content?

Missy starts off her year with an activity during the first week called *Broken Circles* (available at sten.pub/necessaryconditions). *Broken Circles* was designed by Nancy and Ted Graves (1985) to increase and teach cooperation, inspired by a similar task called *Broken Squares* from Pfeiffer and Jones (1970). In this activity, each group has a set of puzzle pieces that, once put together, will form a complete circle for each participant. However, each student starts with mismatched pieces and must swap circle pieces, one for one, with their group-mates until each individual in the group has a complete circle.

Missy's students begin the activity by opening a large yellow legal envelope and taking out various pieces of several circles. The instructions are given (Cohen 1994):

1. This exercise must be played in complete silence. No talking.

2. You may not point or signal to other players with your hands in any way.

3. Each player must put together his or her own circle. No one else may show a player how to do it or do it for him or her.

4. This is an exercise in giving. You may not take a piece from another player, but you may give your pieces, one at a time, to any other members of your group, and other group members may give pieces to you. You may not place a piece in another person's puzzle; players must complete only their own puzzles. Instead, hand the piece to the other player, or place it beside the other pieces in front of him or her.

Students dutifully start moving pieces around and trying out various pieces of their circle together. They make overly expressive eye gestures, pleading for particular pieces of the circle they think will complete their own circle. Remarkably, the rule of silence is unbroken throughout the entire process, except for a few giggles. It takes ten or fifteen minutes for all groups to complete all the circles in their group. Afterward, Missy makes sure to debrief the experience. She asks what takeaways students got from this exercise.

"Everyone had a piece of the circle that others needed," one student replies. Another: "What made it interesting and challenging was that we had to change pieces one at a time. So we couldn't just, like, throw everything in the middle and figure it out." Yet another student: "We really had to pay attention to what everyone else was doing and what pieces they had."

Missy notes a few of these takeaways on the board, carefully phrasing them into norms she wants students to adhere to throughout the school year. These include "Pay attention to what your group-mates are doing," "We all have to work together," and other habits Missy wants to endorse.

Missy starts every year with *Broken Circles*. As a task, it adheres well to our hallmarks of quality tasks: it's universally accessible, it's immediately puzzling and engaging, and it certainly communicates the exact messages about math and about students we like to see. She uses it as a springboard for the rest of the school year. In fact, she enjoys it so much, she has even facilitated it with her fellow colleagues, math teachers and nonmath teachers alike. The inherent lessons about collaboration and groupwork are as important for adults as they are for students.

She does have some advice for would-be *Broken Circle* facilitators, however. She admits that it does require a significant amount of time to cut pieces and sort them into envelopes. She makes sure to have students take apart the circles after each class and keeps the circle pieces in a safe space year after year.

Establishing Groups

There are many models of establishing student groups, and there are convincing arguments to support nearly all of them. Some teachers prefer to group homogeneously according to "ability." The thinking here is that students will be able to work more equitably with peers of "like ability," and the teacher may be able to offer more targeted support to groups of "like ability." Other teachers prefer to group students heterogeneously. In this model, students are expected to learn from one another, using their strengths and knowledge gaps as a potential opportunity for productive groupwork to flow forth. Such grouping will flatten issues of academic status. There is also the practice of grouping randomly or pseudo-randomly (such as, where the students happen to sit in a class of unassigned seats).

We know from research that low-achieving students benefit from a heterogeneous grouping model (Dar and Resh 1986, Kerckhoff 1986). Homogeneously assigned groups do nothing to close achievement gaps (Slavin 1987). There is also an unstated "stigmatizing" when homogeneous working groups are established and routinized. To be sure, there is still much debate about the research on homogeneous versus heterogeneous grouping (see Loveless 1999). It can be difficult to disentangle the countless factors that affect student performance (including the definition of *student performance*, for that matter). It's important to consider, regardless of grouping mechanisms, how students are being perceived and how they perceive themselves.

> "Groupwork *cannot* be something where teachers throw some kids together, give them a task, and then hang out and wait for results."

Rather than get bogged down in research or false-choice debates, Kate chooses to keep her groups relatively fluid and more or less random. About every week, students are working with a different set of kids. She keeps the groups rotating to ensure that students are building relationships with everyone in class, rather than just the few they or Kate happened to choose at the beginning of the grading period. As we'll see, students also consistently assume different roles within the groups so they can build different academic muscles.

Maintaining Groups

In the same way that Kate lays out clear expectations for individual norms, she makes her expectations for groupwork specific and explicit. She describes to students what good groupwork looks and sounds like, monitors student groupwork carefully, and recognizes and publicizes positive groupwork when she sees it. For example, in the fall she establishes the norm of "same problem, same time," which we saw earlier in this chapter. In addition, she provides sample dialogue for students ("Explain that back to me"). She expects students to "work in the middle" of their table to promote shared understanding and positive body language, so she teaches and reteaches that expectation.

As we saw at the outset of this chapter, Kate makes public the behaviors that students exhibit, either by verbal praise or denotation at the front of the classroom. There is no mystery about what Kate expects from her students when they are working together.

Kate credits much of her and her team's expertise in facilitating groupwork to their training in Complex Instruction, a program designed by the aforementioned Elizabeth Cohen and others at Stanford University. Complex Instruction (CI) uses strategies to promote equitable groupwork by recognizing that students need such supports. CI emphasizes the link between groupwork and issues of academic status and how to treat such issues. (See Cohen and Lotan 1997, and Horn 2012 for reviews of the work and research.)

But what about when groupwork goes awry? A colleague of mine once told me that the best time to practice norms is when they're broken. Failing groupwork is a stress test for our norms: it's when they're most tested and most needed. Kate uses a rubric that specifically outlines the behavior for collaboration (Figure 6.5). Although most rubrics you come across are related to the task or content, she employs one that specifies groupwork behavior. At the end of most groupwork sessions, she asks students to reflect on this collaboration rubric. Sometimes the reflection is in a written journal, and other times it appears as a verbal debrief with the entire class. Regardless, with the rubric in hand, students are quick to note when their group and groupwork has fallen short of these expectations. The rubric acts as both a corrective and a lofty goal for productive groupwork.

Collaboration Rubric

The ability to be a productive member of diverse teams through strong interpersonal communication, a commitment to shared success, leadership, and initiative.

	Emerging	E/D	Developing	D/P	Proficient	P/A	Advanced
Interpersonal Communication	Shows little interest in the ideas of others		Listens with partial interest in the speaker's message providing sporadic verbal/nonverbal feedback to indicate some understanding of agreement		Listens with interest to the ideas of others providing verbal or nonverbal feedback to signal understanding or agreement		*In addition:* Thoroughly prepares for conversations having read and researched the topic
Commitment to Shared Success	Provides no positive feedback or unhelpful negative feedback		Provides intermittent constructive feedback to team members		Provides positive and constructive feedback to team members		*In addition:* Actively encourages and motivates others to attain high levels of achievement
Team and Leadership Roles	Has difficulty describing the roles and responsibilities of each team member		Can generally describe what roles and responsibilities each member of the team is expected to perform		Can clearly and specifically describe what roles and responsibilities each member of the team is expected to perform and how they are connected		Uses multiple representations (diagrams, tables, graphs, formulas) to help the audience follow the chain of reasoning

FIGURE 6.5 Kate's collaboration rubric

Group-Worthy Tasks

I'm in a classroom with a teacher who is struggling with groupwork facilitation. He is having students complete a problem set in groups of three or four. His students are supremely disengaged: arms folded, flippant copying of peer responses. It is everything that detractors of groupwork say it is. While the teacher hops frantically from group to group, attempting to get students back on task, I sit down with one of the groups actually working on the problems, although students are working individually and silently.

"Why aren't you guys working on the problem together?" I butt in.

"Because I know how to do it," the boldest student in the group responds. "It's easy."

Although I try to shy away from classifying tasks as "easy" or "hard," this problem set is rote. Each student has notes on the procedures they're supposed to follow. And even if they don't take notes, the steps are up on the board from a demonstrated practice problem.

To facilitate successful groupwork, we must (1) establish ways of working in groups, (2) maintain classroom structures and cultures that continue to support groupwork, and (3) carefully choose the task on which the students are working. Is it a group-worthy task? Oftentimes poor groupwork can reflect a problem with the task as much as facilitation. When a task is rote and requires simple step-following to solve it, groupwork may falter because it is unnecessary. Such a task draws upon the individual strengths of the group members, so issues of academic status jump to the forefront. Some students will blast through the assignment as quickly as possible, whereas others are struggling to understand the steps.

Tasks that are group-worthy hew closely to our hallmarks of a quality task. In particular, the task must be accessible to all students in a group, encourage creativity, and promote individual strengths of the students. Problems that are "open ended" or "open middled" adhere well to this necessary condition. We find ourselves at the intersection of effective facilitation and quality tasks (Figure 6.6).

Consider the two similar yet different tasks in Figure 6.7. Both draw upon the same concept of complementary and vertical angle pairs. The problem on the left is relatively straightforward and could be quickly solved by an astute student, alone. If this problem were assigned as a group problem, the student might quickly find

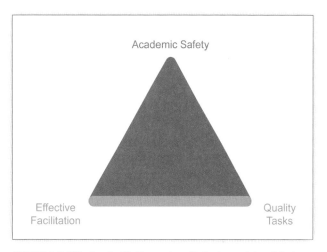

FIGURE 6.6 Effective facilitation and quality tasks are interrelated.

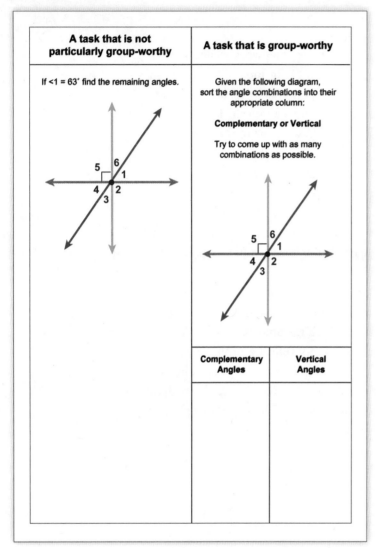

the missing angles, leaving the other group-mates in the dust. The problem on the right requires students to slow down and attempt to capture *all* of the angle pair types. The resultant discussion will be much richer than the one stemming from the problem on the left. It would be challenging for a single student to identify *all* the combinations of angles immediately. Also, there is a potential gray area to wade through. For instance, can we say that combinations of angles can be vertical angles (for example, that $\angle 1 + \angle 6$ is vertical to $\angle 4 + \angle 3$)?

A group-worthy task overlaps with our indicators of quality tasks in general. Chapters 4 and 5 illustrated these indicators and provided some models. In addition, in Chapter 9 we'll see examples and indicators of tasks that are especially good for the practice of problem solving. These rich problems are reliably good group-worthy tasks.

Group Roles

Many teachers make groupwork more productive and equitable by establishing roles. In Kate's math department, the group roles are task manager, norms manager, resource manager, and communication manager, and teachers instruct students about their expectations for these roles in the fall, along with the rest of their working norms. The roles are then described, exemplified, laminated, and taped to worktables so they are handy for student reference (similar to those in Figure 6.8).

Recall from the beginning of the chapter that Kate records and publicly amplifies students' behaviors in her classroom. She also records when individuals exemplify group roles. Sometimes, once students have gotten the hang of it, she'll have the students record that information themselves: "I might ask the communication manager how many times they've heard from each person," Kate says. "Or I might ask them how they are making sure everyone is participating."

Kate keeps the roles rotating more or less randomly. She has the group roles identified on the wall, and she shuffles cards with the names of her students from time to time (Figure 6.9). This system is one way to generate randomized grouping as well as randomized roles for individual students.

I'm always impressed with Kate's intentionality when it comes to facilitating groupwork. In some respects, it almost feels like she writes a whole extra lesson plan: there's the lesson plan intended to deliver the content knowledge to her students, as well as the lesson plan intended to ensure that groupwork is being modeled and maintained. And indeed, in Chapter 8 we'll look at how to build a lesson plan that incorporates these crucial elements. She assures me, though, that once you make group management a consistent part of the classroom, it starts to drive itself. "Once you've been tending to groupwork in your teaching with a lot of intentionality, you just do it automatically," she says. "It's hard *not* to. And you notice when things start to derail, and intervene. It becomes a part of who you are in the classroom."

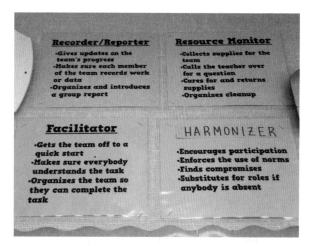

FIGURE 6.8   Group roles are posted on the wall and at each table.

Facilitating Solo Work

Sometimes individual work is more appropriate for the task than groupwork. How do we facilitate solo work (Figure 6.10)? Is individual work even something that needs to be facilitated? What norms are present when students are expected to wrestle with math individually? Effective teachers do, in fact, have some suggestions for facilitating individual work (which, if I'm being honest, surprised me).

FIGURE 6.9   Cards with student names make it easy to change roles and groups.

Hushed Tones

Theresa tells me the most important norm she has for solo work is noise level. "I know a lot of students need near-silence to concentrate fully," she says. "Since we do so much groupwork already, I really want students to think individually from time to

FIGURE 6.10 Facilitating solo work is just as crucial as facilitating groupwork.

time." Theresa talks to her students about the need to carve out a time for relatively hushed work. It's certainly not silent. In Theresa's classroom, you can still hear murmurs and conversations between student and teacher, but clearly a switch has been flipped to solo work time.

Student Choice: Opt-In Work

Brett has students opt in to the type of solo work they'd like to focus on. If there's a concept a student is struggling with, Brett provides work on that topic. It's possible that four kids in a group of desks are all working on varying concepts. During this solo work time, students are encouraged to talk to one another, particularly if they need assistance from someone working on an alternative topic. Brett calls these Choice Days. He has one a couple of times per month. Between these days, he reminds kids to circle or highlight particular problems or concepts they struggle with so they can devote Choice Day time to them.

It's Not So Different

Christine doesn't consider solo work and groupwork all that different in terms of norms. She encourages students to take the same modes of being they have for groupwork into their individual time. "Just because you don't have others to question your answer, you should still think through on your own whether it makes sense; individuals must take on bits and pieces of all of the roles/norms to support a rich, problem-solving, individual thinker."

Christine also has students engage in similar protocols during solo work as they would in groupwork, which are illuminated more in Chapter 7.

Conclusion

Most lesson study structures or teacher observations look only at what's happening in the moment in a classroom. Although the in-the-moment facilitation moves are crucial, it's important to pay attention to the underlying routines and norms that affect student learning. Facilitation underlying the lesson is as important as facilitation within the lesson. To be sure, these teaching moves (if one can call them teaching moves) are more difficult to spot and require long-term attention. Rome wasn't built in a day, and neither are the routines in your classroom. Make your expectations clear, give students a chance to practice them, and continually monitor them from day to day, week to week, and month to month.

Once we have a classroom with well-established norms and routines, we'll have the opportunity to make the most of our short-term facilitation techniques (or facilitation within a task), illustrated next.

REVIEW

- Long-term facilitation moves are as crucial as in-the-moment facilitation moves.
- Norms guide the way a class works, and they exist whether they are acknowledged or not.
  - Make sure you are designing and establishing positive norms; otherwise undesired norms will creep in.
  - Constantly teach norms by making them explicit and debriefing them.
- Groupwork provides opportunities for mathematical brilliance that solo work sometimes can't.

- Students need to be taught how to work together as a group.
- Make sure, if you're having students work in groups, that the task is group-worthy.
- Group roles can help communicate expectations of groupwork.
- Solo work is also an important part of math class and should be facilitated with the same importance as groupwork.
  - Make your expectations of your students explicit.
  - Teach and practice your expected routines.
  - Develop norms.

Facilitation Within a Task

When you try to prove a
theorem, you can almost be
totally lost to knowing exactly
where you want to go. Often,
when you find your way, it
happens in a moment, then
you live to do it again.

—DEANE YANG

In the previous chapter, we looked at effective facilitation over multiple weeks, months, and even the entire school year. In this chapter, we'll zoom in to the smaller, crucial facilitation moves within a single task to ensure that students understand and access math at a deep level.

Divergent and Convergent Thinking

The facilitation of an individual task that promotes student ingenuity and conceptual mathematical understanding is a journey through divergent and convergent thinking (Figure 7.1). At the outset, there is a natural starting point from which all participants begin. This is the part of the task where students identify what they understand about it and begin brainstorming some solution paths or initial estimates, or just start tinkering around with the problem. During this time

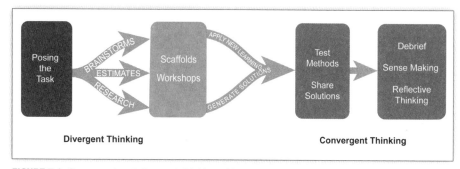

FIGURE 7.1 Convergent and divergent thinking within a single task

of divergent thinking, students or student groups might try a wide range of differing approaches. At some point during the task, students' thinking begins to converge toward solutions, sense making, and consensus building.

Effective facilitation within a task involves attending to both types of thinking: divergent and convergent. Without effective facilitation of the *divergent* thinking phase of a task, the math may become unfocused or aimless. Without effective facilitation of the *convergent* phase of a task, mathematical sense making may not take place.

In this chapter, we'll travel through this framework, start to finish, discussing each key moment along the way:

▲ Posing the task and initial brainstorming

▲ Scaffolding and workshops

▲ Sharing solutions and debriefing

Posing the Task

Few tasks can be given to students with no initial support other than the word *go*. Before letting students begin a complex task, some preface is required. Here are a few proven protocols that can help you launch problems successfully (Figure 7.2).

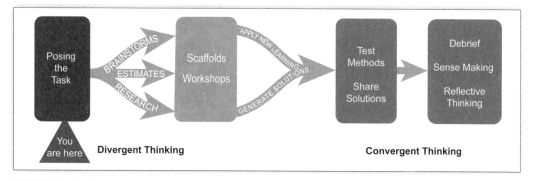

FIGURE 7.2 The first section of this chapter focuses on posing the task and initiating divergent thinking.

The Know/Need-to-Know/Next-Steps Process

The Know/Need-to-Know/Next-Steps process (hereafter shortened to NTK) involves asking students to identify critical information that will help them solve a complex problem. A teacher begins by posing a problem scenario and facilitates the following process:

1. *What do we* know *about this situation?* Individually, in groups, or as a class, students identify the following:

   ▲ Crucial—or potentially crucial—information contained within the problem

   ▲ Key mathematical content students know that may aid in the solution

2. *What do we* need to know *about this problem to solve it?* Individually, in groups, or as a class, students identify the following:

   ▲ Key missing information they will need to complete the task

   ▲ Key know-how they have yet to learn that they will need to complete the task

3. *What are some potential next steps?* Individually, in groups, or as a class, students identify potential next steps to follow. Students need at least one next step to tackle the moment the teacher releases the class to the task. The next steps must be readily understood by each student and each group. We want *something* to build from.

Before teachers undertake the NTK process, they must identify what they hope will bubble up from students. Upon completion, students should be equipped with the following:

▲ The information contained within the problem that will help them solve it

▲ The content knowledge that will help them solve it

▲ The information *not originally* contained within the problem that will help them solve it

▲ An immediate next step that will get them *somewhere*

If students are unable to articulate one or more of these elements of the NTK process, something is amiss.

I'm in Carmen's eighth-grade math class, watching him facilitate the NTK process. In the center of their table, each group has a different coffee mug that he picked up for a few bucks at a thrift store. On his desk rests an oversized novelty mug. All the mugs are more or less cylindrical in shape. He asks,

> How many of your small cylindrical coffee mugs will fit into my large one?

Earlier, Carmen identified the key things he wanted to elicit from students. I glance at a copy of his facilitation notes, where he's written the following:

During K/NTK, be sure to elicit

▲ *Know: shape of the mugs (cylinder)*

▲ *Know: shape of the base of the mugs (circle)*

▲ *Know: One is bigger than the other.*

▲ *Know: We're talking about volume (not area).*

▲ *NTK: dimensions*

▲ *NTK: how to find the volume of a cylinder*

He's not sure every student recalls how to find the volume of a cylinder. For Carmen, the NTK process is as much a fishing expedition as it is a problem-posing protocol. If students seem shaky, he anticipates holding a small workshop or quick refresher lesson on how to find the volume of a cylinder. If students are able to speak to Cavalieri's principle for volume (the volume is the area of the base times the height), he plans to forgo the workshop.

During the lesson, he lands somewhere in between. He felt like a few students were still confused about the fact that the diameter of the cylinders was the base. He told me, "They need to be able to identify that B in volume formulas stands for the 'area of the base.' That's a common mistake I see students make when they see the formula." During the NTK process, he makes sure to highlight that particular trip wire when calculating the B in Cavalieri's principle. Otherwise, he's confident that students will be able to get started on the task. Students have identified some next steps: "calculate the circular area of the cylinder base," "measure the height and radius of the cylinders," and even such specific items as "get rulers."

Now—and only now—is he ready to release the students to begin their work on the problem. Once he does, students get right on the task because they have enough to get started.

Estimate First

In Chapters 4 and 5, we saw how estimation could form a high-quality task in and of itself. Consider including estimation as part of the problem-posing process when appropriate. Having an estimate on hand will be helpful for students to consider whether their answer is reasonable or their result has violated expectations, which we know increases understanding (recall Chapter 4). Here is an estimation facilitation protocol that works well, promoted by Dan Meyer of Desmos and Andrew Stadel of Estimation 180:

1. After posing the problem, prompt students: "Give me an answer that you know is *too low*." Record their answers publicly on the whiteboard. Consider asking why students know their numbers are too low.

2. Prompt: "Give me an answer that you know is *too high*." Record these alongside the too-low answers. Consider asking why students know their numbers are too high.

3. Prompt: "Give me your 'just-right' estimate for the solution." Record these as well. Optionally, create a number line for the low, high, and just-right estimates.

Although it's acceptable to get some estimates on the board and move on, I encourage you to go deeper to get at crucial information within the problem. For instance, if the task requires students to identify the measurement of a missing angle, consider highlighting estimates that stem from an understanding of, say, supplementary or complementary angles.

Going through the estimation process before solving has several benefits. It will lay bare what students know about the task. Through their high, low, and just-right estimates and the resultant discussion, the teacher will obtain an understanding of how students are approaching the problem and what strategies they may try out. Listen for particular vocabulary words or the seeds of a solution strategy during this time.

Estimating beforehand also allows the task debrief to practically write itself: Was your initial estimate spot-on? Did you make a faulty assumption when estimating?

Notice and Wonder

In a Notice and Wonder protocol, a teacher provides an artifact—an image, a video, an audio clip, a text-based scenario—and students describe what they *notice* about the artifact and what they *wonder* about the artifact.

Max Ray-Riek, author of *Powerful Problem Solving*, describes Notice and Wonder as an effective way to generate interest and build mathematical capacity:

> Students are very capable, with practice, of finding important information in math problems (and stories, images, videos, etc.) and making conjectures about that information. It's a matter of helping them get started, valuing their ideas, and helping them stay connected to their own thinking. (2013, 43)

(I would add that students are also very capable—with no practice—of finding information you hadn't even considered.)

These protocols—NTK, estimating before solving, and Notice and Wonder—will become more effective with repeated use. Students become more adept at using them, and teachers get more practice in facilitating them. Now that we've launched the task, honored divergent thinking and brainstorming, and equipped students with enough to get started, we can turn toward facilitating *convergent* thinking.

Scaffolding and Workshops

Part of the challenge of facilitating tasks is knowing *when* to give instruction. Right after the problem is posed? Before the problem is posed? After the conclusion of the class period via online tutorials? My short answer to these questions is this: teach when you need to teach. It could be shortly after students have identified their next steps, it could be thirty minutes into students working on a task, it could even be *not at all*, depending on how students are working and persisting through struggle.

It's also important to ask, *How should I give instruction?* Most of us were raised on only one model of instruction: whole-class lecture. To be sure, sometimes this is the most effective, efficient way to explore content. Often, it's not.

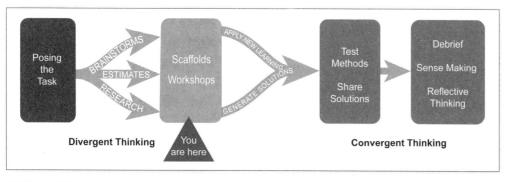

FIGURE 7.3 This next section focuses on the middle of the task, including how to transition from divergent thinking to convergent thinking.

Consider playing with both variables. Instead of delivering instruction to the whole class, try giving it to just a handful of students and allowing them to be your "liaisons." Instead of using only lectures, try another approach. Next, we'll see several models of instruction that break the mold of whole-class instruction.

The Workshop Model

FIGURE 7.4 The workshop model

Students are working through a problem in Brett's class that has them analyzing the cost of a moving truck based on the mileage that a driver travels. Their goal is to determine which would be better from the driver's point of view: to procure a larger, more expensive moving truck that requires fewer trips or a smaller, cheaper moving truck that requires more trips. Students are working in groups of three as Brett moves around the room, asking questions and taking notes.

Students need to generate a mathematical model that adequately describes the situation, and Brett notices a few of the groups struggling. After all, there are several interrelated elements of the scenario to consider: the cost of renting the vehicle, additional mileage, the gas consumption of each vehicle, the number of trips each type of rental truck will require, and the distance between the starting point and the destination. The problem is complex. Some groups are having difficulty staying organized.

Students have been working on the problem for about fifteen minutes when Brett grabs their attention and asks each group to send one representative to a *workshop*. One student per group convenes at a large table circled by enough chairs for everyone to have a seat. Brett asks a few workshop attendees to share what they've done and what they've come up with for their model thus far. Some of the elements of the models align, some differ. In those that differ, he asks additional questions and compares ideas until students feel confident in their answers and/or understand where they went wrong. After about fifteen minutes of discussion, questions, and checks for understanding, Brett dismisses the workshop attendees back to their tables to work with the rest of their group members, who had continued to work through the workshop time.

Once back in their original groups, the students who attended the workshops share their newfound knowledge and understanding of the problem with their group-mates.

At this point, the groups create a model for the scenario and work toward completing the task.

This workshop model is a common tool on Brett's tool belt. "I use small workshops pretty often in my class instead of traditional lecture," he says. "When there's something I want to teach or communicate, I find it works better if I can talk to a small group of kids around a table, rather than to thirty kids all sitting at their desks. I also like it because kids then have to go back and explain the concept to their group members. Kids learn better from each other. And they learn best when they're teaching it themselves."

Brett uses several different types of workshops. Here are a few that he mixes and matches, depending on his purpose.

Sign-Up Sheets

Brett has a piece of chart paper on the wall with the heading *I would like a workshop on . . .* Underneath that, he has written several concepts around the topic for the day:

- ▲ *Finding the slope of a line*

- ▲ *Finding the y-intercept of a line*

- ▲ *Finding the solution to a system of equations*

As students enter the classroom, and throughout the class, they occasionally break off and add their name to one of the columns of workshop options.

While students are working on their task, Brett calls together those who have signed up for the various workshops. Each one lasts ten to fifteen minutes. He'll lead them through a quick discussion of the concept and makes sure everyone understands what it means. He'll guide them through a small practice problem and then have another problem ready for the workshop attendees to solve.

I ask Brett how he's able to get participation from students for an optional lesson. "How do you get students *wanting* more instruction?" I ask bluntly.

"I document it, but I don't really grade for it," Brett says. "If I see that a kid hasn't attended a workshop in a while, I might make him come to a specific one or just check in with him a little more heavily. Or sometimes I'll be like, 'Hey Johnny, you might want to sign up for this workshop,' and give them a slight nudge. But I don't need to do anything like tack on a grade for workshop attendance or anything like that. I've found that—contrary to popular belief—students actually *do* want to learn. When I offer these optional workshops, I have no shortage of students wanting to participate."

All Groups Versus Some Groups

Sometimes Brett makes sure that every group sends at least one group member to the workshop. He does that most often when he would like to go over a new or newish concept. He sometimes sends the workshop attendees back to their groups with a sample problem for the rest of the group to solve (with the workshop attendee's help, of course).

Other times, as he's floating from group to group, he'll make a note of which groups are struggling with a specific portion of a task and ask that those groups send someone to the workshop. This might occur when a concept isn't necessarily new but students demonstrate that they need extra practice.

Product Refinement and Getting Unstuck

Although most of the workshops Brett offers are related to content, he also hosts ones for students to refine their solutions and make their work better.

In this type of workshop, he invites all the attendees (one from each group) to bring their group's work through the problem thus far. He asks a few students to share how their group approached the problem and where they are in the solution. Some groups haven't gotten too far in the problem; others have completed it. In the latter situation, the discussion revolves around the conciseness, presentation, and clarity of the solution. In the former situation, the discussion is around how to get unstuck. In this case, seeing other groups' solutions is enough to get the stuck groups moving in the right direction.

Assigned Versus Self-Selected Attendance

Occasionally, Brett requires particular students to attend workshops. If a student demonstrates a misunderstanding of a certain concept, he'll invite that student to attend a workshop on that concept. Sometimes, Brett's decision is based on a couple of missed warm-ups in a row. Other times, it might be based on a formal assessment such as a quiz or test. Other times still, it's based on the way a student responds to a question. Brett is always concerned about how students see themselves and their status in the classroom, so he'll often mandate that those who have demonstrated understanding attend such workshops also, if only to cloud the perception of who "gets it" and who doesn't quite yet.

The workshop model—in whichever format—is an effective way to transmit mathematical know-how. Many students learn better in smaller settings than in a whole-class lecture.

Make It Visual

One consistent through-line I see in effective lessons is that a concept is visible and visual to students. If your task does not already include a visual element, add one by asking students to draw a picture or come to consensus on a diagram before proceeding with a solution path, even if the solution doesn't necessarily require one. Don't assume when you say "equilateral triangle" that all students will automatically recall and visualize a triangle with three sides of equal length.

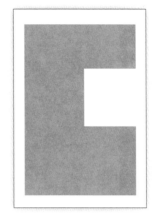

FIGURE 7.5   A nonroutine shape does not have a formula associated with it.

Another make-it-visual hack is to use nonroutine or composite shapes. There isn't a ready-made formula for the area of the shape in Figure 7.5. A task that incorporates such an odd octagon will require your students to think visually.

Here are some additional recommendations for making math more visual:

▲ Use complex/composite shapes.

▲ Draw before solving.

▲ Make use of mini-whiteboards.

▲ Deconstruct the problem using problem-posing protocols.

▲ Ask students to compare drawings.

▲ Use a number line for estimates.

▲ Require the solution to have a visual component.

These techniques are effective but not always applicable. What about tasks that aren't visual in nature? How do we incorporate more visible thinking for non-geometric concepts? Concept mapping is helpful.

Concept Mapping: Connecting Content

One way to incorporate more visual thinking is to link mathematical content via a concept map. Dina starts with the primary topic of a unit and works outward from there. Figure 7.6 shows an example from a unit on quadratic functions. Early in the unit, she posts the essential topic in the center. As she and her students move through the unit, she adds more granular concepts as they come up, such as understanding

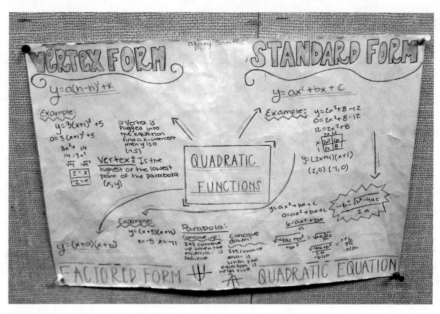

FIGURE 7.6 Concept mapping helps connect content and enhance understanding.

quadratics in standard or vertex form. She posts the diagram prominently, referring to it regularly to ensure students are seeing the connections. This concept map helps Dina's students see math as a connected discipline rather than as a haphazard set of arcane rules to follow.

Concept Mapping: Deconstructing a Problem

Concept mapping may also be used within a task. Jeff is facilitating the following problem:

> You are helping your friend decide which new car to purchase. He or she is considering two options: either a Ford Fusion SE or a Ford Fusion Titanium Hybrid. Your friend would love to get the hybrid but is concerned about the high initial cost. Bearing in mind that he or she would like to keep this car for a number of years and that cost is of the utmost concern, please investigate and determine which car you think your friend should choose.

The task hints at concepts similar to those in our problem with the light bulbs and energy efficiency from Chapter 5—namely, the high initial cost of a hybrid car versus the long-term savings brought about by having better gas mileage. Jeff has students read through and notate the problem before engaging the entire class. He continues the launch of the task by asking students to identify the essential question they are answering: *Which car should we recommend, and why?* Jeff writes this question in front of the class on big poster paper.

From here, Jeff and his students decode the problem. They identify related questions that emanate from the central question:

▲ What are the initial costs of both cars?

▲ What is the gas mileage of each car?

▲ What is the cost of gas?

▲ What are the expected maintenance costs associated with each car?

Jeff and his students now identify additional information. From the "cost of gas" question, he draws additional links to the following:

▲ Do we think gas will get more expensive as time goes by?

▲ Do we need to use different types of gas for the different cars (i.e., regular unleaded or premium unleaded)?

Once the class has a clear visual of all the information in this problem, they discuss the mathematical content, starting with, *What math will help us develop our model, and what variables will the model incorporate?* One student says they will be able to develop an equation for the cost over time based on the initial cost and the cost of gas consumption. Jeff draws a line between these two elements (initial cost and gas consumption) in the visual in a different color and writes "Create an equation." He pushes students a little bit further by asking another probing question. "What will the equation include? What will it look like?" From here, the students identify that the equation will have a slope and a y-intercept: the slope represents the cost over time growing because of gas and maintenance, and the y-intercept represents the initial cost. This information is also included on the chart paper.

Although this process is time consuming, these visuals are incredibly helpful for students. "I get lost easily in math," one student tells me. "I get distracted, I lose my place, I don't understand, and I get lost. When I get lost, I get frustrated. Having a visual helps me keep track or remember what I'm doing."

Making thinking visible can have long-term benefits for students as well. In a classroom where students are experiencing and modeling problem solving visually, students have been shown to improve their metacognition, or thinking about thinking (Ritchhart, Turner, and Hadar 2009).

Sharing Solutions and Debriefing

Students need to communicate their mathematical ideas (Figure 7.7). Whether demonstrating a homework problem from the night before or talking through a complex, in-class task, students can increase their confidence, mathematical understanding, and communication by presenting problems (Figure 7.8). It is important, therefore, that the presenting student speak clearly and the audience pay attention, which can be challenging. Kate holds very high expectations for student presentations and audience participation in her class.

"I always try to sit in a student desk when students are presenting and be as hands-off as I can," Kate says. "Whenever the audience doesn't point out a mistake in a presentation or doesn't ask questions, I just say that the person presenting deserves feedback—even if they don't want it—and we will wait until some of us speak up and give feedback. Sometimes if the audience is having a really hard time with giving feedback, I might say, 'Can someone please ask a question about distributing that needs feedback?' If certain students are taking too much airtime, I'll say, 'If you've already shared, I need you to step down, and if you haven't, we're expecting to hear some thoughts from you.'"

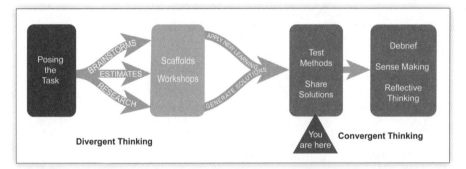

FIGURE 7.7 Now that we've traversed nearly the entire task, we need to start making connections and ensuring deep content understanding.

FIGURE 7.8 Presenting to peers offers students a chance to practice mathematical communication in an academically safe classroom environment.

Prompting students to present to their peers and adults is an effective way of deepening conceptual understanding, but it's crucial to be mindful of the potential trauma it can induce in some students. Many of us remember being unable to solve a problem in front of the class and the teacher becoming more and more impatient.

Here we need to acknowledge the importance of academic safety. In an academically safe classroom where all students feel valued and mathematically smart, student presentations become equal parts sense making and individual celebration. Kate is able to press upon her students because in addition to being an excellent facilitator, she's laid the foundation of a class where student ideas are valued.

We explored concepts of academic safety in Chapters 2 and 3. Consider the following options for sharing solutions and solution methods that can promote social and self-regard.

Video Shorts

Missy wanted to assess students on their presentation skills but was having difficulty giving instructive feedback on presentations while also providing scores and feedback on the actual math content. "It was hard to do both at the same time," she tells me. So, she started employing what she dubs "video shorts." Students have sixty seconds to record themselves explaining the problem on an iPad camera, and then they upload or e-mail it to Missy. Students have whatever medium they were using to solve the problem (for example, a mini-whiteboard, poster paper, and so on) to help explain the problem.

"Then I could go back and watch and rewatch the presentations and give better feedback," Missy says. "Also, students weren't as nervous because they were presenting to an iPad camera rather than to their peers."

Gallery Walk and Sticky Notes: Likes and Wonders

Likes and Wonders is an excellent way to build mathematical understanding while fostering a safe social environment. In Brett's classroom, I commonly hear the sentence starters "I like . . ." and "I wonder . . ." from students. On this particular day, students have completed a problem on large pieces of chart paper and have placed them around the room. Students have two different colors of sticky notes. Their instruction is to "go around the room and add at least one 'I like . . .' and at least one 'I wonder . . .' to each solved problem using the sticky notes." The "likes" include varied responses such as "I like the organization of the problem," "I like how you factored before dividing by x," and "I like that you included units." Some of the "wonders" are "I wonder if this answer is reasonable," "I wonder if you made an error while factoring," and "I wonder if you could have included a diagram." Students return to their original problem and review the feedback from their peers. Brett then gives students a few minutes to make improvements or changes.

Peer Editing

Christine uses a similar approach to have students offer peer-to-peer feedback. She assigns a problem that necessitates a written report, perhaps one page or so. As a teacher with a substantial population of English language learners, she wants students to use complete sentences to reinforce their mathematical reasoning. Upon completion of the written report, she asks them to swap papers and complete a peer-editing worksheet (Figure 7.9).

The worksheet contains some similarities to Brett's Likes and Wonders approach. In this case, Christine has asked students to "list the two items you find the strongest" and "list two improvements you would recommend." In addition, she has some more specific "look-fors" for peer feedback, based on what she wants students to focus on.

Using Likes and Wonders, peer editing, or a similar structure works well within our ecosystem. Peer feedback reinforces our goal of creating a socially and emotionally safe classroom by ensuring that all students have something to contribute and all students have something positive to say about their peers. It helps students be critical of one another's work in a professional manner.

There are also two sneaky side benefits to peer reviews. By having students review and decipher one another's work, they revisit the problem and check their own understanding of it. Students may see in other students' solutions how they ought to have approached the problem or whether they made an error. Peer reviews are also great for reinforcing a

Eagles' Offense – How Can We Improve?
Final Report Peer Editing

Author's Name: _____ Your Name: _____

After reading through your partner's report, please choose the appropriate check box for each question. Then answer the free-response questions below.

Descriptions, Explanations, and Connections

Describe the purpose & goal of the report?

☐ Yes, very clear!
☐ Yes, but could be clearer
☐ Description is weak
☐ Description is absent

Clearly describes thought process throughout report?

☐ Yes, very well described!
☐ Yes, but could be improved
☐ Description is weak
☐ Description is absent

Uses both Algebra & Geometry explanations?

☐ Yes, both are present and connected!
☐ Yes, but no connection made.
☐ Yes, but explanations should be improved.
☐ Only one type of explanation is described.
☐ No, this should be addressed.

Solution is clear and uses "because"?

☐ Yes, very clear!
☐ Yes, but could be improved
☐ Solution does not include "because"
☐ Solution is absent

Representations, Accuracy, and Supporting Work

Uses multiple representations to enhance report?

☐ Yes!
☐ Yes, but not in correct format.
☐ No, this should be addressed.

Defines key math terms?

☐ Define all math terms
☐ Some math terms defined
☐ No, this should be addressed.

Are there accurate units and labels?

☐ Yes!
☐ Yes, but could be improved
☐ No, this should be addressed.

Checks if answers are reasonable?

☐ Yes
☐ No

Please list the two items you find the <u>strongest</u> about this report? Describe why?

Please list two <u>improvements</u> you would recommend to the author? Explain.

FIGURE 7.9 Christine's students use this peer review and feedback form.

common desire among teachers for students to make their work organized and easy to understand. The first few times through a peer review process might result in students noting that they can't decipher their peers' work because of sloppiness or disorganization. Students quickly gain empathy for what a teacher must decipher and will start making their work cleaner and easier to understand.

"Externalizing the Enemy"

One way to amp up the rigor in a task is to "externalize the enemy." This was a phrase I first heard from a colleague of mine, Paul Curtis. This is how he frames it: Typically, the teacher acts as the "enemy." The teacher is the one whom students must impress to receive an acceptable score. Paul talks of coaches, who have a natural *external enemy* in the opposing team. A coach has buy-in for team practices because the opposing team is the enemy his or her own team must face.

Paul applies this model to his instruction. Instead of having students present their work to him, he invites outside panels to see students' work. "The moment students hear that their work will be judged by someone other than me, the level of importance and intensity skyrockets," he says. "You can tell because students become intentional about their work. Even their handwriting gets better, because they know I won't be the one judging it." Sometimes the external enemy is other teachers (math and nonmath instructors), sometimes it's interested volunteer parents, and often it's his administrator. He typically provides the evaluators a rubric (see Chapter 10) and will even go so far as to plant some critical questions that he hopes his students will have to answer.

Now that we've looked at facilitation from problem launch, through divergent and convergent thinking, and into students sharing, let's zoom in further on in-the-moment facilitation moves that could be made anywhere in a task.

Quick Moves

I often hear teaching described as a series of small, subtle moments. How we react to these small moments or off-the-cuff questions can determine the fate of our lessons. Henningsen and Stein (1997) suggest that small teaching moves contribute significantly to high-cognitive-demand classrooms.

Consider how difficult this aspect of our profession is! These small moments require a teacher to (1) hear what a student is saying, (2) process what the student is saying, (3) develop a hypothesis about what the student understands or doesn't understand about the topic, and (4) develop a response that will get the student to go one step further in their understanding, all

FIGURE 7.10 Quick moves are in-the-moment facilitation actions, probing questions, and other immediate strategies. They're perhaps the most challenging aspect of facilitation but quickly become easier with experience.

in the span of a few seconds, while managing the rest of the class too (Figure 7.10). How can we get better at these split-second decisions? The short answer is to *slow down*. Here are five strategies to aid us in these moments. They all boil down to slowing down and getting curious.

Listening and Exploring

I ask Leanne at Weirmont about this seemingly impossible task of slowing down time to craft a quality response to student questions. I'd always been impressed by how she navigated these small moments and answered thoughtfully.

"One thing that helped me is the allowance to explore what students were exploring," she says. "I would essentially just repeat what I'd heard and check to see if I understood them correctly. Then I'd allow myself to think about the idea, even if I wasn't sure what the best response was. There were times when I'd have to work out what a student was saying on the whiteboard before I would respond. Sometimes the ideas forced me to pause and check my own thinking. 'Why was I able to cross out an x in the numerator? What happens if we do FOIL backward?' I had to give myself permission to be curious and want to know more about what a student was communicating."

> How can we get better at these split-second decisions? The short answer is to *slow down*.

Max Ray-Riek of the Math Forum and author of *Powerful Problem Solving* gave a short talk titled "Why 2 Is Greater Than 4" (2011). In it, he suggested that teachers need to listen *to* students' ideas rather than listening *for* a particular response. When teachers are fishing for just the right answer to a question, they're shortchanging students as well as stunting their own facilitation. Teachers searching for a hoped-for response often move more quickly and with less sophistication than teachers who listen and explore ideas with their students. By listening and exploring, teachers are not only honoring students' ideas but are also slowing down their own thinking and communication. In a classic study, Mary Budd Rowe showed that teachers give students an average of 0.9 seconds between the time they are asked a question and the time a teacher intervenes: less than a second of wait time (1974). When you listen and explore, you're naturally going to take the extra seconds that you need to hear what students are saying.

"Permission to Be Inarticulate?"

Students often enter secondary math classrooms with baggage that prevents them from participating for fear of appearing unsmart. Perhaps the biggest singular difference between elementary classrooms and secondary classrooms is that secondary students don't ask questions, whereas elementary students do. That's why I'm always struck when I'm in a secondary classroom where students are willing to admit their nonunderstanding of a topic.

Leanne's class is like that, and it became apparent why after a short while. I began to hear this refrain from Leanne and her students: "Permission to be inarticulate?" It's asked in the way an army private would ask for permission for something, albeit a polite and sanguine army private. They don't really even wait for permission to be granted. It's a verbal starter to let peers know that the student is going to think aloud. If students need clarity on a topic or aren't sure of something, they preface their question or comment with "Permission to be inarticulate?" and then launch into their question, wondering, or conjecture. Of course, after hearing this phrase from students a few times, I hear Leanne say it as well. She's at a crucial part in her exploration of a problem involving a linear equation. She pauses and says, "Permission to be inarticulate right now? What would happen if I made the line more negatively steeper?" She was referring to a line with a negative slope and was making it "more negative," but she didn't let formal math vocabulary get in the way of communicating her idea.

Thanheiser and Jansen (2016) refer to this invitation as "rough draft thinking," implying a first attempt that will be revised going forward. The phrases *permission to be inarticulate?* and *I need to use rough draft talk* are also sentence starters. They get students talking. Although Leanne's students didn't use their sentence starter every time they had a question, it did come up now and again, maybe every other class period. Each time, it unlocked this all-too-rare specimen in a secondary math classroom: public display of struggle and confusion.

"Turn and Talk"

Among the most effective go-to moves Leanne employs is "turn and talk." Rather than asking students to raise their hands in response to a question, or calling on students randomly (which tends to be acutely nonrandom), she asks students to "turn and talk" to their neighbor about the question. Pairing students gives everyone in the class a chance to respond to the prompt while allowing for the conversations to find the cracks in understanding. When students share in the large group after a turn-and-talk, their responses are more thoughtful and organized because they've rehearsed and processed out loud once already.

This is a move elementary teachers have used for decades. Teachers of elementary students are well steeped in the need for all students to engage in a task as well as feel

> When students share in the large group after a turn-and-talk, their responses are more thoughtful and organized because they've rehearsed and processed out loud once already.

validated. A turn-and-talk approach yields more equitable discussion than "Raise your hands" or random callouts. It also provides an efficient way for us to take the pulse of the class by "listening in" while several students talk.

"Say More About That"

Another little go-to move is to prompt a student to "say more about" a topic. We want to identify gaps in understanding while amplifying accurate conceptual understanding. Students can be inarticulate and imprecise when first responding to a question. A question doesn't even have to be about math, and I find myself stumbling through a first response. On a second pass, I might actually articulate something worthwhile.

Leanne often follows an incomplete student response by asking the student to "say more about" the topic. If she's able to, she pokes at a specific word the student said: "Say more about how *steep* the line is," "Say more about what you mean by *slowing down faster*," "Say more about the *symmetry* of the object." The student then can gather him- or herself and respond in a more precise manner. Either way, we're finding the cracks in understanding. And as Leonard Cohen crooned, a crack is "how the light gets in."

"Explain Her Answer"

Teachers and students are used to the tagline of nearly every math problem ever assigned: "Explain your answer." Leanne has an interesting twist on this prompt: "Explain his [or her] answer." A student responds to a question posed by Leanne. Leanne asks another student to explain that answer and whether they agree or whether that is the tack they would have taken. This twist forces students to listen to one another while assessing the veracity of their claims.

Conclusion

The short- and long-term facilitation moves throughout this and the previous chapter are closely linked with the other two elements in our secondary math pedagogy. Effective facilitation can make a quality task better and an academically safe classroom even more welcoming. Facilitation moves help us focus on both mathematical understanding and self-regard for individual, young mathematicians.

REVIEW

- The life span of a quality task involves facilitating toward and through divergent and convergent thinking.

- Tasks must be *facilitated* rather than simply posed.

- Protocols are helpful to decode and highlight information within a task.

  - Know/Need-to-Know/Next Steps

  - Incorporate estimation before setting off on a task.

  - Notice and Wonder

- Small workshops are an effective way to communicate mathematical knowledge, and there are several models of workshops.

- Effective facilitation requires making learning visual and visible for students.

- Concept mapping is a way to enhance understanding of a certain topic and the connection between topics.

- At the conclusion of a task, some solution sharing and sense making is crucial to close the lesson.

- In-the-moment facilitation moves are among the most difficult to master as a teacher.

- One of the most important facilitation moves teachers can make is to authentically listen to their students.

- Try to get your students talking to one another throughout a task.

PUTTING THE
PIECES TOGETHER

Now It's Your Turn

My favorite basketball player growing up was Mark Price of the Cleveland Cavaliers. All of my peers were Michael Jordan fans. In the late 1980s and early 1990s, it was practically a given that you rooted for Michael Jordan and the Chicago Bulls. Whereas Jordan was known for his majestic dunks and jaw-dropping athleticism, Mark Price was known for his shooting and free-throw percentage. While my friends were bragging about MJ's slam dunk championships and actual championships, I proudly heralded Price's three-point shooting titles and how he retired with the highest career free-throw percentage. I had a Mark Price jersey from Team USA—not the famous Dream Team, mind you, but rather the team that came *after* that team. The one with Mark Price.

I really wanted to be like Price. But to be completely honest, I didn't practice free-throw shooting that much. I spent more time watching Mark Price than actually practicing. And so, tragically, neither my fandom nor my jersey made me as good as Mark Price at shooting free throws. I missed seven of ten free throws in my seventh-grade basketball tryout and never bothered to play the sport again. You can watch basketball all day long, but if you don't get out there and play and practice, you're never going to improve. As I discovered.

"Learn by doing," the popular adage goes. Knowing the research and hearing the stories that constitute our secondary math pedagogy of academic safety, quality tasks, and effective facilitation is one thing. It informs our practice. But in the end, our practice is our practice.

We now turn from our three pillars of pedagogy to the nuts and bolts of everyday instruction. How do we interweave these actions around academic safety into a lesson plan? How do I develop a classroom atmosphere that hones persistent problem solving? How can we hold in both hands quality tasks and mandated assessments? How do I create a physical environment that aids effective facilitation? How do I put this all into practice? The next few chapters and the appendices will help us make that turn.

Planning the Lesson

When the Lesson Goes Wrong . . . and Very, Very Right

"We're seeing mathematical history being made here today," a classmate muttered out the side of his mouth.

—JERRY FARLOW, *PROFESSOR PICKLE AND THE OMICRON AFFAIR*

Remember Brett's *Energy Efficiency* problem from Chapter 5 (and Appendix G2)? Jaime facilitated this problem a few years ago to introduce systems of equations. His students knew how to model linear functions and could sketch a graph based on equations. Finding the intersection of two linear functions seemed like a logical next step. At least, that was Jaime's plan.

Jaime intended for students to use two linear functions to determine *when* the energy-efficient light bulb becomes the more cost-effective option. One group of student mathematicians wanted to check the *overall cost savings*. That is, in the expected life span of one energy-efficient light bulb, what would be the savings compared with using incandescent bulbs? Note the plural here: *bulbs*, not *bulb*. You see, not only does an energy-efficient light bulb use less energy, but it also lasts a lot longer than an incandescent bulb. You have to replace incandescent bulbs more often than energy-efficient ones. This was an unexpected yet welcome layer of complexity, and yielded a problem that was different from the one he anticipated.

"I didn't discourage students and say, 'Hold on, let's just stick to the question I had in mind,'" Jaime tells me. These are mathematicians, after all! And mathematicians pose new and interesting questions. So he let them run with it.

The group researched the expected life span of an incandescent light bulb. From here they modeled a *linearly increasing step function* (Figure 8.1). The students' solution was probably better and more representative of the actual cost savings than Jaime's anticipated solution of mere linear equations. What a brilliant idea!

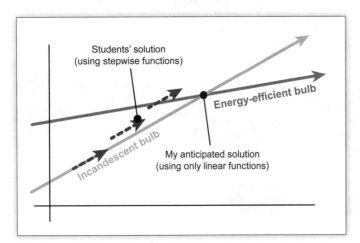

FIGURE 8.1 One group of students saw a solution method using an additional constraint I hadn't anticipated.

Jaime still held a workshop on finding the intersection of two lines, teaching the mathematical concept of a system of equations. Students constructed linear equations based on research and on information that Jaime provided. When students presented, he introduced the vocabulary of step functions.

Even though the results from one group were unanticipated and Jaime had to adjust his plans, the outcomes of this lesson couldn't have happened without his careful *planning of the lesson*. He had thought through the task, the facilitation, and the academic safety of the classroom during his planning phase. Paradoxically, the better a lesson is planned, the more freedom you'll have to take detours from those plans should the situation arise. Teaching is like jazz: you plan and plan and practice and practice the piece so you can deviate from it and improvise.

Many teachers I talk to are wary of letting go, of letting students take problems in unexpected directions, for fear the lesson's direction will become haphazard and miss the mark. In this chapter, we will allay these fears and see how to put the pieces of our mathematical classroom together to plan a lesson. Rather than planning a lesson in a scripted beat-by-beat, minute-by-minute breakdown, we will approach it through the lens of our pedagogy and seek to understand how students will experience it. Once we've planned our task, facilitation, and academic safety, we can rest assured that even a lesson plan that goes awry can still go right.

Selecting and Planning the Task

Most schools and districts adhere to some sort of scope and sequence, a plan of which standards to teach when. Although some districts allow for more wiggle room than others, generally we let the standards guide our task selection and design. We start lesson planning by thinking deeply about our standards, carefully selecting an aligned task, and then checking for and ensuring quality.

Check for Quality

In Chapter 5, we examined ways of creating, finding, and adapting tasks. How can we be sure that a task meets the high standards we've set? Recall our hallmarks for quality tasks, which should do as much of the following as possible:

- ▲ Spark curiosity and foster engagement

- ▲ Yield creativity

- ▲ Promote access from all students in the classroom

- ▲ Require and convey deep, crucial mathematical content

- ▲ Connect and extend content

Although it is difficult to find a task that meets all five of these hallmarks at once, we can do some back-of-the-envelope calculations to see if it passes muster. In the same way we can employ a scoring guide to assess student work, consider an informal scoring guide for a task (Table 8.1).

We're not trying to be hyper-scientific here. We simply want a quick check to make sure we're employing high-quality tasks. If you total up the cells of the scoring guide and end up with something around five to ten, the task doesn't pass our check for quality and should be scrapped or adapted. If a task lands in the ten to fifteen range, you can give it the green light for further planning.

Over time you'll develop a feel for and get better at predicting the quality of a task. In fact, it might be worth spending a few minutes predicting where a task will land, followed by reflection afterward. If you and the other people in your department want to assess and ramp up the quality of your tasks together, I recommend conducting a task sort as a group. The gist of it is this: find a few tasks and rank or sort them according to quality with colleagues, followed by a conversation about how you calibrated your rankings, or about where you had differences of opinion. Although the exercise itself is valuable, the *conversation* is where you'll develop common understandings of what

Hallmarks of Quality Task	1	2	3
Sparks curiosity and fosters engagement	I'm not immediately curious about the task scenario.	I'm intrigued by the task scenario and would consider working through it, if I had the time.	I am compelled to attempt this task.
Yields creativity and leads to new ideas	The task is straightforward; students don't have the opportunity to test out ideas.	Students will have the opportunity to create new artifacts or test out ideas within this task.	Students will naturally create a new, never-before-seen mathematical artifact while completing this task.
Promotes access for all students in the classroom*	Some students will not understand or be able to access this task.	Every student will be able to engage with the task on some level.	Every student in the classroom will be able to access and be challenged by this task.
Requires and conveys deep, crucial mathematical content	The task is unaligned to crucial content and/or is rote or procedural.	The task is aligned to crucial standards for my course.	The task necessitates the use of mathematical content on a deep and permanent level.
Connects and extends content	The task basically "stays in its lane." It doesn't require or hint at other content.	The task draws upon content from previous or different content areas.	Students will notice that the task draws upon content from previous or different content areas.
Total =			

TABLE 8.1

*This row is non-negotiable. A quality task *must* be accessible.

makes for a quality task. You may wish to have an external tool for calibration, such as the scoring guide in Table 8.1. Or you may wish to simply sort the tasks from "highest quality" to "lowest quality." Table 8.2 includes a more structured and hashed-out protocol, but feel free to make edits as you see fit.

Task Sort Protocol

Prework

Facilitator identifies four to six tasks or problems. These may be from common assessments, from textbooks, or a mixture of the two. Ideally there will be a variety of types of tasks (word problems, card sorts, multiple-choice problems, and so on).

Protocol

- The facilitator hands out paper copies of each task to pairs of participants and asks them to sort out the tasks from highest quality to lowest quality. Each pair must come to consensus for their rankings.

- Once every pair has their rankings, the facilitator asks each duo to share their rankings, making notes on a whiteboard or poster paper.

- The facilitator asks and the group discusses the following questions:

  ▲ *On which problem or problems do we have similar rankings? On which do our rankings differ significantly?*

  ▲ *Why do you think that is?*

  ▲ *What was it about this task that yielded such calibration?*

- The facilitator asks and the group discusses the following questions:

  ▲ *On which task or tasks does it appear we are not well calibrated?*

  ▲ *Who had it ranked higher than the rest, and why?*

  ▲ *Who had it ranked lower, and why?*

  ▲ *After hearing one another, are there any tasks that you would consider moving in your rankings?*

- Facilitator debriefs the conversation. Each participant completes the sentence by filling in the blanks: "I used to think _____, but now I think _____."

TABLE 8.2

These conversations and protocols around task quality are challenging and delightful. I always find it fascinating to hear what teachers value in a mathematical prompt. It's also rare to get through these conversations without at least one comment along the lines of "I like this task, but here's how I'd make it better." This is music to my ears. Once I hear that, I know participants are thinking critically about task design and will begin looking at their own tasks with a critical eye.

Once we identify a high-quality task, we begin planning it out.

Do the Task Yourself

The first and most important thing you can do when planning a lesson with a quality task is attempt the task yourself. Once a task meets our standards, dig in and explore it as a student would. You'll find the nooks and crannies where students may get stuck, and you'll figure out how to get unstuck. Lose yourself in the problem and see if you can find your way back. As you're working through it, keep an eye out for the following:

▲ Potential stumbling blocks

▲ Opportunities to highlight concepts

▲ Multiple solution strategies

▲ Opportunities for visual representations

Working through the problem ahead of time will also get you comfortable with a task should students take it in another, unanticipated direction. Next, we'll see how it can be helpful to have a list of probing questions to get students unstuck or to clarify misconceptions; this would be an excellent time to consider these questions.

Many of the tasks presented in this book are more complex than they seem initially. Make sure you give them a go before your students do. It will be crucial when planning the facilitation.

Planning the Facilitation

Teaching is a constant negotiation of planned and unplanned moments. We want to be able to plan for as much as possible while still being flexible enough to change course on the fly as needed. Planning the facilitation of a lesson involves identifying key moments throughout the class period that may yield high-leverage opportunities for understanding. Although every task is different, there are several generalizable moments to consider when planning a lesson. Figure 8.2 shows the moments in a typical day's lesson that we'll plan out. Remember, this is only a model structure of a lesson. You may wish to deviate from this structure where appropriate, just as a jazz pianist may wish to change keys for a few measures.

These moments as well as our three-legged pedagogy appear in a lesson plan template in Appendix G1. Most lesson plans emphasize only the standards and the linear

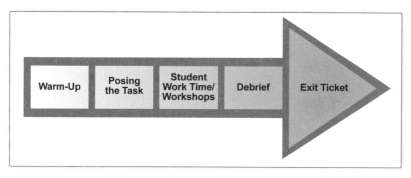

FIGURE 8.2 A typical lesson adhering to our pedagogy

Please see Appendix G.1 for a full-sized version of the *Necessary Conditions* Lesson Plan Template.

agenda items. This new kind of template is intended to get you thinking about short- and long-term facilitation moves, promoting mathematical social and self-identity alongside the beat-by-beat moments of a class period.

Planning a Warm-Up (Bell Ringer)

Every great classroom I've been in consistently employs warm-ups. Their content varies. Sometimes they are specifically about the content of the day (or the previous day). Other times they are meant to get every student engaged in mathematical thinking that's not specifically related to the day's content (such as a Math Talk) but gets students in a mathematical frame of mind.

Some of the best warm-ups offer a bridge between prior content and what's in store for the day's lesson. Consider a calculus class in which the previous day focused on summing the area under a curve using various techniques (right-hand sums, max sums, trapezoid sums, and so on) toward approximating a definite integral. Today, the teacher wants to transition to anti-derivatives to calculate the precise integral. A Which One Doesn't Belong? task might do the trick (Figure 8.3).

Students notice differences in each of the four graphs, especially regarding the area under the curve. They have seen the left two and upper-right examples before. But the bottom-right graph is new in the sense that they have yet to learn how to calculate precise areas under curves using anti-derivatives. Nevertheless, they will still notice that the area provided by that graph is the best representation, that

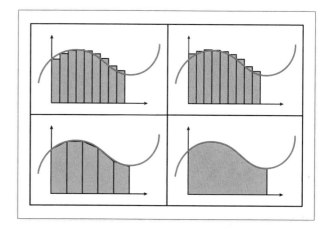

FIGURE 8.3 A Which One Doesn't Belong? task may serve as an excellent warm-up, engaging all students while allowing teachers to do some quick formative assessment.

the amount of area under the lower-right curve is between the others, that there are no discrete shapes and it's smooth, and so on. What an excellent way to recap prior know-how while laying the groundwork for the day's activities!

Many of the shorter tasks we examined in Chapter 5 serve as excellent warm-ups: Which One Doesn't Belong?, Estimations, Always/Sometimes/Never, and Number Talks.

Task Models for Warm-Ups

- Which One Doesn't Belong?
- Estimations
- Always/Sometimes/Never
- Number Talks

Now that we've engaged students' brains, it's time to plan task facilitation, starting with the launch.

Planning to Launch the Task

A task requires more than just posing it to generate momentum toward problem solving. The launching of the task should yield the following:

▲ Curiosity and a desire to get started

▲ Key information and variables about the task scenario

▲ Key prerequisite content knowledge

▲ A clearly articulated question

▲ A shared understanding of the problem

▲ Initial estimates of what the solution might look like

▲ Immediate next steps

Engage students to develop these elements of the task and record them visually when appropriate. These guideposts orient students while they work and give them reference along the way. Recall from Chapter 7 some of our problem launch strategies: the Need-to-Know (NTK) process, estimating first, and Notice and Wonder. Consider which of these might be most appropriate for the task at hand. Generally, the NTK process is good for making sense of a problem with a lot going on (such as a complex modeling task); estimation is good for building buy-in, number sense, suspense, and curiosity; and Notice and Wonder is excellent for tasks with a visual element. But these are broad-brush generalizations, and each task might be best served by a different launch process or a combination of several, depending on your goals and your students.

Understanding a problem and developing strategies for a solution reflects the work of a mathematician. During this vital sense-making phase, clarity and specificity are crucial. Although some ambiguity can be productive—and sometimes essential—and lead to rich discussions, confusing vocabulary, a lack of shared understanding, or unspecific next steps can cause frustration. Table 8.3 may help you determine when you have enough information with enough specificity for students to get started or whether you need to keep probing for additional information or specificity.

Element of problem launch	You may need to elicit more specificity from the students.	You have enough to move into the next phase of the task.
Key information and variables about the task scenario	"At the corner of the shape . . ." "Plan C is more expensive . . ."	"Point C on the bottom, left-hand side of the shape." "Plan C costs an additional three dollars a month."
Key prerequisite content knowledge	"We did something like this last week." "Slope." "Volume."	"Last week we defined standard deviation—how far something deviates from the rest of the sample." "Find the slope from two points." "Find the volume of a sphere."
Clearly articulated question	"What's the biggest number of parking spaces?"	"What is the maximum allowable number of parking spaces, given our constraints of cost and space?"
Shared understanding of the problem	"Does everyone understand?"	"Harold, can you put the question in your own words?"
Initial estimates	"Forty-five?"	"I know it can't be less than twenty because that's less than the initial amount."
Immediate next steps	"Draw a picture." "Get supplies." "Create a model."	"Draw a picture of the garden with dimensions." "Get chart paper and rulers." "Create an equation: • Slope is the amount per customer. • The y-intercept is the initial cost."

TABLE 8.3

Planning for Student Work Time: Teacher Monitoring (Look-Fors)

Once we've established key variables, a guiding question, and immediate next steps, students begin working. Within the first few minutes, ensure all students and groups are getting started on a solution path. Once students are working productively, what is our facilitation role? What should we be looking for? What should we plan to do?

It's essential to build in time to listen to student thinking and assess their current understanding. Floating from group to group and eavesdropping yields critical data about what students know and don't know about the problem or the content. It's possible that you'll want to jump right in and intervene. You may also want to plan some probing questions to help students who head down an unproductive path.

When planning how you'll facilitate the lesson, it's helpful to think through the common misconceptions students may have, and what questions you'll ask in response. The folks at the Mathematics Assessment Resource Service (MARS) at the University of Nottingham have excellent models of anticipated hang-ups in their planning guides for "Formative Assessment Lessons" (map.mathshell.org/lessons.php). For each task, they thoughtfully describe "common issues" and accompanying "suggested questions and prompts" to help students get unstuck. This is a useful practice, akin to our "hint cards" from Chapter 5, when we want to help students advance in a task via their own thinking.

When planning, you also may want to anticipate topics and prepare resources for small or whole-class workshops. In Chapter 7 we saw how Brett used sign-up sheets for targeted workshops, which he had planned ahead. Based on the conversations students are having, you'll want to be ready to host a small group for a quick workshop or engage the whole class in a discussion. Is there a common point of struggle for several groups or students? Are different groups beginning with differing assumptions or trending toward wildly different solutions? Are groups failing to apply prior concepts that are required for the completion of the task? These are good indicators to plan a workshop.

Also, plan how you'll record what you observe. For example, students will demonstrate ingenuity that you'll want to highlight in the share-out—either to illustrate a mathematical concept or to assign academic status, or both—and document for your records. In Chapter 6, we saw how Kate used a document camera to display how she tracked the norms each group was displaying—both positive and negative (though mostly positive, it should be pointed out). Other teachers use a clipboard and float around, jotting down opportunities to highlight positive work-time behaviors, mathematical thinking, and ideas for next teaching steps.

While students work, you'll want to employ the strategies described in Chapter 7, including listening to student conversations and becoming genuinely curious about what they have to say mathematically. Plan to use some of our sentence starters such as "Say more about . . ." and "Permission to be inarticulate. . . ."

Consider even your body language and physical placement in the room: what do they say about the dynamic in the classroom? There is a stark difference between a teacher peering over a desk and a teacher sitting in groups, asking questions, and listening to responses. Where do you plan to be? How will you ensure that you're not using your physical presence only in a small area of the room? When you place yourself right in the action, you transform the classroom from a teacher-dominated environment to one of shared responsibility for learning.

Planning for the Share-Out

After work time and workshops, students near a solution. Having them present their mathematical ideas puts responsibility on students while potentially assigning them academic status. To that end, it's critical that a teacher normalize student presentations. The more they become routine in the classroom, the more academically safe and productive the presentations will be (Figure 8.4).

To help plan the solution/methods sharing, consider this first: *why* are the students presenting their work and ideas? Perhaps you want to highlight differing methods that lead to the same answer, so students can make connections. Maybe you want to hear students articulate the mathematical concepts from their own mouths. Perhaps the share-out is an exercise in assigning academic status. We want to make sure we know why students are presenting their work, because that will help the presentations stay focused.

The presentation style may differ, depending on what the purpose of the presentation is. Students may present a full, formal solution to a problem or task. Or you may want to highlight a specific method a student chose. Brett is continually looking for solution methods he didn't plan on. "Because I pull a lot of my lessons from a curriculum, it's in a certain linear order. So, unfortunately, I get sort of locked in to a particular method of how to solve a problem. I want to make note of when students go outside the box when they solve a problem in a way I didn't anticipate."

FIGURE 8.4 When planning for presentations, consider how and why students are presenting and how you will prepare them.

When you plan your share-out, think about how solutions will be presented. What protocols or sharing formats will ensure that students are invested in their own and each other's solutions? How much time do you anticipate having for presentations? Table 8.4 will help you think through these critical *why* and *how* questions during your planning.

Why are students presenting?	Who is presenting?
• To highlight the mathematical concept germane to the task • To compare and connect differing solution methods • To assign academic status • To practice presenting complex ideas in front of peers • To discuss the most challenging parts of the problem and discuss how they got unstuck	• One student or group • A few, select students or groups • A few, random students or groups • Every student or group
How are they presenting?	To whom are they presenting?
• Planned and rehearsed problem and solution presentation • Gallery walk • Swapping papers	• Entire class • Select peers • Partner • The teacher

TABLE 8.4

Thinking through these questions will also help you plan the debrief portion of the lesson.

Planning the Debrief and Connections

After (or as) students present solutions and methods, make sure that important concepts shine through. During the "debrief and connections-making" portion of the lesson, you'll help students clarify their own understanding of the math concepts embedded within the problems and identify generalizations we can make about the content. Students acquired some new knowledge throughout the lesson; we want to amplify and solidify that learning here.

It's the trickiest part of facilitation, and one that gets better with practice and planning.

During the debrief, we ask questions to clarify the math content from the day's lesson. It can be challenging to design productive questions when planning, let alone when you're winging it. Because you've already worked through the task in advance, though, you'll have an idea of where the mathematical sticking points are in the task or concept. Consider starting there when you plan. What makes this task or concept difficult? As a teacher (or as a student), where have you typically seen pitfalls? What connections can you draw to previous content? Is there anything in this content that hints at the next day's lesson? Here we also must take to heart Leanne's practice of slowing down and listening to students. Ask students to be precise with their answers to your questions. Don't fret over a few seconds of processing time. Plan your questions, but allow student thinking to influence your plans.

If you're not sure where to start, you might begin with debriefs in lessons where you've had students estimate ahead of time. Revisit the initial estimates after they've worked on the problem. Were their estimations spot-on? Did they skew too high or too low? Why might that be?

In Chapter 4, I discussed one of the biggest violations of expectations my students had: scaling area and volume at the same rate as the side lengths. During the debrief, I would really try to hammer this learning home. Initially, students estimate that when you double the perimeter of an object, you double the area. Once students calculate the area and reflect on their predictions, the debrief practically facilitates itself: *they* are the ones asking why their estimates are so far off.

Consider the following approaches and questions when planning the debrief:

▲ Does your solution align with your initial estimate? Why or why not?

▲ What in this task did you recognize from previous lessons?

▲ What made this problem particularly difficult?

▲ What allowed you to "break through" in this task?

▲ What words or concepts were confusing?

▲ What did you like about [another group's or student's] solution?

Regarding this last bullet, you may plan to facilitate a gallery walk (Chapter 7) with sticky notes of "likes" and "wonders." When analyzing peer work, students engage in sense making. The best debriefs are owned by students.

Planning for Closure: Exit Ticket

In the last few minutes of class, after the conclusion of the day's main activities, plan to give students one or two problems or a reflection question related to the day's content. The goal of these questions is more formative than summative in nature. You want to see if the concepts *stuck*. In this respect, these one or two problems are as much for the teacher as the student. An exit ticket prompt can also be as simple as *What did you learn today?* Mr. Rogers–style.

Peter is a teacher in California who concludes almost all his lessons with the same exit ticket. He has a designated wall space by the door divided into four quadrants with a small icon in each (Figure 8.5). The icons represent four different pieces of formative feedback:

+   One thing that could be made better

!   One thing you want to make sure you don't forget

-�ϙ̇-   One thing that became clear today—a light-bulb moment

?   One thing you still have a question about

Students write a piece of feedback for at least one of each of the four categories on sticky notes—one per note—and place them in the appropriate quadrant on the wall as they exit the classroom for the day. Peter then collects the small pieces of feedback to check for student understanding and to help design the next day's lesson. The entire feedback session takes only a couple of minutes, but it gives Peter invaluable feedback on how to improve and useful information about what his students learned that day.

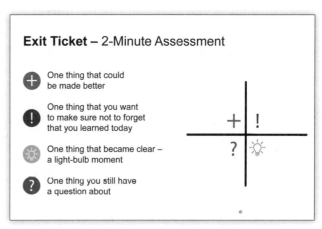

FIGURE 8.5 Sample four-quadrant exit ticket

Planning Homework*

The practice of assigning homework is fraught with controversy. Some teachers maintain that homework is critical to honing the math skills students learned in class that day. In addition, students need to get used to doing homework outside of class time, because that's a huge part of college. Other teachers maintain that homework doesn't enhance learning and only serves to kill mathematical excitement. Research studies of elementary students suggest that the practice of homework serves to exacerbate preexisting learning gaps: diligent students or students with a strong home support system will receive high grades, whereas students who lack a support system are penalized (Organization for Economic Co-operation and Development 2014). In high school environments, this disparity is further complicated by after-school activities—either extracurricular commitments or work.

One teacher I know assigns homework that requires no numerical calculation. Typically, her homework consists of things like "Find an example of a parabola and take a picture" or "Ask a professional how they use math in their work." Other times she'll have students do a mini Notice and Wonder as homework: "Given this scenario, come to class with one question about it. Be ready to discuss."

I hope you weren't looking for a concrete answer to "the homework question" in this section. Every classroom and every student is different. I've been in effective classrooms where the teacher is dead set against assigning homework. I've been in effective classrooms where—with support—the teacher assigns homework consistently. The "with support" aspect isn't to be overlooked. Secondary students lead busy and ever more challenging lives, and homework can be another hurdle. Nevertheless, the primary suggestion I would offer is to *make homework work for your students*, not the other way around. Make sure you have a well-articulated reason for assigning homework. Acknowledge its pitfalls and consider modifying assignments for some students. If you're not going to assign homework, acknowledge its intended benefits and work to accrue those benefits in other ways.

Planning for Academic Safety

Lesson plan templates typically include ample space for planning the task and planning the facilitation. They do not typically account for academic safety, despite how much we now know about its effect on students' ability to learn math. As we discussed in Chapter 3, insufficient attention or passive attention to academic safety preserves the status quo. We must be proactive. To adhere to the third pillar of our pedagogy, we need to treat it in a lesson plan just as we do the facilitation and the task itself.

Planning to Identify Moments of Brilliance

As you work through the task, what are some of the potential pitfalls and some of the opportunities to demonstrate brilliance? Is there a portion of the problem where novel thinking, risk taking, or other habits of a mathematician may crop up? What are some paths a student might take? What thinking might you have an opportunity to celebrate? Jot these ideas down as part of your lesson plans. (See Figures 8.6A and 8.6B)

In Chapter 13, we'll see the value of using common planning forms within a department. If you've created a list of mathematical "smartnesses" à la Ridgeland teachers (Chapter 3), I recommend incorporating those into your lesson-planning template to keep them front and center while planning.

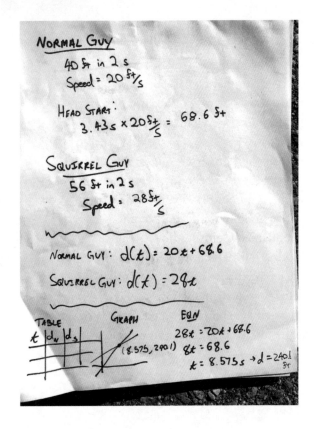

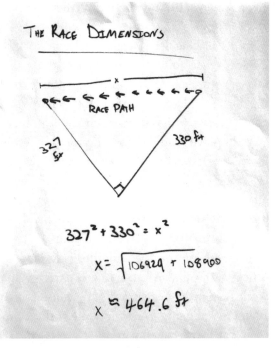

FIGURE 8.6A, 8.6B When planning this task, the teacher tries several different methods. Working these solutions helps him anticipate potential student thinking to highlight.

Planning for Peer Assignment of Academic Safety

How will you facilitate peer encouragement to reduce gaps in academic status? It's one thing if a teacher gives students specific mathematical praise, but to achieve a truly academically safe classroom, students must actively participate in the passing along of academic status. When planning, consider providing time and space for peer appreciation and encouragement. In Chapter 7 we saw the "likes and wonders" protocol for solution sharing. Similarly, a gallery walk of solutions allows students to give praise to one another vis-à-vis their mathematical work.

One of the ways that Leanne subtly encourages students to recognize one another is to notice when students do so and thank them as they exit the classroom. If a student shares a positive word with another student, Leanne takes note and, in a quick aside, thanks the student for contributing to a safe classroom environment. She shows that she notices and values such language and that there's a place for it in her classroom.

Dina often closes her class period with three questions (Figure 8.7). The first question pertains to the germane content of the day, for example "How do you write the equation of a line when you're given two coordinates?"

The second and third questions serve to bolster students' mathematical identities.

▲ "Who deserves praise today?"

▲ "How are you using your agency this week?"

Dina asks students to think for about a minute before sharing their specific praise with the entire class. One student remarks, "I want to praise Zariah for asking a lot of questions and pushing our thinking." Another student offers praise for a student who helped him get unstuck. For the last question, about agency, Dina has students share with one another how they're using their agency this week. Eavesdropping on one of the groups I hear, "I know I need to come in for tutoring."

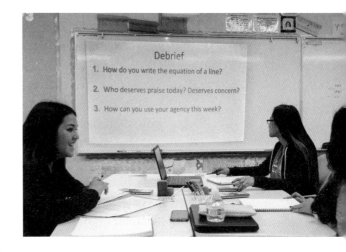

In just a few minutes, Dina has recapped the important content for the day, prompted students to contribute to peer assignment of status via praise, and given students an opportunity to reflect on their needs and behaviors. Given that Dina closes most lessons similarly, students are adept at assigning and being assigned academic status.

FIGURE 8.7 Three typical debrief questions for discussion in Dina's class

Planning for Equitable Facilitation

As you plan your lesson, think carefully about what structures or protocols you will put in place to ensure you elicit ideas and responses from every student. We want to make sure that each student gets an opportunity to share mathematical ideas. Table 8.5 offers two quick protocols that ensure that every student has time to think and has an opportunity to share.

Think-Pair-Share	Think-and-Go-Around
• Give students one minute to think silently about the prompt.	• Give students one minute to think silently about the prompt.
• Students discuss their response with a partner.	• One student in a group shares his or her response.
• Partners share insights with the entire group or entire class.	• The student to the left of that student shares his or her response, and so on until every student has had the floor.
	• (Optional) Students may respond to the conversation after every student has shared.

TABLE 8.5

You may also consider grouping during the planning phase. Haphazard or non-strategic grouping can lead to issues of academic status and inequity. Throughout the course of a class, each student should have the opportunity to work with all their peers. Some teachers have a tightly regimented rotation schedule to ensure every student is grouped with every other student for some amount of time over a semester. Others group randomly, changing groups often enough that students are sufficiently mixed and remixed. Attending to equity means promoting heterogeneous grouping early and often. Provided we are using our norms and other facilitation strategies, grouping should allow for equitable facilitation.

On the first day of school, Brett has every student use a permanent marker to write their name on one card from a deck of playing cards. Throughout the year he uses the cards to randomize his calling on students: playing cards are easy to shuffle. He also makes sure he gets through the entire deck of students before the class ends. This eliminates the potential for unintended bias while ensuring he interacts with every student. Some teachers use wooden craft sticks for similar purposes, drawing one (and eventually all) from a can (and then replacing them so students are never truly "off the hook").

Planning Modifications and Accommodations for Students with Special Needs

When planning lessons, we must consider students with special needs. In addition to individually designed modifications necessitated by students' Individualized Education Programs (IEPs), there are other ways we can modify tasks and our facilitation to yield academic safety and set students up for success.

Give students the task ahead of time. Allow students to obtain a "sneak preview" of sorts. They may take the problem home or to their specialist and read through it ahead of time. They may want to underline challenging vocabulary or highlight crucial information. They may want to rehearse what they'll say. This preparation time is a great way to increase students' access to the problem.

Provide a pre-annotated template. In Appendix H, I provide a problem-solving framework. For students with special needs, consider providing one that is annotated with key variables identified. Remember: you're not solving the problem for students, nor are you doing the thinking; you are just creating a path for students to travel.

Host small, heterogeneous workshops. During a complex task, host a small workshop of four or five students, some of whom may have special needs. Use these small groups to clarify difficult concepts and allow students to ask genuine questions.

Communicate with parents early and often. Whether it's to brag about a student, to pass along crucial information (such as news about an upcoming test), or to specify what the student needs to work on, be sure you're in frequent contact with the parent or guardian. Partner with them to learn and share information about the student that may not show up on an IEP or a standardized test score. How does the student respond to challenge? What are some warning signs I need to be aware of? When has the student connected with a teacher in the past?

Lose the deficit mindset; acquire a surplus mindset. The most important thing you can do for students with special needs is to see them as a valuable part of the class and as budding mathematicians. In Chapter 3, we learned how teachers at Ridgeland identified and communicated mathematical "smartnesses" to each and every one of their students. Students with special needs are rarely told that they are smart mathematically. Identify what makes them excellent students and invaluable members of your classroom.

Conclusion

Many schools and districts require teachers to submit lesson plans a week or so in advance according to their pre-approved lesson-planning documents. I distinctly recall filling these templates out the way students fill out packets of busywork. I knew they weren't going to be used, looked over, or learned from. They were more an accountability mechanism than a template to help teachers think about their lessons deeply.

My hope in this chapter and going forward is that you'll take a fresh look at your lesson planning. It's through deliberate lesson planning that we can integrate our three elements of a successful secondary math pedagogy. In the succeeding chapters, we'll zoom out from a singular lesson to consider the arc of the school year, followed by approaches an entire math department can take.

A reminder: in Appendix G of this book, you can find a lesson plan template that supports the approach we've taken here, including a few that have been filled out to serve as examples. However, I recommend you adapt the template to best fit your classroom and school needs. As you take ownership over your lesson plans, how will you attend to all three elements? Task selection? Facilitation? Academic safety?

REVIEW

- When planning a lesson, take into account all three pillars of our pedagogy: academic safety, quality tasks, and effective facilitation.

- We plan scrupulously partly so that we can feel comfortable deviating from our plans.

- Check the task for quality ahead of time by using our scoring chart and by doing it yourself.

- Generally, a full lesson ought to have these well-planned elements:

  - ▲ Warm-up

  - ▲ Task launch

  - ▲ Student work time

  - ▲ Solution or methods sharing

  - ▲ Debrief

  - ▲ Closing

- If used, homework ought to be meaningful and accessible for students.

- Plan for moments to call out mathematical brilliance to assign status.

- Be sure to plan each lesson with appropriate accommodations for special student populations, including students with special needs.

- Consider using the lesson-planning template in Appendix G.

Problem Solving and Pedagogy

Theresa's classroom walls are adorned with an array of student work, norms, and classroom procedures. In addition, she has a poster titled "Problem-Solving Strategies," which includes strategies ranging from "Draw a Diagram" to "Walk and Talk" to "Reread the Problem." The entries are written in several different handwritings. "Every time we do an activity that involves significant problem solving, we debrief it," Theresa tells me. "We always debrief the math stuff in the problem, but in addition we will debrief the actual problem-solving strategies we used. I ask students to recall their experience and what they did to get unstuck. Every time we do this, we get to reinforce a couple of these strategies and add a couple of new ones as well. The list is still growing.

A problem well put is half-solved.

—JOHN DEWEY,
"THE PATTERN OF INQUIRY"

"The thing that surprised me most," she continues, "was how important these 'nontraditional' strategies became to students. Most math textbooks teach you to use math-specific techniques toward problem solving like 'guess and check.' Those are fine, but what *really* seemed to work well with students persisting were things like 'Take a breath' and 'Take a two-minute break.' My kids discovered that those small breaks did just as much to help them persist as any strategy you'd find in a textbook."

I think about times I became frustrated with a math problem in high school and college (or, often these days, with the Sunday *New York Times* crossword puzzle), when I was stuck seemingly beyond all hope. Often what got me unstuck wasn't a new piece of know-how, but getting away for a few minutes or an hour. I have a vivid memory of a physics problem I abandoned after becoming frustrated, only to wake up in the middle of the night with a new, successful approach.

Theresa honors the authentic ways in which people solve problems and puzzles in her math class, and she draws upon this ever-growing list of strategies throughout her lessons. They've paid dividends! When I'm in her classroom, I see a lot of positive indicators of problem solving: students don't give up quickly, and they employ the strategies described on the poster, often using several (which, as it turns out, is one of the strategies: "Try another strategy").

Math educators have the opportunity to teach a real, transferable skill to all students, regardless of their future career choices. The nature of mathematics—the creativity, the connectedness of the content, the challenge, and the satisfaction of a completed problem or proof—makes problem solving a natural fit. We can impart the disposition and skills to solve complex issues and problems. We can make these experiences pleasurable and joyful for students so they seek out problem-solving opportunities for themselves. As George Pólya put it in *How to Solve It*, "Such experiences at a susceptible age may create a taste for mental work and leave their imprint on mind and character for a lifetime" (1944, v). Theresa agrees: "Part of the value of mathematics is that it's a natural fit to develop problem-solving skills. What other subject gives you such a robust opportunity to practice perseverance and problem solving?"

Unfortunately, this opportunity is often removed and replaced with the exact *opposite* experience. Textbooks and teachers often stymie the potential for problem solving by breaking complex tasks into discrete steps ahead of any student think time (Meyer 2010). The "problem solving" in a typical textbook example is more of an exercise in determining which formula or which predetermined method to use (Figure 9.1). Inserting the steps or formulas into a problem dampens the potential for deep problem solving. Worse, students use that experience as their framework for how to "do math," and the cycle repeats itself the next time they see a complex task.

The entirely hands-off approach to problem solving can be just as destructive as the over-scaffolded one. I've been in classrooms where frustrated students complain that their teacher "won't tell us what to do." The students know that the teacher knows

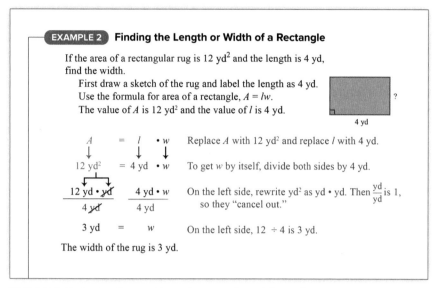

FIGURE 9.1 Textbooks often provide overly prescriptive solution paths.

how to solve it; he's just withholding that information to make them suffer. Problem-solving experiences need to be *facilitated*, not just passively assigned. Teaching them isn't a "hands-off" experience, and teachers need to aid the problem-solving *process*. And it *is* a process. Teaching the problem-solving process requires structures, mindsets, and support. It needs just as much facilitation as any scripted lesson.

The teachers highlighted throughout this book invest in the problem-solving process when teaching mathematics. In this chapter, we'll make the implicit explicit. We'll look at instructional techniques for facilitating the problem-solving process while ensuring that students are the ones solving problems. We'll see how developing and honing problem-solving dispositions and skills go hand in hand with the three pillars of our pedagogy: problem solving requires tasks that require problem solving, adept facilitation to ensure that students are solving problems, and academically safe environments that enable all students to engage in problem solving. These elements can help us design meaningful and long-lasting problem-solving experiences for our students.

Problem Solving, Defined and Recognized

One of my favorite stories of mathematics and problem solving is about Andrew Wiles, the mathematician who was the first to prove Fermat's last theorem. To hear Wiles tell it, he became singularly obsessed with this theorem from the seventeenth century:

For all integers $n \geq 3$, there is no solution to the following equation

$$x^n + y^n = z^n.$$

It's a seemingly straightforward equation. What makes it particularly vexing is how similar it is to the Pythagorean theorem, for which there are many solutions:

$$a^2 + b^2 = c^2.$$

Wiles worked on Fermat's theorem for seven years before finally developing what he thought was a successful proof, in 1993. It was big news—the *New York Times* published a story about it on their front page—but there was an error in the proof.

Rather than give up, Wiles enlisted the help of a Cambridge mathematician, Richard Taylor, to "repair" the proof. After another year, they used Wiles's original framework and (finally) came up with an ironclad proof to this age-old mathematical mystery.

In his tireless quest for a solution to this problem, Wiles displayed the ideals of problem solving in math. He persisted for a long time through great challenge. He tested and refined his ideas. He recognized when there was an error. He enlisted the help of a peer and collaborated.

Problem solving is the process by which one approaches, navigates through, and solves complex tasks. It is riddled with paradoxes. It is both internal and external. It requires deep contemplation and outward discussion. It can be incredibly frustrating and eminently satisfying. It relies on past knowledge and can reveal new knowledge.

"God, This Is So Confusing."

How would one recognize this kind of problem solving in a classroom? What does effective problem solving look and sound like? Table 9.1 provides some "look-fors" for problem solving. Discourse and body language are your first and best clues.

Signs of good problem solving	Signs of a lack of problem solving
• Discussion about the mathematical parts of the problem (understanding the problem) • Students looking at the same document • Multiple passes at a problem • Scratch work	• Students asking for a formula right away • Blank papers • Folded arms (body language)

TABLE 9.1

Let's look more closely at discourse. At Ridgeland High School, students are working on a task where they must find missing angle values in a diagram of crisscrossing lines. They're sitting in groups of three with their papers in front of them. They're struggling with the task.

STUDENT A: Since they're parallel, maybe we can use co-interior or something . . . The two insides are supposed to be equal if we're using colinear lines.

STUDENT B: Can we put a transversal in?

STUDENT C: Putting a transversal line in . . . I think it would change what [angle] 2 and [angle] 3 would be . . . I think . . . God, this is so confusing. . . . Okay, so we know the lines are parallel and we know [angle] 2 and [angle] 3 . . . so 360 minus 125 . . . 125 plus 103 equals 228 . . . and the angles we have are now 228 . . . So 360 minus 228, so we know that x and [angle] 4 both together equal 132 . . . So that's all we know so far.

STUDENT B: You would think it would be easier.

STUDENT A: Should we use our *one question*? I think we should.

STUDENT C: But we should try and go through the rest. And then come back to it. Okay?

In this short conversation pockmarked by silent moments of intense concentration, you see the hallmarks of effective facilitation as it relates to problem solving. The group is stuck, so they consider a new approach: drawing a transversal passing through the parallel lines. They also voice their frustration ("This is so confusing" and "You would think this would be easier") without getting discouraged. Finally, they come to a consensus that they should use their "one question," but before they do, they want to try the rest of the problems.

The *one question* refers to the one question they are allowed to ask their teacher during this time. They know they'd better make it count. This is a subtle but effective way of encouraging problem solving. The students define their question before they ask it. They ensure that this is indeed the problem about which they want to ask. They know it's possible that the correct method will become apparent to them after solving a similar problem, so they try that first. Through her use of *one question*, their teacher has encouraged them to persist through this otherwise difficult problem.

These are the sounds and sights of productive problem solving. The experiences are both spontaneous and carefully crafted by the teacher. The task yielded the need for just-out-of-reach information; the teacher designed a "one question" norm for the classroom, prompting students to work through the rest of the problems before returning; and their group norms paved the way for students to aggregate their group know-how as well as knowledge gaps. All the elements are here: tasks, facilitation, academic safety.

Developing a Problem-Solving-Centric Environment

Although each of the three elements of our pedagogy is necessary for an effective classroom, all three are particularly crucial when it comes to problem solving (Figure 9.2). Challenging problem-solving activities will test and refine these elements, so we pay acute attention to them now.

Academic Safety as a Requisite for Problem Solving

Creating and nurturing the academic safety required for students to engage in problem solving is challenging. Students must feel as if they have a *mathematical* strategy or insight related to the specific problem at hand. At this point, they must be able to draw on their mathematical smartness.

Students must also believe that all this work is going to be worth it in the end. The struggle that they experience through the problem-solving process needs to have some value attached, preferably intrinsic in nature.

Finally, students must also have the willingness to *scrap* a failed solution method. This is perhaps the single most difficult aspect to convey about problem solving: that a successful solution may involve trashing a previous attempt. It takes academic safety for a group of students to toss out their prior work without anyone feeling criticized or diminished. Look for ways throughout the school year to highlight, promote, and celebrate failed first attempts, and be willing to talk about your own.

Let's take a deeper look at ways to create academic safety during problem solving.

FIGURE 9.2 Developing a problem-solving environment requires particular attention to each of our three pillars of pedagogy.

Academic Safety: Equity and Access to Problem Solving

Problem solving is a skill that develops slowly over time. Students will struggle at first. This is true for students of all backgrounds. Students of low socioeconomic status (SES) may be particularly vulnerable as you transition from a teacher-directed classroom to one that incorporates more problem solving. Scholars think that students from a working-class background may be more used to direct commands and given less autonomy in their daily lives. For this reason, the thinking goes, complex mathematical tasks may be initially challenging to the point of frustration. Personally, I'm more inclined to believe it's an issue of access. Students with higher SES are given more complex tasks—more cognitively demanding tasks—partially because of teacher experience in areas with high SES and partially because of the low expectations teachers have for students of low SES (Means and Knapp 1991).

Regardless of the reason, students of lower SES often have had fewer prior opportunities to engage in complex math tasks and may become quickly frustrated in the problem-solving process. This initial frustration does *not* suggest that students of low SES can't engage in problem solving. On the contrary, we know all children can become adept problem-solvers, given the support and the right expectations. For students who struggle in problem solving—regardless of SES—consider providing more structure, protocols, and templates to aid them in what may be their first foray into true problem solving. Appendix H contains a template for a problem-solving framework that will aid in the process.

Like any muscle that goes unused, problem-solving skills can atrophy. They can practically become vestigial by the time students reach secondary grades. Be patient, provide support, start slowly, and debrief every problem to communicate the math.

Facilitation: Making the Time for Problem Solving

The process of problem solving itself is a slow one. It's important to recognize that up front so that you can allot sufficient time for it. My recommendation to teachers incorporating problem solving is to double the amount of time you think it will take. If you think a task will take one class period, be ready for it to take two. I've seen problem-solving warm-ups spiral away from the intended five minutes and take the entire class period. This is a good thing! Provided students are engaged with the problem and continuing to work through it, I'd suggest taking all the time needed. Just be prepared for it to take longer and structure your weekly agenda accordingly.

Facilitation: During Those First Few Minutes, Let Go for a Bit

Once everyone is clear on the problem and once crucial information about the task has been displayed visually, it's time for the students to begin the nitty-gritty work of problem solving. Now it's time to turn the problem over to them so they can begin working. These first few minutes of student problem solving can be tricky to navigate but are crucial to the process.

▲ **Check for understanding of the problem.** Check in on each group or student individually to make sure they at least understand the problem. Look for evidence on their paper—underlined words, pictures—that suggest they know what the problem is asking. Use this time to check in on each student. Don't ask, "Do you understand?" or "Any questions?" because you'll probably get a passive "yes" or "no" regardless. Ask a specific question about the task to check for understanding.

▲ **Don't jump in too quickly.** I've seen teachers get antsy when students can't figure out a task right away. Within a few minutes, the teacher will readdress the entire class with, "I see a lot of folks struggling with X. Why don't you try Y?" Try to resist that urge. Also, consider checking the clock, and don't allow yourself to make suggestions until after at least, say, five minutes have passed. Teachers drastically overestimate how much time they've allowed students to struggle before intervening. What feels like ten minutes is usually much less in reality.

▲ **When you help, offer strategies, not solutions.** Ask students to draw a picture of the scenario, or to highlight important (or confusing) words. Refer them to their estimates. Have them try a "smaller" problem (for instance, find the *fourth* term, rather than the *nth* term).

▲ **Monitor groupwork and group norms.** If you're employing a groupwork routine (such as in Kate's class in Chapter 6), examine evidence for positive group norms. Pay attention to body language and facial expressions. Make sure that every student is attending to the task and group members are attending to one another.

▲ **Start planning for previously unplanned facilitation.** It's possible you'll need to host a workshop you hadn't planned on. Perhaps the task has acute challenges you weren't aware of and you'll need to host a quick huddle. Consider facilitating a small workshop (Chapter 7) with select students rather than interrupting the entire class for a mini-lesson. You don't want to impede students' progress in problem solving by taking over: it detracts from the task itself and establishes a dangerous expectation that you, the teacher, are the actual problem-solver.

Problem-Solving Tasks

Let's now consider task selection and design to enhance students' problem-solving skills and dispositions. When choosing a problem-solving task, it's crucial that the teacher be able to articulate the following:

- ▲ The math content required to solve the task

- ▲ The mathematical dispositions the task will engender

As always, to know and articulate the content and mathematical dispositions that are required, solve the task yourself ahead of time. Even if you're aware of the solution, you might not recognize where potential traps may lie. So, try the problem. Use lots of paper. Write down the challenges and the mathematical dispositions this problem will build or show off. You'll want to capture this information for the debrief when you're explicitly communicating to students the math within the task. Throughout your work, think about whether this task makes for good problem solving, because not all tasks do. Recall our indicators of quality tasks:

- ▲ Spark curiosity and foster engagement

- ▲ Yield creativity

- ▲ Allow access from all students in the classroom

- ▲ Require and convey deep, crucial mathematical content

- ▲ Connect and extend content

Many of these can be applied to a good problem-solving task. I would add another, squishy condition:

- ▲ A problem-solving task ought not be immediately solvable.

In other words, the task should allow and *require* a bit of struggle from students. This might be implicit in our stipulation that a quality task "requires deep content," but it's worth being named explicitly here. To build students' problem-solving muscles, we need to give them tasks that ensure those muscles get worked. We *want* students to try out a few of the facilitation strategies listed above, and that requires a task complex enough to need them. The task must be truly "problematic" (Cai and Lester 2010).

Perhaps knowing what is truly a problem-solving task is more readily understood by describing what it *isn't*. Card sorts make up one category of our models for quality tasks. These tasks are excellent at producing discourse and engagement from all students. They are certainly a quality task. However, they don't inherently require problem solving, because they are immediately solvable (in the sense that students can develop an answer for at least one of the four elements in short order).

A task I quite like that builds problem-solving muscles is *Leo the Rabbit* (Youcubed).

Leo the Rabbit

Leo the Rabbit is climbing up a flight of 10 steps. Leo can hop up only 1 or 2 steps each time he hops. He never hops down, only up. How many different ways can Leo hop up the flight of 10 steps? Provide evidence to justify your thinking.

Having seen this task facilitated in classroom a few times (and having attempted it with my own daughter), I know that certain patterns reliably emerge. Participants draw a diagram of the ten steps at some point. Participants make a table at some point. Participants get frustrated at some point. To successfully solve the problem, it helps to get organized and go back and check your work. These are all part of the problem-solving process and are the kinds of skills we hope to develop in students!

Problems that rely on some sort of combinatorics such as *Leo the Rabbit* make for excellent problem-solving opportunities because they engender so many of these habits. In *Powerful Problem Solving*, Max Ray-Riek asks students to "Notice and Wonder" the following scenario (2013):

Wooden Legs

Wendy builds wooden dollhouse furniture. She uses the same kind of legs to make 3-legged stools and 4-legged tables. She has a supply of 31 legs.

In this problem teachers are encouraged to provide physical manipulatives to aid in the problem-solving process. Typically, when a physical object helps students understand and solve the problem, you've got a great problem-solving task.

Noah's Ark is a teacher-developed problem shared by Fawn Nguyen that has yielded very positive feedback from teachers and students (Figure 9.3).

Noah's Ark

Mr. Noah wants his ark to sail along on an even keel. The ark is divided down the middle, and on each deck the animals on the left exactly balance those on the right—all but the third deck. Can you figure out how many seals are needed in place of the question mark so that they (and the bear) will exactly balance the six zebras?

FIGURE 9.3 *Noah's Ark* task

This task is lovely for all grade levels. I've seen it facilitated with seventh-grade and pre-calculus students, and it's delightful each time. Students will take several tacks initially but tend to create algebraic models—whether they know it or not.

"I love this problem," Brett tells me. "The use of pictures helps students conceptualize the idea of variables. They always struggle and then have a 'breakthrough moment.' . . . In addition, there are several ways to look at the problem. The share-outs are always really rich. [It] gets the students talking math without them realizing they are talking math."

That's a good problem-solving task.

Modeling Tasks and Problem Solving

Tasks where students have to develop a model are excellent for developing problem-solving chops. Students will typically have to make and articulate assumptions to build the model. Real-life scenarios often facilitate assumption making because no physical scenario can be perfectly abstract. Students must identify and select the most appropriate variables.

Problem-based learning (PrBL) or *Three-Act Math* tasks are great examples of modeling tasks. These similar task models require students to assess the information in a scenario, assess what's missing or needed to resolve the question, and enact a potential solution path. Along the way, students make and declare assumptions—through research, given information, or intuition—and must construct convincing arguments for their solution paths.

Conclusion

One common frustration I hear from teachers is that students aren't naturally persevering through challenging tasks in their classroom. They say students give up easily and just want to be told how to complete a task. Therefore, the teacher is resistant to including more complex tasks. In such a case, I agree with the diagnosis but disagree with the treatment. That students don't persevere through challenging work is precisely *why* we need to give them many opportunities to hone their problem-solving abilities. If we want them to become persistent problem-solvers, we need to provide problem-solving tasks while creating an environment that celebrates challenge. We also need to make sure we're facilitating in a way that maximizes a student's ability to solve problems. We can't give up on problem solving! We need to demonstrate patience and persistence as well.

Math teachers have opportunities to advance or hinder students' abilities to problem solve in a greater context. We've repeatedly seen teachers select tasks and facilitate them with an eye toward academic safety, which enhances students' abilities and desires to persist through challenging problems. One of the great joys of teaching secondary students is seeing them learn how to problem solve through difficult situations. Whether it's finding the biggest possible value for *x* or figuring out how to pay for college, problem solving is a lifelong skill that we have the privilege of bringing out in students.

REVIEW

- Problem-solving activities offer opportunities to test and refine students' problem-solving abilities.

- Mathematicians may take years to solve a problem.

- When we're engaged in deep problem solving, our pillars of pedagogy are absolutely essential.

  ▲ An environment of academic safety is essential to promoting problem solving.

  ▲ A classroom problem-solving experience must be facilitated effectively rather than passively assigned.

  ▲ A good problem-solving task mirrors our hallmarks for quality tasks with the addition that a problem-solving task shouldn't be immediately solvable.

- Problem solving and the cognition it requires is an essential skill for students that will pay dividends that transcend your math class.

- Pay particular attention to students who may be new to a problem-solving environment.

10

Assessment

Children, wake up
Hold your mistake up
Before they turn the
summer into dust.

—Win Butler

We're hanging out in Kala's trailer classroom on a sunny Wednesday afternoon. It's lunchtime right now, and as is the norm in Kala's class, her room is filled with students eating lunch and talking about the news of the day at Samueli Academy. I'm looking at some student reflections that have been posted on the wall and ask Kala about them. "Actually, I have to go run some copies. Sandra, would you mind telling him about your portfolio?"

Kala exits the room, and Sandra—a tenth grader—starts explaining her portfolio. "At the end of every unit we collect some of our work in a portfolio and assess ourselves," she says. "We also write a reflection on how we grew and where we struggled during this unit. Ms. Gabler [Kala] likes to read a few of them aloud that are inspirational and post them on the wall."

I ask Sandra if she'd be willing to show me her portfolio. She walks behind Kala's desk and opens the file cabinet. She carefully thumbs through the dozens of manila folders before she finds hers. Once Sandra finds it, she opens it up and starts spreading her old work on the table. "This is from last year. Ms. Gabler keeps our portfolios from one year to the next." Sandra trails off as she starts examining her old work more intently. She squints at one of the pages quizzically and then exclaims, "Daaamn! I've groowwwwwwn!"

Sandra shows me one of her very first work samples. It's from a problem-of-the-week she turned in about a year and a half earlier, as a ninth grader. "Look at this!" she exclaims. "All I did for this problem was make a table and put a number down." She says it in a get-a-load-of-this-guy tone. Sandra compares her ninth-grade work with a more recent work sample, which has extensive pictures, complete sentences, formulas, and other things we would expect from a budding mathematician. In this moment, Sandra is both surprised at and proud of her growth over the past year and a half. She's beaming.

▲   ▲   ▲

As we aspire to a pedagogy of academic safety, quality tasks, and effective facilitation, we run into systems of assessment that work to counteract each of those three elements. Standardized assessments are usually filled with low-level or rote tasks. The proctoring of a standardized assessment certainly cannot be classified as effective facilitation. And the results of the standardized assessments reinforce students' negative attitudes about the subject and about themselves. Much of this system, sadly, is intractable. Rethinking assessment practices is an exercise in figuring out what we as teachers can and cannot control. As we'll see at the end of this chapter, though, there may be more room than we think for teachers to advocate for change.

Math is the most tested secondary subject. A district is worried about low test scores, so they constantly give benchmark assessments that look like the accountability test. Teachers are worried about their students' performance on benchmarks, so they give more rote tests and quizzes that look like the benchmarks. It's a cycle.

In addition to the destructive assessment practices foisted on students by states and districts, it's important that we look inward at the assessments we design and assign in our own classrooms. It's standard practice for teachers to implement end-of-unit assessments or mid-unit assessments, not to mention semester and end-of-course exams. These tests often look conspicuously like the practice problems contained in a textbook or like the questions that constitute the mandated assessments we complain about.

Teacher-developed assessment systems are generally lacking in both quantity and quality of data: the only artifact we capture is the final grade on the test. An 87 is entered into a grade book. Rarely does the number describe what the student under-stands about a specific piece of content. It's just placed in the grade book alongside other numbers from other assignments, until the numbers are "averaged" to generate a numerical score at the end of a grading period. But what does that number mean?

I never took a course on assessment in my preservice teaching program. Nor did I learn how to incorporate meaningful data into my instructional practices. Early in my teaching career, I remember standing in the teachers' lounge copying pages out of our issued textbook. I'd use scissors to cut out my favorite problems and use clear tape to tape them onto another piece of paper, which I'd copy again. This Frankenstein's monster of a page constituted my assessment materials. Later in my teaching career, we were given a CD-ROM of a bank of problems that looked like the problems given on the mandated assessment. The teacher could simply input a standard and type the number of questions he or she wanted on the assessment. These were the tools in my assessment toolbox.

Fortunately, I have since learned how to use models and systems of assessment that not only adhere to our ecosystem of a rich mathematics experience but also provide meaningful insight into how teachers can improve their instruction. This kind of assessment requires time: time to design the assessments, time to partition the data in a meaningful way, and time to process the data in a way that is instructive for our practice and for student learning. It requires effort and organization. It requires deliberate teaching practices. But it's worth it, because when we do this work, we get to see our students beam and hear them say, "Daaamn! I've groowwwwwwn!"

Assessment in a Learning Environment

The purpose of summative assessment—a quiz, a grade on a homework assignment, a state-mandated test—ought to be to provide meaningful, actionable data. With good enough data *and* thoughtful analysis, teachers can learn about their students and their practice. The same is true for students: given quality data and the methods to interpret the data, they too can learn how to improve. Assessment is just as much a part of the learning environment as tasks and lessons.

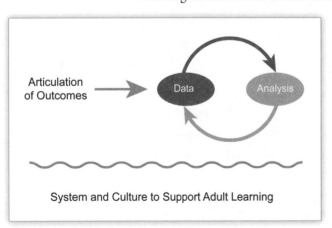

FIGURE 10.1 A holistic system of assessment that promotes student and adult learning

To achieve such assessment, a classroom, department, or school requires the following essential ingredients (Figure 10.1):

▲ Articulation of meaningful student outcomes

▲ Collection of meaningful data

▲ Meaningful data analysis

▲ A system that supports assessment and learning

We will explore each of these ingredients from multiple angles and see how they connect to our classroom pedagogy. The final ingredient, a system that supports assessment and learning, is touched on throughout this chapter but is given a fuller treatment in Chapter 13, where we will discuss many matters of systemwide alignment, including assessment.

Meaningful Outcomes

The following is a prompt I often give teachers as we begin a day of professional development:

> Concerned about budgetary matters and middling test scores, your superintendent has decided to eliminate math from the curriculum after sixth grade.
>
> Fortunately, he has granted a brief meeting with his most talented and passionate math teachers: you! You are to give a sixty-second elevator pitch to persuade him to keep math as part of the secondary education experience. Good luck!

The prompt is intended to help us take a step back and think about a few questions we rarely consider: *Why math? What is the purpose of math instruction? If math is little more than arithmetic and we have calculators in our phones, why do it?*

Given time to think about this prompt, math teachers never fail to put together a compelling case for the value of secondary mathematics beyond the actual content: math helps us become creative problem-solvers, math helps us communicate abstract ideas, and so forth. Too bad students are not traditionally assessed on these valuable skills! Students are assessed on whether they got the correct answer and whether they showed their work. And they're assessed only once per unit (twice if makeups are allowed).

If we are going to reinvent the dynamics of our secondary math environment, we must radically rethink what outcomes we value and how we assess them. If we want to say that we are attending to the mathematical identity of our students, we can't assess them only on math content. We need to assess aspects of mathematical identity. Other outcomes matter, and our assessment ought to reflect that.

Here are three options for identifying meaningful student outcomes.

Schoolwide Learning Outcomes

Schoolwide, the faculty of Samueli Academy (not just the math department, I should note) has developed and defined a set of outcomes they want all their students to demonstrate. All educators at Samueli teach and assess students on these skills and dispositions, resulting in systemwide coherence. In math class, these outcomes help guide teachers to assess what's important.

The outcomes Samueli Academy uses are as follows (Figure 10.2):

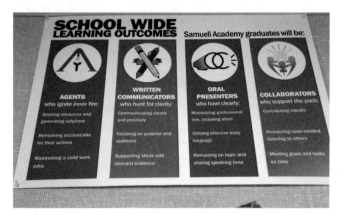

▲ Agency

▲ Written Communication

▲ Oral Communication

▲ Collaboration

FIGURE 10.2 Schoolwide learning outcomes at Samueli Academy

Every assignment is assigned a particular number of points based on the type of activity. For instance, an individual quiz may yield a maximum of ten Content Knowledge and Thinking points and five Written Communication points. A group task may be awarded five Collaboration points and five Oral Communication points. This system better aligns the task to the grade and gives teachers more meaningful data.

Mathematical Smartness

In Chapters 2 and 3 we learned how teachers at Ridgeland High School explored the discipline of mathematics, used the results to assign academic status to their students, and revisited and emphasized these indicators throughout the year to reinforce their value. Teachers also integrated this work with their assessment practices so they could actually value what they told students they value. For example, after a complex task or at the end of an assessment, students reflect on how well they embodied the habits of a mathematician using the following prompts:

▲ I persisted through challenging problems.

▲ I communicated ideas as cleanly as possible.

▲ I demonstrated creativity.

▲ I tried several approaches to the problem.

▲ I encouraged my peers.

▲ I found meaning in my work.

The written responses enhance conversations around academic safety. By giving this type of assessment, teachers are explicitly communicating what it means to be a mathematician and honoring the thoughtfulness of their students.

Common Core Standards of Mathematical Practice

Although the Common Core State Standards for Math provide a comprehensive, vertically aligned set of content standards, the authors also took the time to communicate dispositions of mathematicians vis-à-vis the Standards for Mathematical Practice (SMPs). Given their application vertically from kindergarten through high school graduation, the SMPs emphasize mathematical habits over time, very much in tune with a more comprehensive system of assessment. The standards are as follows (NGA/CCSSO 2010):

- ▲ **SMP1** Make sense of problems and persevere in solving them.

- ▲ **SMP2** Reason abstractly and quantitatively.

- ▲ **SMP3** Construct viable arguments and critique the reasoning of others.

- ▲ **SMP4** Model with mathematics.

- ▲ **SMP5** Use appropriate tools strategically.

- ▲ **SMP6** Attend to precision.

- ▲ **SMP7** Look for and make use of structure.

- ▲ **SMP8** Look for and express regularity in repeated reasoning.

Whether we use these Standards for Mathematical Practice as written, or adapt or develop our own, using a discipline-specific list of habits and practices as lesson objectives and outcomes will change how we gather and use assessment data.

Meaningful Data

When we hear about data in school, our minds invariably conjure up images of spreadsheets of student proficiency data on standardized tests. Possibly we think about attendance data or demographic statistics. These are certainly the easiest sets of data to collect, but they're not always instructive for making instructional decisions.

Todd Rose, in *The End of Average* (2017), points out that typical assessment systems attempt to aggregate first, then analyze. Schools compile proficiency scores and attempt to draw conclusions about how to improve performance. In the aggregation, much of the individual student data are lost before the analysis occurs. A system of assessment for learning does the opposite: it analyzes student work, then attempts to look for patterns, and only then aggregates based on the analysis.

When viewed through this lens, artifacts of student work can act as data just as proficiency scores do, except they can tell you more about what a student truly knows and can do.

Rich Tasks and Artifacts as Data

We've seen the positive effect that high-quality tasks can have on the learning environment, including the facilitation of a lesson and the social and emotional well-being of students. Rich tasks also unlock a universe of assessment that can reinforce our messaging around math while giving us better insight into what students know and can do. The amount of information a low-level task gives us is quite limited. Solutions that rely on recall or regurgitation are narrow in scope: there's only so much a teacher can glean from a two-step math problem, a multiple-choice clicker answer, or a memorized definition.

But as we begin implementing the types of tasks we've seen throughout this book, we start generating artifacts that reveal much more about what a student understands or doesn't understand about the topic. Complex problems that adhere to our markers of quality tasks inherently require more brainstorming, more discussion, more writing, more representations, and more hypothesis testing, all of which yield more information about student thinking. The richness of the student work produced correlates with the richness of the task. We'd be remiss if we didn't take advantage of this opportunity to learn about our students' thinking.

Meaningful Data Analysis

We've got these rich tasks and voluminous piles of complex student work—now what? I find it helpful to think of these artifacts in the way an anthropologist might behold an artifact. We have much to learn from them, so we should treat them accordingly. Complex artifacts require more than a numerical grade based on a teacher's intuition. In this section, we'll get a tutorial on rubrics and see how teachers and departments ensure students are honored for their work while they gather data that inform crucial instructional decisions.

Quality Rubrics

Let's consider for a moment how much information we lose when we use only numerical grading. A student may receive an 80 on an assignment, but what does that mean? Does that mean the student got eight out of ten answers correct? Does it mean the student got the answers entirely correct but didn't "show his or her work"? Does it mean the student turned in the assignment two days late? All the crucial information about what a student knows and can do is lost the moment the assignment is handed back and relegated to a crumpled paper at the bottom of a locker. In the teacher's grade book, there sits an 80 and nothing else. That's the only information we have about that assignment.

In contrast, rubrics capture specific data about what a student knows about a concept and how he or she performs on an assignment. Language arts teachers have long understood the power of a quality rubric, teasing out specific skills and concepts. Perhaps a student demonstrates satisfactory use of punctuation yet struggles with developing a thesis. That information would be lost if we "averaged" those scores together into one mushy number. By using a rubric instead, we can record what the student did and plan the instruction he or she needs next. Effective math teachers employ robust rubrics similarly.

For example, as Brett develops a quality task and plans the facilitation, he crafts a rubric built from the desired outcomes of the task—both mathematical content knowledge and long-term habitual skills. His basic rubric template consists of four columns moving from left to right to represent increased proficiency. The rows consist of specific skills, concepts, and demonstrated items, called *indicators*. The result is a matrix of outcomes that, once used to assess a piece of student work, provides much more information than a simple numerical score. (Figure 10.3 shows one example.)

One student may be able to demonstrate the mathematical concept at hand but requires additional support in articulating the concept. Or a student may know how to find the slope of a line given two points of the line, but not the *y*-intercept.

Rubric Energy Efficiency

	Emerging	E/D	Developing	D/P	Proficient	P/A	Advanced
Content/ Problem Specific	Solution does not contain an equation that models the cost of energy use over time Did not support your prediction by using one other mathematical model (substitution or elimination)		Solution contains an incomplete equation that incorrectly models the cost energy use over time Supported your prediction by using one mathematical model (substitution) in addition to graphing		Solution contains an equation that models the cost of energy use over time, given the assumptions about element price Supported your prediction by using two mathematical models (substitution and elimination) in addition to graphing		Solution contains an explained equation that models energy use over time, given the assumptions about element price Supported your prediction by explaining how you used two mathematical models (substitution and elimination) in addition to graphing
Reasoning & Proof (General)	Provides incorrect or incomplete solutions without justifications		Provides partially correct solutions without logic or justification		Constructs logical, correct, complete solution		Constructs logical, correct, complete solution with justifications
Communication & Representation (General)	Uses representations (diagrams, tables, graphs, formulas) in ways that do not apply to the task or are incorrect		Uses representations (diagrams, tables, graphs, formulas) that though correct, do not properly demonstrate the chain of reasoning; extraneous representations may be included		Uses multiple representations (diagrams, tables, graphs, formulas) to properly demonstrate the chain of reasoning		Uses multiple representations (diagrams, tables, graphs, formulas) to help the audience follow the chain of reasoning

FIGURE 10.3 Brett's rubric for energy efficiency includes general and specific indicators.

Or a student may have demonstrated the work impeccably but turned it in a day late. These data give us a much richer understanding of a student's understanding and mindset.

A quality rubric ought to articulate what students understand or don't understand about the math at hand, reflect how students demonstrate or don't demonstrate habits of mathematicians, and give students an explicit pathway toward improvement and exceptionalism. Fulfilling all three roles requires the rubric to describe quality *specific indicators* unique to the task, as well as *common indicators* that supersede individual tasks.

Specific Indicators

A specific indicator assesses mathematical concepts embedded in this particular task. When you're planning a task and identify the crucial mathematical content you want students to walk away with or demonstrate, you have found your specific indicators.

For example, in Figure 10.3, the specific indicators for Brett's Energy Efficiency task are in the top row. These indicators include the crucial mathematical content within this task, as well as related content from previous lessons. In some cases, the indicators reference the problem scenario specifically; others reference the mathematical content. Specific indicators should give the teacher and student specific data around the mathematical content that might need to be redressed.

Common Indicators

Common indicators could potentially span multiple tasks and multiple units. They are the "meaningful outcomes" discussed earlier and are general enough to be applied throughout the school year, or even over the course of multiple years. They are larger goals, rooted in the mathematical practices and habits of mind. Common indicators describe a holistic view of mathematics and of the student as a mathematician.

To identify and develop the common indicators in a rubric, consider the task that students are performing alongside the desired general outcomes of your math classroom. Which outcomes could align particularly well with the task at hand?

For example, Brett's rubric in Figure 10.3 contains common indicators related to his desired outcomes, listed along the rows "Reasoning & Proof" and "Communication & Representation." These indicators are assessed in the Energy Efficiency task as well as other tasks throughout the year.

Assessing students repeatedly on the same common indicators over time gives a more accurate view of how they are doing in a course and provides a more robust data set for teachers and students to analyze. It also allows for explicit messaging around growth and effort. By assessing the same indicator throughout a school year, students can demonstrate growth as well as gain better understanding of themselves as mathematicians and what professional mathematicians actually go through in solving challenging problems.

Rubrics Versus Checklists

Watch out for *checklists* masquerading as rubrics. A rubric ought to demarcate what makes particular aspects of work or ways of working *quality*, and it ought to provide specific feedback about where a student is and where he or she needs to go to improve. A checklist usually provides little information beyond whether a student completed the task and achieved the correct answer. The numerical scores affixed to the checklist items don't yield much information about what the student knows and can do.

Figure 10.4 is an example of a checklist, not a rubric, despite the title. The teacher who employs this checklist will learn little about what the student knows other than a binary—the student either "got it" or didn't. The student learns little about what he or she needs to do to improve. Often such checklists have an arbitrary point system (usually totaling up to a multiple of ten) and do not span more than one score column. In this example there is no spectrum of development provided. What does a "correct explanation" mean? If a student arrives at an incorrect answer, is it because of a computational error or a conceptual one? All these crucial data are lost the moment the teacher scores the work. Consider instead a rubric that provides useful information and data for the teacher and useful feedback for the student.

Rubric: Pythagorean Theorem Problem	Points:	Possible	Student
1. Student provides correct answer: **15.7**		2	
2. Student provides Pythagorean Theorem to solve: $a^1 + b^2 = c^2$		2	
3. Student correctly labels the sides of the right triangle.		2	
4. Student uses correct units: **centimeters**		2	
5. Student shows all work necessary.		2	
	Total	10	

FIGURE 10.4 This is an example of a checklist, not a rubric, because the indicators are based more on completion and compliance.

In Brett's rubric (Figure 10.3), we can identify which column the student work resides in, establish that base level of understanding or quality of work, and see a pathway for the student to improve. A clear rubric adheres to the concept of a growth mindset in a way that a static checklist cannot. Students see the value in improving their work when given an indicator that ascribes value to improvement.

Rubrics also help remove some of the mystery behind how tasks are graded. Brett says, "You know how math teachers are always insistent that students show their work? I feel like it's incumbent upon me to show my work as well. Using a rubric and citing examples on the work that point to the rubric indicators is my way of doing just that."

Scoring Versus Grading

At the end of the day, or the end of the assignment, or grading period, or semester, schools usually require teachers to input numerical grades. So how does an assessment system that relies on rubrics, indicators, and rich tasks align with a school system that requires a numerical end point? In many respects, it doesn't and can't. However, innovative teachers continue to find ways to "hack" their district's system of grading.

When it comes to rubrics, Christine first retrofits her indicators to align with her grade book: "proficient" is worth a score of eight out of ten, and "advanced" is considered ten out of ten. Then, to adhere to the concept of growth mindset and continual improvement, she allows students to redo their work so they can move farther to the right on the rubric (Figure 10.5), thereby obtaining a higher score.

Richy, a student in Christine's class, describes what happens when he gets a score on an assignment back. "[Christine] hands us back the rubric with the highlighted sections where our work landed. There's also a grade highlighted or written down. We usually have a discussion with her or with another student on what it would take to move into the higher column. Then she leaves it up to us on whether we want to go back to our work and make those improvements.

"It gives us a chance to understand where we went wrong as well as what we did right. Sometimes it helps to talk to another student to figure out why they got an 'advanced' when I only got a 'proficient.'"

The metacognitive act—understanding why their work is in one column of the rubric and what it will take to move to a higher column—naturally results in more permanent learning. This is a far cry from simply allowing test corrections or retakes, which emphasizes redoing rote procedures and correcting computational errors as much as conceptual ones.

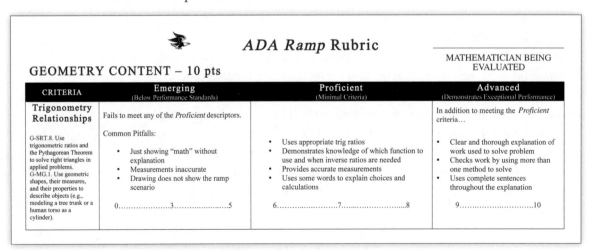

FIGURE 10.5 Christine's rubric for her *Are We Compliant?* project

In addition to collecting the numerical grade, Christine takes note of where the students are in the rubric indicators in tandem with the numerical grade. For example, she can show me where Richy has scored on certain common indicators, measured on performance assessments (PA) throughout the year (Figure 10.6). She shows me that in the first six weeks, Richy turned in an assignment that fell into the "proficient" category for Reasoning and Proof. The second six weeks shows that category as "advanced" for Richy. Because Christine has captured that data over time, she knows and can describe with evidence how Richy has grown in certain outcomes throughout the year. If she needs to return to the student work to refresh her memory or clarify the changes in Richy's work, she has it captured right next to her data as a link. It's incredibly helpful and much more useful than having only six-week numerical scores.

	A	B	C	D	E	F	G	H	I	J	K
1	Student Name	Student ID		PA: 1st Six-Weeks	Link to Student Work	PA: 2nd Six-Weeks	Link to Student Work	PA: 3rd Six-Weeks	Link to Student Work	PA: 4th Six-Weeks	Link to Student Work
2	Richy	203010	Math - Problem Solving	D		D		D		P	
3			Math - Reasoning and Proof	P	[link]	A	[link]	A	[link]	P	[link]
4			Math - Connections	E		E		D		D	
5	Jess	203221	Math - Problem Solving	E		D		A		P	
6			Math - Reasoning and Proof	A	[link]	A	[link]	A	[link]	P	[link]
7			Math - Connections	D		D		D		D	

FIGURE 10.6 A spreadsheet shows students' progress in rubric domains over the course of a year.

"Where do you find the time to do this assessment work?" I ask Christine. "I mean, you're collecting a hundred pieces of student work, analyzing them in-depth, giving them a numerical grade, and then collecting the data on which column they finished in."

"It's certainly a time-intensive process," she says. "Part of moving toward a more thoughtful system of assessment required me to think about what I could give up. I took a little off the top of many of my assignments. I give fewer homework assignments now, fewer packets. I don't give as many daylong quizzes. Also, it's worth noting that these tasks that I use to grade with rubrics often span a couple of days. It's not as if I'm taking their warm-ups and grading those with a rubric. And besides, the English teacher down the hall does this with essays all the time."

I hadn't thought about that until Christine mentioned it. My colleagues teaching English consistently grade essays, give meaningful feedback, and score with a writing rubric. I have a new appreciation for their workload.

Robust assessment allows us to—and perhaps necessitates that we—grade *fewer* things. Our feedback will be more insightful and instructive for students. Consider the difference in the potential for feedback if we assign three robust tasks versus a thirty-question multiple-choice assessment. Provided the tasks are of high quality, we may better understand where students are struggling while giving more meaningful feedback.

Teaching Rubrics and Teaching with Rubrics

Today, Brett is giving his class a task that involves creating a graph with a linear function, in the context of gas mileage and gas usage over distance. Before he gives the task, however, Brett leads a discussion of the specific indicators on the rubric students will be using for the task ahead, which he projects so everybody can see them (Table 10.1).

	Emerging	Developing	Proficient	Advanced
Math Content (Displaying Graphs)	Graph is difficult to interpret and/or its formatting is indecipherable.	Graph shows gas usage over time, but is scaled in a misleading or confusing way.	Graph shows gas usage over time and is properly scaled.	Graph shows gasoline usage over time, properly scaled and annotated.

TABLE 10.1

Each student has a small whiteboard and dry erase markers. "This is going to be our rubric for the task I'm about to give y'all. I'd like you to draw an example of work that would reside in the far-left column, the 'emerging' column." Students giggle as they attempt to draw graphs that are intentionally incomprehensible. Brett circles around the room and finds a whiteboard that is the right amount of legible and incomprehensible from a student named Denise, and he snaps a picture of it with his phone. "Thank you, Denise. Denise has excellently provided us an example of what an 'emerging' graph might look like. I'll add that to our slides." Brett quickly uploads the photo to the slide deck he's projecting so the entire class can see. He then proceeds to do the same with the "developing" column, followed by the "proficient" and "advanced" columns. Throughout the process he facilitates discussions of what "properly scaled" and "annotated" might mean, using the examples his students have provided. By the end of this process, he has examples constructed by the students for each of the four columns for this rubric. He then gives them the task.

While the students are working on the task, he quickly puts the pictures he's taken on his computer and orients them underneath the rubric. He then displays his rubric with examples on the projector. Students are now quick to check their graphs along the spectrum and ensure that they are high quality.

"I rarely even get 'emerging' or 'developing' work anymore because the process is so public and so intentional," Brett says. "We still go through the song and dance of having those columns in the rubric, but I almost never need them."

Brett's right. We need to be public, intentional, and specific when introducing rubrics to get the results we want. Students come to class ill equipped to fully understand and process rubrics. Like cave fish that have spent so long in the dark they've evolved out of the ability to see, our students have experienced years of numerical and haphazard grading that has dampened their ability and desire to improve. For this reason, the rollout of rubrics ought to be thoughtful, strategic, and caring, as Brett demonstrated.

Although the indicators of a rubric must be clear to the teacher (who ostensibly wrote them), they can often be unclear to students at first. For any student for whom English is a second language, a paper of dense text, rows, and columns can be overwhelming. Here are a few quick tips when deploying rubrics.

▲ **Start small.** Early in your use of rubrics, consider restricting your number of indicators to one or two. This focused scope allows both teacher and students to get used to the language and implementation of rubrics. Moreover, shorter rubrics take less time to create, and you might be more likely to stick with them.

▲ **Give the rubric early in the task.** A rubric ought to serve as a series of signposts to guide students toward quality work. Making your expectations public and explicit demystifies the work you're expecting students to produce and the content you're expecting them to display.

▲ **Provide examples across indicators.** Brett demonstrates how to help students determine what the indicators mean in terms of their own work. If you're strapped for time, feel free to fabricate student work, starting with what you created when you worked through the task initially.

▲ **Give students time to reflect on the rubric and their work.** Many teachers choose to have students perform a quick self-assessment on the rubric before they've turned in their work. Or they ask students or groups to swap work and peer-assess each other and give feedback. This cognitive process of peer assessment and self-reflection gives students a deeper understanding of the rubric and the content therein.

Examples of rubrics with *specific* and *common* indicators are provided in Appendix I.

Student Portfolios and Reflection

Systems of assessment and grading—even ones that employ quality tasks and rubrics—have an inherent flaw: they fail to recognize growth, let alone celebrate it. Assessments are typically snapshots in time of what a student knows versus what he or she is "supposed" to know. And the list of concepts a student is supposed to know is constantly growing over the course of a year and career.

Consider a fictional student for a moment. Figure 10.7 shows the profile of this student who is learning mathematical concepts at a steady rate. It looks like this kid is learning quite a bit!

However, when we consider the ever-growing list of stuff the student is supposed to know, his grades won't tell that story of growth. Figure 10.8 shows us this same student profile with the added layer of the amount of math material the student is tested on.

Now he's a student with some passing grades, some failing grades, and an overall middling assessment profile. It's difficult to tell that student to "have a growth mindset" when his growth isn't being honored. To convey academic safety along with quality tasks and effective facilitation, we require a different kind of assessment system, one that celebrates growth. Enter *student portfolios*.

At the beginning of this chapter we were introduced to Sandra and her teacher's system of *student portfolios*. Once a month or so, Kala will assign and collect a complex task. She collects this work in plain manila folders, one for each student.

At the end of each semester she hands back the folders of student artifacts to their authors and gives the following prompts:

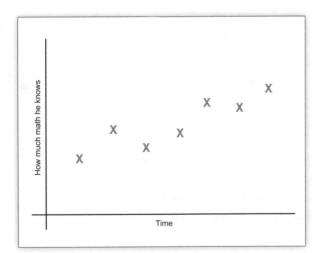

FIGURE 10.7 This graph shows the profile of a student who is learning steadily. The points represent periodic assessments of what a student knows at a given point in time.

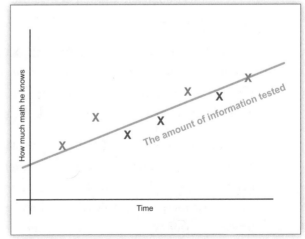

FIGURE 10.8 Because tests assess an ever-increasing amount of information, a student's mathematical growth may be hidden.

After looking through your old assignments and portfolio from first semester, answer the following reflection questions:

1. Which assignment from your math portfolio are you most proud of? Why? (Problem-of-the-Week, portfolio, test, other)

2. Which assignment from your math portfolio are you least proud of? Why?

3. Describe a specific example of how you've *grown* as a math student. What did you get better at? What evidence do you have? In what ways did you improve?

4. "Everyone can do math." Do you believe this is true of yourself? How about of others in the class or your group? Explain how your opinion about this statement has changed since the first day of school, when we introduced the idea.

Having a folder filled with a student's work is required for this intensive, metacognitive activity. That Kala holds on to these portfolios over the course of several years offers additional depth to this practice. There was also something special about the way Kala's student Sandra was so comfortable opening Kala's filing cabinet behind her desk to find her old work. She knows exactly where it resides, and she has ownership over her portfolio. Sandra's reflection is shown in Figure 10.9. I encourage you to read it fully. (Go ahead, I'll wait.)

In just a few sentences, Sandra communicates what it means to have a growth mindset better than any inspirational poster, research paper, or plea I could give. These reflections are like oxygen to me. And we wouldn't have access to these reflections had Kala not specifically solicited them.

What does a teacher need to design a portfolio system? Surprisingly little to start, because portfolios overlap significantly with our pedagogy. Table 10.2 provides some technical elements and some suggestions for resources and tools.

This year I learned the difference between knowing how to do something and understanding something. This is because most of the stuff I learned this semester was new and I didn't really understand it, so I knew that to get a good grade I would have to understand what was being taught, not just know it. An example of this was when we were learning how to do rotations, I didn't know how to do it at all so I looked it up online, asked for help from teachers, asked for help from peers, and most importantly, after I learned it, I made sure to practice it....Everything in this unit was challenging, but my mistakes gave me the drive to move forward and work harder.

Some people see how I'm able to do the math, or they see my grades and they say, "Oh, you must be some kind of genius." That's not true, I'm no where near genius, I'm just a hard worker. If I don't understand something, I ask for help, if I'm not good at something, I practice more, if I need to do something, I put my all into my work. If this is what you call being a genius, then everyone has the ability to be one if they just tried a little harder.

FIGURE 10.9 Sandra wrote this reflection after looking back at her student portfolio.

Element of a Portfolio System	Suggested Resources and Tools
Complex Tasks	*Three-Act Math* tasks (Chapter 3)
	Would You Rather . . . tasks (Chapter 3)
	Problem-Based Learning tasks (Chapter 3)
	Problem-Solving tasks (Chapter 8)
A place to store the student work	Physical folders or files
	Google Docs/Google Drive (For paper-based work, take a photo and upload.)
Student reflection materials	Rubrics
	Reflection prompts
Periodic times to revisit the work during the school year	End of the semester
	End of each grading period
	Student-teacher/student-parent-teacher conferences
	End of the school year

TABLE 10.2

The word *portfolio* perhaps isn't the best word to describe this collection of student work. An artist's or a Web designer's portfolio typically contains their best, most polished work. These student work portfolios naturally contain messy work or artifacts that may or may not represent their best selves. Think about Sandra's realization of how much she'd grown: she had to flip through her old, less sophisticated work to realize her own growth. Perhaps *time capsule* is a better metaphor than *portfolio*. On the other hand, if we think about how one of the things a mathematician does is make mistakes and learn from them, this collection of artifacts perfectly fits that bill: it's sufficiently representative of this student as a mathematician. Perhaps *a mathematician's portfolio* is the perfect term.

Now that we've given students the opportunity to learn from their own work, we will see how the educators at Bell Academy analyze student work for their own learning.

Analyzing Student Work

Bell Academy is a diverse, comprehensive middle school near Detroit, Michigan. I've been coaching the teachers over the course of a school year, and they are as passionate about their students as any I've ever met. They meet every Wednesday afternoon as a staff and have dedicated this time to analyzing student work. Teachers use pieces of the work as artifacts, the way an anthropologist might, to deduce what students understand about concepts and what pathways the teachers might take going forward.

Analyzing student work constitutes the entirety of their teacher-led professional development time. This is remarkable. As I sit in on one of their sessions, I notice that every staff member is fully engaged, using the student work to design probing questions that might uncover a student's deeper understanding or lack of understanding about a topic.

On this particular day, Jessica has brought student work to analyze. She'd asked her students to design floor plans for a house based on particular requirements and then calculate the area, among other things. Jessica shares two samples of student work, and a facilitator leads the staff in a structured conversation ranging from student understanding to the design of the task, using the protocol in Table 10.3 (also available in Appendix J).

Student Work Analysis Protocol

Prework:

Presenting teacher collects two artifacts of student work based on rich task. The teacher brings one "high" and one "medium" artifact to the session. The designation isn't particularly significant. We just need enough work to be able to learn something about what the student knows and can do.

Protocol:

- Presenting teacher describes the task the student work came from. (2 minutes)

- Participants analyze and annotate the work silently. (5–10 minutes)

- Facilitator asks, "What did you see in the student work?" Participants describe evidentiary items they saw in the work. (5–10 minutes)

- Facilitator asks, "What do you think the student thought he or she was working on, based on the evidence we see?" Participants talk about the work from the student's perspective. (5–10 minutes)

- Facilitator asks, "What questions are you left with after this discussion?" Participants share questions they have for the student and/or presenting teacher. (5–10 minutes)

- Presenting teacher reflects aloud on the conversation. (5 minutes)

TABLE 10.3

After the session of looking at student work is over, I ask Jessica about the process and what she does with the feedback. "It forces me to slow down and really consider what my students understand," she says. "In the past, even when I would assign a complex problem, I'd just assign a score based on a scoring guide—give it seven out of ten—and move on to the next paper. I'd be looking for what the student did wrong and deduct points accordingly. By having discussions like these, we're really able to get into what the students know and are able to communicate."

I ask Jessica what specific improvements this process has led to. "Sometimes the big takeaway is *How could I have designed the task better?* For instance, today, with the floor-plan task, it became clear that I didn't ask very deep questions. Despite the fact that I had them designing something, it was a lot of calculations that could be plugged in with a formula, which is what the students did. So even with the student work that was exemplary, I wasn't too sure of what the student could really *do* with the mathematics." I continue to probe, asking what she'll do differently next time, based on this realization. "I want to include more language like *maximize* or *minimize* or give students something more substantial than just *calculate*," she says. "Maybe I'll ask something where one room has to be a certain proportion

> "Wednesday afternoons are now my sanctuary in the midst of a busy week. I get to be a professional."

to another. By having students design the floor plan and *then* calculate the area, the creativity in the task occurred before the math did."

These kinds of insights cannot occur with a multiple-choice exam—whether designed by a state or a teacher. The best actionable information such an exam can yield is that X percent of students answered questions about Standard Y incorrectly, and therefore require additional class time. Sessions of looking at student work honor students and their mathematical ingenuity while giving teachers time to attend to task design and facilitation.

Although the primary beneficiary of these sessions is the presenting teacher, there are significant benefits for all participants. The most urgent and immediate benefit is that teachers are held accountable for implementing quality tasks in their classroom in an authentic way. To have a conversation about a piece of student work, the work in question must be robust. The task ought to adhere to one, if not several, of our criteria for high-quality tasks.

Another benefit is the natural alignment in practice that occurs with such conversations. Teachers come to the table from different content areas and are able to see what students in lower or higher grades are working on. Although it's not labeled a "vertical alignment meeting," one outcome is that the conversation leads to understanding of the kinds of tasks students are asked to perform before and after they are in a particular teacher's class.

There is also a deeper benefit of such sessions. Analyzing student work together cultivates a spirit of professionalism and camaraderie. That teachers are willing to spend an hour once a week after school on a content area that isn't theirs is remarkable. A staff of teachers willing to do such intellectual work to better the teaching practice of their peers is, without exception, a cohesive staff. In Figure 10.1, we saw that a strong staff culture undergirds the activities around assessment. At Bell Academy, we can see how this strong staff culture is created and nurtured.

I ask Jessica why on earth she is willing to spend an hour analyzing work that isn't from her grade level. Wouldn't she prefer to knock out an hour of grading on her own? Wouldn't it be more productive to have an extra hour for lesson planning?

"That's what I assumed at first," Jessica says. "I remember the first time we met, all I could think about were the millions of things I needed to do before tomorrow morning. But once we got into it, I found myself captivated by the intellectual curiosity that was occurring. It's rare that we spend time being intellectually curious, either about our practice or about what our students understand. Even though I wasn't presenting student work in that first session, I walked away with tons of ideas for my own practice. At this point, Wednesday afternoons are now my sanctuary in the midst of a busy week. I get to be a professional."

That's the testimony and that's the challenge with such planned sessions: keeping the time sacrosanct. I've talked to countless teachers and instructional coaches who aspire to do some sort of deep analysis of student work, but for various reasons, it falls by the wayside, often for legitimate reasons. There are always other things to do. It's easy to forget the Important for the Urgent. There must be significant buy-in from the staff to undertake such intellectual work, and there must also be structured time allotted for such professional development. This must be a time reserved for student work analysis—not tutoring sessions, or lesson planning, or grading papers. Sessions of student work analysis work only when everyone buys in and everyone is fully present.

Transparently, student work analysis is my go-to professional development activity. It's something I recommend for all schools, all grade levels, and all content areas. It's excellent for schools moving from good to great or from great to outstanding.

Toward Better Summative Assessment

Thus far in this chapter, we've taken on some rather big ideas. We've gotten into the weeds of assessment while discussing departmental approaches. These ideas are worth knowing but may take time to implement in your classroom. Now let's spend some time considering the semi-regular assessments we assign. What does a quiz or a test look like when we're honoring our pedagogy? What are some practical ways we can make our testing environment and materials better? This section will give some suggestions for changes you can make on your tests tomorrow.

Performance Assessment

Perhaps the most straightforward change we can make is to incorporate more quality tasks into our assessments. In fact, some teachers' summative assessments consist exclusively of complex tasks. Courtney is a teacher in California whose tests consist entirely of three or four complex questions, rather than dozens of rote ones.

"I have a better understanding of what kids actually know about a topic when I ask them these types of questions, rather than a multiple-choice test," she tells me. "Sure, I don't have as many questions, but there's so much work on the page with each problem, I can figure out what they know and what they're still struggling with. And that's kind of the point of tests, isn't it?"

Courtney uses a rubric to assign a grade to each problem, but also to notice and synthesize patterns where students are demonstrating misconceptions. In speaking with Courtney, I ask, "Doesn't that take a long time, though?"

"Not really," Courtney replies. "I mean, it does, but it's always taken a long time to grade tests. In the past I'd have forty questions, but I'd—of course—want to give partial credit, so I'd check their work and give partial points. It was kind of the worst of both worlds: I was assigning rote multiple-choice problems but also scanning their work for calculation errors. It actually takes me less time to grade these performance assessments than my more traditional tests."

Performance assessment is a type of summative assessment that relies on student demonstrations of knowledge on a few complex tasks (or even one), using well-designed rubrics. In a paper produced by the Stanford Center for Opportunity Policy in Education, Linda Darling-Hammond and Frank Adamson wrote, "[P]erformance tasks allow students to engage in more challenging activities that demonstrate a broader array of skills, including problem framing and planning, inquiry, and production of more extended written and oral responses" (2010, 8–9).

There is no distinction between our hallmarks of quality tasks and the attributes of good performance tasks. Both elicit student ingenuity and access along with deep mathematical thinking.

Courtney again: "I've even just given a *Three-Act* task [see Chapter 3] as an exam question. It might seem odd to use *Three Acts* as a model of assessment task, but *that's* the kind of stuff I want to assess!"

But Really, What About the State Tests?

All right, fine. Let's consider the question: *What about the state-mandated assessments that my students have to take? I appreciate using complex tasks for assessment, but at the end of the day, my students need to be able to do the rote calculations demanded by a standardized test.*

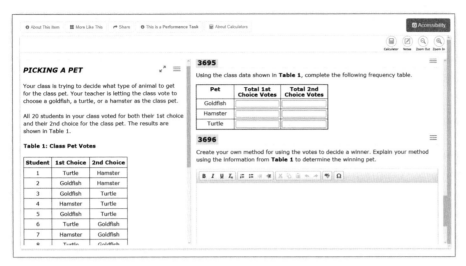

FIGURE 10.10 A sample assessment item from the Smarter Balanced test

This is a common concern. However, I'd challenge the premise of the question. Standardized-assessment items look different today from how they did when you and I attempted them in school. Rote questions on exams are on the wane as assessments are modernized. As standardized tests aligned with Common Core State Standards proliferate, the kinds of questions students are asked have changed as well. Consider this item from the CCSS-aligned Smarter Balanced test (Figure 10.10).

This task requires students to understand a real-world scenario on a deep level, synthesize data, develop a model, and communicate that model using words and mathematical notation. Granted, this is one cherry-picked item, but it's representative of the direction in which next-generation assessments are headed. A teacher who has asked only rote questions on his or her assessments is not preparing students for questions such as these. When teachers suggest they don't have time to implement complex tasks because they need to prepare their students for standardized exams, I'd argue that we can't prepare students for standardized exams *without* implementing complex tasks.

I also have an unsubstantiated pet theory I'd like to share. When I began teaching using complex tasks such as the ones described throughout Chapters 2 and 3, I began to see my students' test scores improve on the Texas state-mandated TAKS test. I compared them with the same grade level for the entire population of the school, and sure enough, my students' scores were better—not hugely better, but slightly better. And I wasn't goosing my stats with an honors course or anything. Now here is my pet theory: when students work on complex tasks, they improve their literacy as well as their math proficiency. Our school had a high population of ELL students. By giving my students many opportunities to decode a complex problem, decipher it, and understand the context, I helped them learn to work through a wordy problem, which is an essential skill on standardized tests. Like I said, it's only a theory, but it makes sense. Had I offered only rote computational problems, my ELL students would have never been exposed to the highly wordy nature of math assessment problems.

Toward Better Teacher-Designed Tests

When you think about it from a distance, the way in which secondary math teachers often assess is confusing at best, counterproductive at worst. Typically, teachers give a series of lessons for days or weeks leading up to the Big Test. Teachers work incredibly hard to make these lessons engaging and interesting. They employ many of the suggestions contained within this book, whether choosing a high-quality task or using facilitation moves that increase engagement or understanding. However, at the end of the unit or end of the week, teachers do a 180, shut down the learning environment, disallow discussion, tell students to put away their notes, and give the Big Test, which consists of thirty-five multiple-choice and short-answer questions. Even in dynamic learning environments, the assessment looks nothing like the instruction that's been happening until this point. Teachers can design the richest tasks and get universal engagement, but at the end of the day, a large percentage of a student's grade is based on how they do on the Big Test—and students know this.

What kind of mixed message does this send? We want students excited and engaged by math, but the stuff they are most accountable for is unexciting and unengaging, often consisting entirely of rote or dry word problems. So how does our dynamic secondary math pedagogy that employs high-quality tasks, ensures effective facilitation, and keeps the social and emotional safety of the student at heart interact with summative assessment?

Our goal should be to blur the lines between our pedagogy and our assessment. Martin-Kniep and Picone-Zocchia argued, "Assessment is at its best when it is ongoing and most difficult to distinguish from the teaching that is occurring" (2009, 66). Given our pedagogical model, the natural end point of this statement would be to scrub day-consuming, silent, sit-and-do exams from our teaching calendar. Scrapping the Big Test would represent a radical departure from the way we've traditionally taught math, toward one that's more in line with the work of a mathematician.

In reality, it may be difficult, impossible, or perhaps inadvisable to eliminate tests and testing entirely. So, what can we do to ensure that we're giving *better* tests and quizzes? Here are a few test-design strategies that better reflect our desired outcomes:

Make tests and quizzes shorter. Consider asking just a few questions so as not to take up the entire class period, which will yield time for additional learning or better understanding of new or prior concepts. Also, shortening quizzes will help minimize the effect of the students-finishing-quickly phenomenon where some students finish in half the time as others, which results in wasted class time and puts a spotlight on students who may take longer to complete the assessment. Shorter, more regular tests and quizzes can be more effective.

Incorporate high-quality tasks into your tests. Whether it's one or two assessment items or all the assessment items, consider embedding tasks that adhere to our hallmarks of quality tasks into your test. A teacher may wish to eliminate five to ten rote assessment items in favor of one rich task.

Assess the key standard for the week and the key standard from the previous week. Make sure you're not checking for understanding only on the most recent math concept. That way the standard isn't assessed on a one-and-done basis. It's possible that a student may understand a prior concept better after having practiced the most recent concept.

Allow for collaboration and student discourse on at least a portion of the test. Some teachers divide their tests into two parts: an individual section and a group section. The individual section would contain more traditional aspects of assessment. The group section would contain tasks that are aided by or require the input of peers. Students are allowed to share ideas and strategies fully during this section. Making this section the first portion of the test may also serve as a review, reminding students of concepts they've learned throughout the unit.

Allow retakes and award full credit for retakes. This policy can be a point of contention among math teachers. By allowing students to retake assessments—the thinking goes—we are training students to *not* prepare for exams, which, like it or not, is a part of their schooling. This argument assumes that having students come in during their lunch period or after school to retake a test isn't a punishment. Instead, allow for full credit on retakes to communicate to students that their work (and the content) is still valued and valuable. Some teachers choose to have students complete some sort of additional reflection along with their retake. Whatever route you choose to go, it's important to emphasize a growth mindset. It's difficult to encourage growth mindset thinking when a student's grade is irrevocably wrecked by an exam score.

Becoming an Agent of Change

Designing a system of assessment that supports and enhances both teacher and student learning is no small undertaking. Many of the strategies outlined in this chapter are work intensive and require a sustained focus on improved outcomes. For example, learning from student work (as the teachers at Bell Academy do) necessitates additional and specific time in the workday for meaningful analysis. Still, despite limited resources and the current test-heavy environment many students endure, there is a growing understanding at many schools and districts that more robust and insightful assessment is needed, and teachers are working to bring that change.

For example, at Sioux Falls New Tech in South Dakota, teachers were worried that over-assessing students was consuming valuable class time and only reinforcing the stratification associated with test scores. They brought to the district a proposed assessment plan that included performance assessments, analyses of student work, and a collection of student data against external rubric indicators. Their plan aligned with the district scope and sequence and included the tasks teachers were going to implement, the dates they would implement them, and the means by which they would calibrate and assess the work produced. The district was delighted that the school was so proactive and granted them a waiver, allowing teachers to bypass the regular monthly benchmarks.

> The district was delighted that the school was so proactive and granted them a waiver, allowing teachers to bypass the regular monthly benchmarks.

In many districts, officials are just as aware of the destructive nature of standardized tests as teachers are. District officials are former teachers, current or former parents, and/or former students themselves. The understanding that rote assessments can be harmful is nearly universal. The challenge lies in breaking the cycle. As much as there is a shared understanding that assessment acts as a negative feedback loop in education, there is just as much decision paralysis about what to do about it. Change requires a fully fleshed-out alternative proposal of action that will ensure that students are progressing along in their standards.

The staff at Sioux Falls demonstrated that this goal could be achieved while using a system of assessment that enriched their classrooms. Immediately, this shift freed up several class periods for more meaningful work, including the facilitation of high-quality tasks that yielded rich artifacts as data, just as teachers discussed in their proposal to the district.

This isn't to say that every school system will ease up on benchmark requirements if asked, but it's a possibility if teachers and administrators develop a fully fleshed-out plan of action complete with assessment tasks, dates when they will occur, and the means by which teachers will use and communicate the data they collect. Once you develop this robust assessment plan, bring it to the appropriate district authorities and begin that conversation. Your audience may very well understand the "why" of a better system of assessment; it's up to you to bring them the "how" and the "what."

Although systemwide change is our goal, it's more likely that a math department or an individual teacher will rethink their assessment practices on a smaller scale. Bell Academy teachers chose to analyze informative assessments during their weekly professional development meetings. Individual teachers such as Jessica use their planning periods and inservice time to take deep dives into student understanding. Every context is different, but the potential for a rich, positive assessment system is available to us. Our ecosystem of an effective math classroom demands it.

Conclusion

As we continue to put the pieces of our pedagogy together, the issue of assessment is unavoidable. Regardless of how you choose to tackle it—with rubrics, student portfolios, departmental conversations, or some combination—keep our three elements of successful math classrooms as your North Star. Ask yourself these questions for every assessment: *Is this activity and the feedback I give communicating the work of a mathematician? Is it accessible? Does it encourage a growth mindset? Am I providing challenging, quality tasks? Am I facilitating in a way that will deepen student thinking?*

These questions may seem daunting. It's one thing to espouse these values around pedagogy; it's another to work within a school system that pushes against it. So don't try everything all at once. Don't go all in. Try a few of these assessment practices and see how they go. Start small. Enlist the help of your peers. Assessment can be fraught, but it can also unlock tremendous opportunities for student and adult learning.

REVIEW

- Assessment has traditionally been destructive to student and teacher learning, drawing from rote tasks and aggregated data.

- Teacher-designed tests can be just as damaging as standardized assessments in communicating math messages to students.

- An effective math pedagogy demands an assessment system that honors student and teacher learning and growth over time.

- To start, determine the desired outcomes for your classroom or department.

- Develop rubrics that elucidate a progression of indicators toward desired outcomes.

- Many high-quality tasks are interchangeable with quality assessment materials.

- Use quality tasks that align with your outcomes for assessment.

- Deep analysis of student work can both inform the teacher on key instructional choices and offer better insight into student learning.

- A robust assessment system can lead to systemic change.

The Physical Environment

Design is not just what it looks like and feels like. Design is how it works.

—STEVE JOBS

The physical environment your students experience is tightly linked to both facilitation and academic safety. Your classroom can make for a warm, inviting space that aids in the facilitation of groupwork. It can also make for a cold, sterile environment that makes individualized work the norm. Although it's not determinative, a good physical environment can pave the way toward good pedagogy.

Teachers of elementary students know the importance of thoughtfully using classroom space, and it's something we secondary teachers could stand to learn. Having had the luxury of spending time in elementary classrooms as a coach, guest teacher, and parent, I've seen the positive effects a well-crafted physical environment can have on elementary students. At the secondary level, I've seen the significant effects of a middle or high school teacher who takes environment into account. It's more than just colorful posters on the wall; it's how and where materials are stored, how the desks are arranged, the type of furniture purchased, the technology used. A thoughtful arrangement of the classroom can minimize disruptions and leave more time for math. And sure, it's a little bit about colorful posters.

A classroom's physical environment and resources must serve to aid our pedagogy. Consider these questions:

▲ How will the physical environment allow for collaborative problem solving on complex tasks?

▲ How will the physical environment encourage routines that make for smooth transitions?

▲ How will the physical environment be welcoming to students?

Although there are constraints in any classroom, this chapter will outline some best practices and name some best materials to meet these goals.

Classroom Materials: The Essentials

I tend to see similar materials across successful classrooms. Some are costly, and others are much cheaper. Here are the essentials:

Whiteboards Brett calls the mini-whiteboard "the best piece of technology in [his] classroom." It's hard to disagree with him when I see his students use them to share solutions, agree or disagree with statements, and jot down their scratch work (Figure 11.1). And they don't cost much. Although one can purchase mini-whiteboards at retail prices, Brett chooses to purchase panel whiteboard material at Home Depot and have them cut there. He's able to get a class set of mini dry-erase whiteboards for less than fifty dollars. Bang for buck, it doesn't get much better than that.

Giant Poster Paper or Butcher Paper. To get into complex mathematics and the communication of complex mathematical ideas, you need a lot of space to write. When students present their solutions to the class (or via gallery walk, as in Chapter 7), they'll need ample space to convey

FIGURE 11.1 Dry-erase whiteboards allow for quick sketching and fluid thinking.

their ideas. They may need to draw diagrams or make a table. For this reason, having giant poster paper is essential. My personal preference is for giant poster paper that adheres to the wall, but sticky chart paper can get quite expensive. In lieu of these giant notepads, consider butcher paper. It does take a bit more grunt work to create manageable sections for student work and to stick them to the wall for presentations, but it's a considerably cheaper option.

Document Camera. A document camera or projected iPad allows presenters to project live images of paper documents and other physical objects and manipulatives, with no special markers or equipment needed. The seamlessness with which presenters can project their work allows for immediate workshopping on a concept or presentation of a solution to a problem.

Calculators. Depending on the activity, calculators—standard and graphing—can be invaluable tools for understanding. Teachers must be judicious about when to have calculators at the ready. Some wait until students have shown sufficient work or brainstorming. We don't want the calculators to facilitate the thoughtless banging away of numerical calculations or the intense step-following required to successfully find the intersection of two lines on a graphing calculator. Once a student has demonstrated how to set up or solve a particular problem, however, a calculator can streamline the arithmetic work that accompanies many complex problems.

Dice and Cards. Dice and a deck of cards serve as random number generators. Random number generation is helpful when one needs to come up with random numbers within a task (say, to generate random coordinates on a plane or tally up probabilistic events). They can also be useful for facilitation. For instance, a teacher could draw a random card from a deck to determine which group will present a solution or to determine a randomized selection of students to attend a small-group workshop. Although many of us are familiar with six-sided dice, gaming stores and online retailers have n-sided dice available for purchase (that is, dice with a varied number of sides to select from).

Additional Resources. Later in this chapter, you'll find a checklist of additional materials and classroom resources that support a positive math experience.

Modular Furniture

Over the past twenty years, the tech industry has changed the way we think about work spaces. The old assembly-line model has given way to a more fluid, open, and dynamic physical work space.

Classrooms are just now catching up to the twenty-first century in terms of furniture that enables contemporary work. In the past, classrooms typically came equipped with desks that were difficult to move and practically begged for individual work, what with the attached work surface on the right and the basket for books underneath: educational, one-armed bandits. These desks were designed for a twentieth-century learning environment. They are excellent at keeping individual students' work to themselves. They save space with a convenient basket for books. (They're not so convenient if you're left-handed, but that's only 10 percent of the population, right?)

These desks are still prevalent in classrooms across the country and make for an adventure in groupwork. In the first chapter of this book, I described how Leanne at Weirmont had to rotate and position the desks to make a sort of pinwheel so students could work together while not getting stuck. It'll be a while before these desks are fully phased out, because furniture is often low on the priorities of schools and these chairs are indestructible. Leanne and thousands of other teachers make do.

Still, many schools have been able to invest in furniture that better reflects the modern work space and better supports collaboration and discourse when appropriate. At its best, classroom furniture should be able to do the following:

- Allow for various groupings

- Create a "clean" look to the classroom

- Give ample space for walkways and movement

- Provide work space large enough for collaboration on large poster paper

- Provide work space small enough for student discussion while they work on smaller paper

- Be moved around easily to accommodate different lessons

Although achieving all of these goals seems ambitious, companies have begun manufacturing such furniture for the classrooms, just as they did for tech companies decades ago. Steelcase is a furniture company that has applied design thinking to education spaces. The result is student furniture that meets all the goals listed above.

On any given day at New Tech High in Napa, California, you'll walk into a classroom and see teachers having a small workshop with a few students, teams working collaboratively on a poster problem, and other students working diligently on individual items. The next day, or perhaps later in the same class period, the class will move the desks to allow for a whole-class lecture, when that is the most appropriate instructional format. This is the flexibility modular furniture allows and that our pedagogy demands.

At Samueli Academy, students and teachers particularly enjoy the Steelcase Verb desks (Figure 11.2), which have a whiteboard and whiteboard holder built right in. Students can perform collaborative problem solving seamlessly with these holders. The dedicated place for a whiteboard invites visual learning and collaboration. Without any prompting from the teacher, students grab the whiteboard and start demonstrating problem solutions to their peers. These desks even have little slots for holding writing utensils or calculators.

FIGURE 11.2 Steelcase Verb desks have a place for built-in whiteboards for display.

The desks are also well equipped for individual work. The same whiteboards can act as visual barriers. The scene evokes memories of those "folder forts" we used to build in elementary school during spelling tests.

Modular furniture is expensive, sometimes prohibitively so. Most teachers work with the furniture they're assigned. They push desks together; they pull them apart. This is part of the daily routine that secondary teachers go through when they want to have a dynamic classroom. Until Weirmont High School is able to invest in new furniture, Leanne will work her (and her students') arm muscles by moving her twentieth-century furniture to fit her twenty-first-century pedagogy.

Creating a Pleasant Physical Environment

We don't often have the luxury of choosing the building or classroom in which we will help develop mathematical thinkers. But we do have opportunities to create a more *pleasant* physical environment: the kind of work space that facilitates peaceful discussions and deep, contemplative thought. We can do this by maximizing the amount of (or simulating) natural light and using noise reduction techniques.

Natural Light

Maximizing the amount of natural light should be a goal of teachers when setting up their classrooms. Studies show that natural light produces a more positive and more productive work environment. Similarly, studies show directly that exposure to natural light has positive effects on learning, attitudes toward school, behavior, and attendance (see Edwards and Torcellini 2002 for a comprehensive literature review). Classrooms with high amounts of natural light also benefit from a reduction in flickering or incandescent light, which can cause eyestrain.

It's not always possible for teachers to be in control of the amount of natural light they have access to. In lieu of natural light, consider lamps that serve as a natural light substitute.

Sound Reduction

Classrooms that are too loud can make concentration difficult for many students. Secondary classrooms are often built to maximize the number of bodies that can be reasonably put in a room, not for acoustics. The floors and walls in secondary classrooms can harshly amplify sound waves and allow them to reverberate. The best strategy for noise reduction is to use effective facilitation strategies, such as those found in Chapter 6 (developing a norm around talk volume) and Chapter 7 (using small-group workshops). One of our goals is to maximize student-to-student mathematical discourse, which naturally increases the volume in a classroom, so it's important that we teach students to use appropriate voice levels in their groups.

One antidote to a classroom whose walls and floors deliver a harsh reverberation of sound is simply *stuff*. The more objects within an acoustic space, the more places sound waves can go to be dampened and die. In particular, rugs with their high surface area and soft fabric absorb sound efficiently. Putting up foam posters or felt is a way of adding color to a room while reducing sound. Provide as many escape hatches and captures for sound as possible.

Starter Supplies

Let's talk teaching supplies. Although every physical space and content area has different needs, a starter set of teaching supplies will make your daily lesson planning much easier. Rather than having to run to an office supply store at night to purchase three dozen dice because you are teaching a lesson on probability the next day, keep your supply closet well stocked with the items listed in Table 11.1 on the following page.

I left a few blank spots so you can write in your own. Once you have a list like this, you can take advantage of cheap buys when they're on clearance or at a thrift store, rather than after a long day of teaching.

Starter Supply List	
Dry-erase markers and erasers	Scissors
Dice	Compasses (Staedtler brand recommended)
Patty Paper	A few decks of cards
Glue sticks	Reams of graph paper
More dry-erase markers	Sticky notes
Poster Pads	Rulers
Protractors	Pennies
Golf pencils and erasers	Colored pencils
Measuring tape	Yardsticks
Yarn	Tape (Scotch, masking, and painter's)
Even more dry-erase markers	

TABLE 11.1

Modern Computing Technology

Access to technology has never been more ubiquitous in classrooms across the country. Computers have become as much a part of the classroom experience as calculators were thirty years ago, and as the chalkboard a hundred years ago. Often computers arrive in the classroom as part of a bond or district initiative to give students more access to twenty-first-century technology. Although such ambitions are noble and potentially effective, teachers are often at a loss about how to best navigate this new dynamic.

Initiatives that seek to push technology and Internet access to students often do so without a purpose or plan. Technology becomes the *thing* that the kids are learning about, not content. Rarely are teachers consulted or given training on what they are supposed to do with student laptops that allow them to have the world's information at their fingertips.

I've seen countless (and at this point, predictable) such cycles: A district passes an initiative to get technology in the hands of students. Thousands of computing tablets or laptops get purchased over the summer. By fall, these devices are issued to students. Teachers aren't sure exactly what to do with them at first. Sometimes the school purchases an instructional software package, also at great cost. That package then becomes the purpose of the laptops: to host the instructional software, the effectiveness of which is debated. At some point the laptops become a classroom management issue as students find ways around firewalls and Internet blockers. Or students get off task and use other apps. Sometimes the laptop breaks or loses functionality and a replacement must be procured. Even when everything is working perfectly, students can mindlessly click through instructional software tutorials and make haphazard guesses at online quizzes until they achieve "proficiency" and can move along to the next lesson. I've had students tell me point-blank that they just keep taking the same computer assessment over and over until it gives them a green check mark, allowing them to move on and receive a passing grade.

At this point, mathematics has ceased to be the learning outcome; navigating the instructional software is the new learning outcome. It's difficult to see how such environments promote quality tasks, effective facilitation, and academically safe environments. It is possible, however. Instructional software and Internet access can have positive outcomes on learning math, so long as they're approached purposefully and with intention.

Making Instructional Software Work for Students

Classrooms that employ instructional software effectively use it to complement their stellar pedagogy, not as a replacement. There are benefits to using well-designed instructional software, including

- ▲ the ability to keep track of student understanding,

- ▲ coherence in standards that accompany professionally developed software, and

- ▲ time for students to get individual assistance in a nonthreatening atmosphere.

There are also significant potential pitfalls that instructional software helps teachers fall into, including the following:

- ▲ Students rarely engage in mathematical discourse.

- ▲ Students are constantly presented with rote, low-level, or unengaging math tasks.

▲ Teachers may not develop close relationships with students if kids are plugged into screens during the entire period.

▲ The data captured are incomplete (see Chapter 10 regarding data).

Staff at Bell Academy use instructional software flexibly to reinforce procedural skills and keep tabs on their students' progress. Typically, teachers will employ a rich, complex teaching task (such as those outlined in Chapters 4 and 5) and follow that up with an appropriate activity on the instructional software. You can see this in a snapshot of their weekly schedule (Table 11.2).

Monday	Tuesday	Wednesday	Thursday	Friday
Complex Problem (Day 1)	Complex Problem (Day 2)	Instructional Software (Day 1)	Instructional Software (Day 2)	Problem-of-the-Week

TABLE 11.2

On Monday and Tuesday, teachers use a complex teaching task to illustrate or explore a new concept, typically in groups. On Wednesday and Thursday, they'll have students use their laptops to work through the instructional software to reinforce concepts from the task, as well as fill in any gaps that may have cropped up. On Friday, they'll shelve the laptops again as they work through a rich problem-of-the-week.

This weekly schedule allows teachers to maintain the elements of an effective classroom while gleaning the benefits of instructional software. Students get time to work in groups on Mondays, Tuesdays, and Fridays and time to work independently on Wednesdays and Thursdays. Teachers at Bell Academy also will swap days around, depending on the content, task, or outside events (such as pep rallies, snow days, and so on).

Even so, teachers at Bell Academy offer a word of caution. They had to (and have to) fight for such a flexible schedule. Early on, they would get reprimanded by the district for not following the instructional software to a T. The district spent a lot of money on the hardware and software, and districts don't like to think that their money was ill spent. Sadly, this stance is typical of districts that make such a financial investment: we bought this stuff for your classroom, so you ought to be using it to its maximum. Bell Academy consistently has to provide data, lesson plans, and reasoning why they're not using the software five days a week. Fortunately, for the past few years they've been able to do that, reaping the benefits of our pedagogy and those offered by instructional software.

Making Internet Access Work for Students

A colleague of mine offered a warning a few years ago: "When you give students laptops with Internet access, everything about the class has to change. You can't teach the same way, asking the same type of questions." He's right. At the point of this writing, a student can type an equation into Google or Wolfram Alpha and receive a solution for x. In fact, students can dutifully type derivatives and integrals into Wolfram and receive answers. A worksheet asking students to calculate ten different definite integrals becomes an exercise in transcription.

So how can we use the Internet to learn mathematical content, rather than just look it up and copy it down?

Project-based learning (PBL) is one pathway toward effective use of the Internet as a tool. In Chapter 5 we saw how Christine had students research the Americans with Disabilities Act to determine the specifications for wheelchair ramp compliance. In this case, the students' online research necessitated mathematical investigation, rather than supplanted it.

PBL units can also include authentic data as the artifact of study. Data from local and federal agencies are often freely available online:

Authentic Data Sources

National Oceanic and Atmospheric Administration (NOAA)

National Center for Atmospheric Research (NCAR)

The Census Bureau

Environmental Protection Agency (EPA)

World Food Project (WFP) and Mobile Vulnerability Analysis and Mapping (mVAM)

In lieu of using previously collected data, some teachers make data collection a part of their PBL units. I've seen students design surveys using Google Forms to collect data on a variety of issues, from community needs to favorite after-school activities. After the creation and implementation of such surveys (which in itself necessitate learning what makes a good survey question), students can conduct statistical analysis on the responses. A high school statistics class may explore whether a statistical finding is significant according to its p-value. A middle school classroom may determine the median of a dataset.

Teachers also may wish to take a more curated approach to Internet access by using select online activities specifically designed for students. When assessing the effectiveness of the Internet-aided activity, our triad still applies. Ask these questions of the activity:

▲ Does it reinforce messages around academic safety? (Chapters 2 and 3)

▲ Is this a high-quality task? (Chapter 4)

▲ Does it allow for effective facilitation? (Chapters 6 and 7)

The same questions I posed in Chapter 7 (*Who is talking? What are they saying?*) also still apply. The best technology-aided activities evoke the same delight and discourse that the best pencil-and-paper activities do. For example, Internet-enabled activities can be a boon when exploring spatially heavy topics, such as geometric constructions. It's possible to drag a point around a screen and see what happens in a way that is impossible with paper and pencil.

The programmers at Desmos (www.desmos.com) understand this advantage well. They have enabled their online calculator to handle "sliders." That is, a variable may be defined and assigned a range of values. Learners can drag the slider to different values and see the resultant change on the graph. This interactive feedback yields a delightful and connected experience. Students do not need to draw an entirely new graph to see what a small change to the slope does; they may simply drag it a few pixels over and reflect on the change in the graph (Figure 11.4). Or, students can move a slider around to see the effect of dilating a particular object on a coordinate plane. The possibilities for investigation are endless, and still require a facilitator to help make sense of the activity.

FIGURE 11.3 A student comparing two parallel lines uses the Desmos graphing calculator.

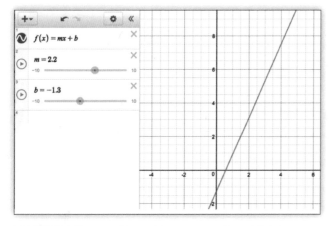

FIGURE 11.4 Desmos sliders enhance sense making while being a delight to use.

Desmos has begun applying the "ahas" provided by a dynamic graphic calculator more broadly, and now hosts a cache of high-quality, online activities that maintain their commitment to pleasurable, playful, and connected mathematics. In addition to the *Polygraph* activity mentioned in Chapter 5, the teaching faculty at Desmos has developed lessons across all secondary grades that adhere to our hallmarks of quality tasks. In addition to the excellent lessons they develop in-house, Desmos also relies on the math teaching community writ large via a searchable "activity builder."

Recently, I asked some teachers to give some quick feedback on a slew of tasks I sent their way, including some from Desmos. It wasn't terribly scientific, but I did ask, just on a gut-feeling level, about the quality of about twenty different tasks that they employed in their classrooms. Among the highest rated were Desmos's *Function*

Carnival (Figure 11.5) and *Central Park* (Figure 11.6). The teachers I polled said that students were immediately puzzled by the scenarios and wanted to keep refining their solutions until they got them as correct as possible.

When incorporating technology into the classroom, teachers need a keen and skeptical eye.

▲ Is the technology provided in service to the math (rather than the other way around)?

▲ Does the technology enable mathematical discourse or hinder it?

▲ Will this technology result in my desired outcomes?

▲ What are the potential pitfalls that could result from this technology?

Teachers also need to consider the long-term effect of technology on their classroom and the potential unintended consequences of students having access to computing and technology:

▲ What expectations am I setting up by having technology in the classroom?

▲ Do I have the agency to change things around if I see it isn't working?

▲ Beyond student achievement data, how will I know that the technology is resulting in better math outcomes?

▲ How will I roll out technology in a measured, manageable way (as opposed to that of the ensuing chaos from a dam breaking)?

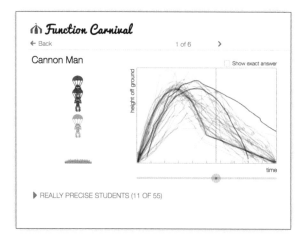

FIGURE 11.5 Function Carnival is one of Desmos's highly rated tasks.

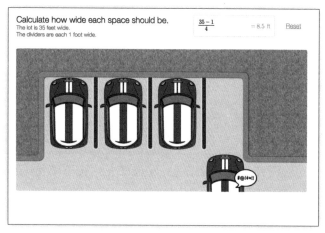

FIGURE 11.6 Central Park is another highly rated task from Desmos.

Technology has the power to disrupt a classroom, positively and negatively. Be sure to consider these questions and be intentional about its deployment.

The Prominence of Student Work

Although classrooms differ wildly in their physical space, furniture, access to technology, and a host of other variables discussed in this chapter, there is one consistent feature I see in every effective learning environment: the prominent display of student work. Whether the teacher has thirty-year-old student desks or every student has access to a Google Chromebook, effective teachers have work displayed prominently (Figure 11.7). And to be more precise, the work that's displayed is often the type of work worthy of our student portfolios from Chapter 10, or problem-solving tasks from Chapter 9. In other words, teachers don't just post tests that receive high marks. Instead, the type of work displayed celebrates students' work through a challenging task.

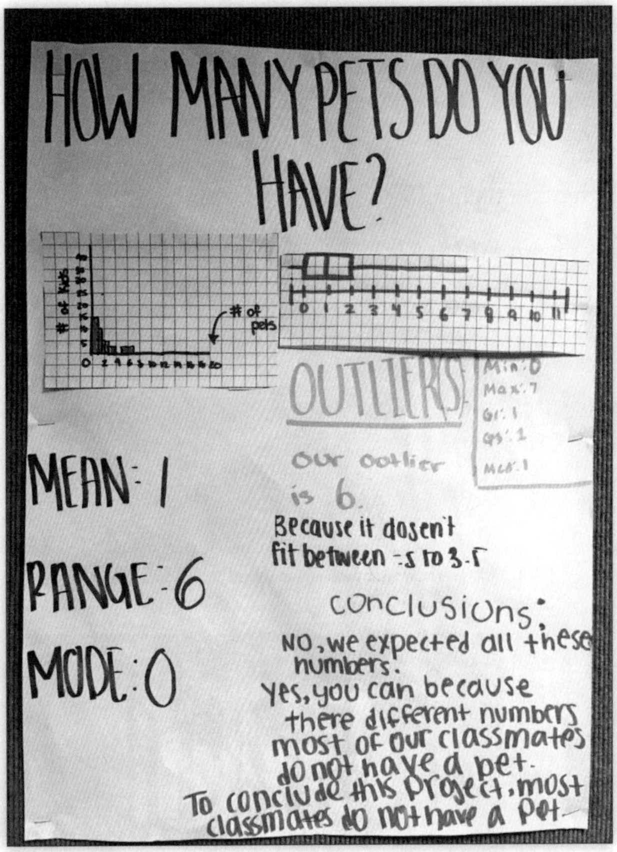

Granted, this pattern is more correlation than causation: prominent displays of student work are probably a lagging indicator of a successful classroom rather than a leading one. Regardless, student work speaks to the type of tasks teachers are assigning their students and the value they put on the work students produce.

FIGURE 11.7 Student work adorns the walls of effective math classrooms.

Conclusion

Designing a welcoming educational environment doesn't *feel* like something a secondary educator ought to be too concerned with. But in the most effective classrooms I've been in, teachers make the physical environment as pleasing to be in as possible. And creating a welcoming, effective physical environment doesn't mean to just "add more posters" or buy a plant to make the room more colorful (though they couldn't hurt). It means considering the look, feel, sound, and malleability of the classroom in a way that speaks to our pedagogy. Most important, the way you set up your classroom speaks to your values as an educator.

REVIEW

- The physical environment and supplies we provide students can streamline our facilitation while promoting a safe atmosphere conducive to challenging work.

- As much as you can, encourage as much natural light as possible and seek ways to minimize harsh, distracting noise.

- Identify necessary and useful supplies ahead of time to save on the midyear stress of purchasing materials, and possibly to save money by looking for deals.

- Modern technology can be a boon as well as a hindrance to mathematical understanding; be intentional about rolling it out, and be sure you know its purpose.

- Display student work and student thinking prominently.

ZOOMING

OUT

From the Lesson to the Year, from Classrooms to Systems

n 1957, Dutch teacher Kess Boeke published *Cosmic View: The Universe in 40 Jumps*. Starting from a single scene—a woman holding a baby—he zooms out by a factor of ten on every page. On the subsequent page we see and read about a whale. On the page after that, he zooms out by another factor of ten, describing and revealing a picture of a military base. With every page he zooms out another factor of ten until we're 100 million light-years from where we started, the original scene only hinted at by a point in the midst of galaxies beyond our imagination. *Cosmic View* was the inspiration for the famous film *Powers of Ten* (1977), which zooms out to 100 million light-years and zooms in by powers of ten to a single proton.

We started our journey with a single student, Damien, in Chapter 1. We panned our camera sideways across the classroom, zooming in to single moments with an eye toward individual students. We stopped the camera at different aspects of effective math classrooms—our three-legged pedagogy. Starting in Chapter 8, we began putting the puzzle pieces together to develop a full picture of lessons in effective secondary classrooms. In Chapter 12, we will zoom out, moving from structuring a single lesson or single unit to a coherent, cohesive yearlong approach to math. In Chapter 13, we'll zoom out farther from a classroom to a math department, learning how teams of teachers improve over time. We'll see how systems affect students and how teachers can affect systems.

Now we shall continue to look for representatives of the living world in all succeeding scales. Rather strange coincidences will occur in the following pictures: unexpected things coming together on the hand of this child!

— KESS BOEKE, *COSMIC VIEW: THE UNIVERSE IN 40 JUMPS*

CHAPTER

12

Structuring the Year

My mathematical mind can see the breaks. So I'm gonna stop riding the brakes.

—BRITT DANIEL

"I don't start with content," Missy begins. She catches herself. "Actually, let me take that back. I start with *real* content. *Real* math." I ask her what she means by "real" mathematics. "I use the start of the year to showcase the best of what mathematics has to offer," she says. "I do that through activities that give students the message that they are smart in math and can be successful in my class." I find this interesting. Most scope and sequences suggest beginning the year with rudimentary content that is supposedly necessary for the course: a geometry textbook will often start with a unit on vocabulary, an eighth-grade textbook will begin with a recap of arithmetic and order of operations. Missy's goal for the first unit of instruction in her algebra class is different.

Whereas an initial unit of an algebra class might be titled something like "Chapter 1: Introduction to Functions," Missy titles her first unit "Unit 0: Mathematical Smartness." The unit consists of four or five problems (it varies, depending on the schedule and the year). The problems adhere to several of our hallmarks of a quality mathematical task from Chapter 4. They aren't, however, explicitly tied to the upcoming algebra content for the school year. Rather, they introduce the mathematical dispositions she wants her students to experience. To Missy, it is more important that students begin the year with engaging activities that showcase the discipline of math. She's less concerned about priming students for upcoming investigations into equations in point-slope form and more concerned about getting students excited for her classroom.

One of Missy's favorite mathematical tasks for the beginning of the year is Hotel Snap. This activity was the brainchild of middle school teacher Fawn Nguyen, and was later adapted and published to NCTM's Illuminations website. Missy immediately found this lesson engaging and wanted to incorporate it into her class. She didn't let the fact that NCTM lists the standards as sixth grade deter her one bit. The task was engaging enough, accessible enough, and complex enough that she wanted to use it in her class.

In Hotel Snap, students construct "hotels" out of Snap Cubes. Each type of hotel room is worth a different monetary amount: a corner room is worth more than an inside room, a higher floor is worth more than a lower floor. There are also constraints to ensure the hotel is structurally sound: it must be able to stand on its own. Students keep track of the value of their hotels and try to maximize their worth. Working in pairs or triads, they use the Snap Cubes to build, unbuild, and rebuild through multiple attempts. A full description of Hotel Snap can be found in the Problem-Based Learning section of the Task Library pages 316–319.

Missy follows Hotel Snap with a debrief discussion that ties back to the title of the unit: Mathematical Smartness. She asks students what kinds of thinking and working they engaged in throughout the activity. Missy records these responses at the front of the room:

We tried multiple designs before we got our best solutions.

We talked to each other throughout the activity.

We were focused.

We used our hands as well as our brains.

Each group took a different approach.

These behaviors and mindsets that Missy records are exactly the behaviors and mindsets she wants to see from her students throughout the year.

The day after the Hotel Snap debrief, Missy gives students *Leo the Rabbit*, seen in Chapter 9. Once again, she records the behaviors and mindsets the task yielded that day. By the end of the week, she has a documented list of mathematical attributes that students have demonstrated and practiced. This is the foundation on which her students will construct their mathematical identities.

All of the tasks Missy provides in her first week of classes adhere particularly well to the following two descriptors of a quality task:

▲ They yield creativity.

▲ They can be accessed by all students in the classroom.

By focusing on tasks with these two traits, Missy lays the foundation for her course and for what mathematics can be. Students who enter her class on Day 1 feel welcomed, regardless of their past experiences. For some, it's a fresh start. For others, it's a new way of experiencing the fun and beauty of math. For most, it's both of these.

And about the actual algebra content in her course: isn't she starting off "behind"? Missy isn't too worried. "I know we spend a week at the front of the year not seemingly doing algebra. It's true: compared with other algebra teachers in the district we kind of start a week behind. But we always make up that ground throughout the year because we've laid the groundwork for things like groupwork and having students believe that they are smart mathematicians, which is kind of new for some kids. And it's not as if we're *not* doing math. These are probably the *most* 'mathy' things we can do!"

Missy devotes the first week to building a foundation, but she builds on that foundation all year long through high-quality tasks, effective facilitation, and tending to the social and emotional safety of her students. She continues to offer her students opportunities to engage in rich tasks and develop their mathematical smartness throughout her units of instruction and within her assessment practices. Starting from the first week, Missy structures her year so that students will exit knowing that they are smart and capable mathematicians.

Planning Your Year

Over the course of this book, we've zoomed in to look at individual elements of effective math classrooms, including lesson planning and assessment strategies. Now we are going to zoom out and look at the entire school year. Individual lessons, activities, and interventions are a net positive, but a long-term approach can truly change how students experience mathematics. It requires yearlong commitment to improve outcomes: commitment to the tasks students are working through, commitment to improving facilitation, and commitment (to the point of vigilance) to treating social and emotional safety. Finally, it takes commitment to put these together in a coherent narrative.

It's challenging to plan through these issues on a day-to-day basis. Even the act of selecting a task requires a significant investment of time, and teachers must work through the task as part of planning to facilitate it with students. These two acts (selection and solution) can consume the entirety of a teacher's planning period. Where does one then find the time to take care of the additional duties of an effective teacher: calling parents, planning for differentiation, entering report card information? How do we plan for quality when we also have the very real need to get things done?

There are no easy answers to this challenging question. A short answer that might get me in trouble is to do *some* planning over summer vacation, although even the word *planning* doesn't convey the light touch I have in mind. Consider reading some books that are delightful and contain materials for use. For instance, Paul Lockhart's *Measurement* (2014) is at once a joy to read and chock-full of interesting mathematical investigations. "Planning" in such an instance might be dog-earing a page with an interesting math question. Or it could be simply keeping an eye out for potential mathematical scenarios, as described in Chapter 5. Let me be clear: summer vacation is a time of renewal, and renewal is imperative. I'd argue it's possible to experience renewal and also keep your mathematical radar open for ideas and joyful math problems.

It is unreasonable to ask a professional to change much more than 10 percent a year, but it is unprofessional to change by much less than 10 percent a year.

It's also important to set reasonable, realistic goals for planning. I'm reminded of one of Steve Leinwand's "Four Teacher-Friendly Postulates for Thriving in a Sea of Change" (1994). His third postulate says, "It is unreasonable to ask a professional to change much more than 10 percent a year, but it is unprofessional to change by much less than 10 percent a year."

I ask you to keep this "10 percent rule" in mind as you consider planning your school year. Were you to adopt all of the strategies outlined in this book all at once, you might burn out or perhaps not sleep for a year. And I'm the last person to recommend not getting sleep. Rather, consider your current practice—your tasks, your facilitation, and the academic safety of your classroom—and think about what a 10 percent change would look like. Ten percent is a rough estimate, and implementation varies, depending on what you choose to try. Still, a 10 percent change in task usage, for example, would map out to one day every other school week if we were to think about it in sheer calendar-ese. That seems manageable.

During the school year, as much as you can, plan ahead as far as possible, perhaps even for the entire year. Although it's certainly possible to develop tasks and establish structures during the school year, it's difficult to tackle these demanding mental exercises with the knowledge that in thirty minutes the bell is going to ring and your classroom will be inundated with twenty-five to thirty teenagers. The longer view we have of our classroom, the more we may be able to mentally devote to its improvement. Here are some ways to do just that.

Tending to the Social and Emotional Well-Being of Your Students

Throughout this book, we've seen ways of attending to students' mathematical identities (Figure 12.1). Some of these are strategies that require thoughtful planning, such as assigning status intentionally (Chapter 3). Other suggestions are baked in to the day-to-day ways in which you treat your students, such as authentic caring (Chapter 3). As you think about your year, consider which intentional strategies you'll employ, and in which areas you want to demonstrate more day-to-day building of academic safety.

Regardless of which strategies you employ, you'll want to collect information (data) on how students are experiencing your classroom and seeing themselves as mathematicians. Consider asking them informally (we'll see an example of a lunch panel in Chapter 13) or formally via a survey of mathematical mindsets, such as the Community School did.

FIGURE 12.1 It's important to take stock of each and every student's well-being regularly throughout the year.

Mathematical Mindset Survey

The Community School is in Spokane, Washington. Each year, the teachers identify one key focus area for the entire staff to work on. This year, they have identified math as their primary focus. This decision was a result of some test score data, but also the general sense identified by their math teachers that students seemed disengaged and rarely wanted to work on challenging, complex problems.

The teachers at Community wanted to understand more about the underlying issues before trying to solve them. They began the year by designing a survey for their students that asked about their mindsets around math. The survey included free-association exercises, agree/disagree statements, short answers about what they believe mathematicians actually do, and other questions that would uncover what students think about math and what they think about themselves as mathematicians. The survey was given in the form of an anonymous Google Form. The responses were revealing, if unsurprising. In response to the prompt, "Do you think you are good at math? Why or why not?" they received the following:

▲ I believe I'm okay at but increasing in knowledge everyday. why? well because some problems i do know and some i don't. The ones i don't know increase my knowledge when i give them a try.

▲ I think I am decent at math, when i apply myself.

▲ no because I don't have a lot perseverance, but I'm working on that.

▲ Yes. I like math, so I don't give up. I'm good at puzzles and figuring stuff out.

▲ No because it doesn't interest me. I am also afraid of being wrong.

▲ no because I don't have patience and i learn math better when it's an actual class that's not on the computer.

These were just a few responses out of the hundreds they received, but they're a representative selection. More to the point, there was an Agree/Disagree/Unsure prompt that went with "I think I am good at math." Thirty-nine percent of students agreed that they were good at math. Twenty-four percent agreed that "Math is fun."

The survey data helped the staff of Community better understand their students' mindsets. From here, they were able to design an action plan. They started by employing a strategy that felt quickly implementable: Number Talks (Chapter 5). They spent the first few months of the school year building up each student's sense of mathematical self by encouraging multiple ways of looking at a problem and ascribing value to all of them.

As they continued to analyze the survey results, Community staff members felt like they needed to go further. After reaching out and looking at the data, they decided to do the work of assigning academic status (Chapter 3). By iteratively surveying the students' mathematical mindsets, teachers were able to sustain messaging around academic safety. Throughout the year, the staff designed strategies to address specific gaps and shortcomings they saw in the survey data.

Planning Tasks Throughout the Year

Planning one's units of instruction involves making value choices. A commitment to student-centered and content-centered learning leads to an exercise in prioritization, whether determining the relative importance of a content standard or discovering an acute gap in student understanding. Prioritizing one understanding over another is difficult to square with district scope and sequences that frame standards or lessons as one-time events. In these documents, once a standard is "covered," it is time to move on to the next standard. Rarely do district scope and sequences allow for additional exploration of crucial content, or for teachers to adjust their plans based on student need.

A teacher with agency, however, knows what concepts might require additional prioritization and is empowered to make instructional decisions in response. And if the teacher does not know, he or she can look at data from the prior year's test results according to standard or have a five-minute conversation with a teacher from a grade level above. Either way, the teacher learns which concepts might require additional class time.

Bell Academy teachers work together to prioritize units of instruction using a template consisting of "power standards," essential questions, real-world applications, and performance assessments. Their power standards are more general concepts and clusters of related standards, rather than precise, singular standards: think big topics such as Exponential Growth and Decay and all the substandards therein. The teachers then rephrase the power standard in the form of an essential question. They also identify "authentic applications" of the essential question, where possible. Finally, they design performance assessments grounded in the authentic applications, which help them understand what students truly know about a topic (Table 12.1).

Power Standards	Essential Questions	Authentic Applications	Performance Assessments
Create linear equations from given scenarios.	What information in a scenario is important and mathematically viable?	Price/cost models, linear rate models (distance versus time)	Create a linear model for a business that must purchase inventory and sell it back to break even and make a profit.
Solve a system of equations, using an optimal method (graphing, substitution, elimination).	How can we compare two linear models and identify certain break-even points?	Break-even situations (energy-efficient machines), comparative rate problems, cost-profit analysis	A potential car buyer is deciding between an expensive hybrid car and a cheaper conventional car. Use a system of equations to model the cost over time, based on gas mileage and gas prices.
Understand how to model and calculate exponential growth and decay.	What makes exponential growth and decay different from linear change? How can we make predictions using an exponential model?	Populations of species, computing technology advancement	Identify an endangered species and model its population over time. Write a paper describing when the population caused the species to be considered endangered.

TABLE 12.1

The process of identifying the outputs (performance assessments) helps them prioritize the inputs (lesson planning and class time). To be sure, this approach is not a free pass to skip teaching particular content or standards wholesale. Prioritizing standards is an acknowledgment that because of importance or needed additional instruction, certain standards may require more time than others and may have to be addressed in multiple ways. Once we have our standards prioritized, we can design, find, and adapt our "anchor problems."

Anchor Problems

Anchor problems are opportunities for students to showcase what they've learned about a topic—or several topics. Think of these as the most critical problems you'll assign the entire year, and the ones you'll spend the most time planning for and assessing. If a student can demonstrate proficiency on these, say, ten to twelve problems, you'll be sufficiently convinced they know the material and will have the evidence to prove it. These tasks may serve as "portfolio problems" (Chapter 10) and serve to readdress the mathematical habits of mind.

When talking to teachers about selecting such high-quality tasks, I'm often asked an urgent question: *I'm teaching this concept next week. Got any good ideas?* This question is problematic. A hastily designed or selected task can result in poorly designed facilitation of the task, and it can be difficult to find a high-quality task under time pressure.

I prefer a more intentional approach. Rather than thinking about a particular standard around which to select or design a task, consider the next *several* standards. Instead of lesson planning for this coming Monday, think about the next several weeks—or preferably, the entire year.

Nearly every school and district offers several days of inservice at the beginning of the year. Sadly, many of these inservice days do not meet the needs of teachers. Although going over new rules and procedures for the year is important, schools should also allow for inservice dedicated to teachers honing their craft. Of course, I'm not advocating for a blank check of free time for instructors either. Left to our own devices, we would likely head off to our rooms to plan the Urgent, but not necessarily the Important. Instead, I encourage schools to yield inservice time to departments so teachers can work together to identify important keystones of their classes. In Appendix K, you'll find a sample inservice agenda.

Given a three- or four-hour window of inservice time, consider selecting or designing ten to twelve high-quality tasks to facilitate during the year. I encourage teachers to go one step further: put these tasks on the calendar. Although they may get moved around because of a number of unforeseen circumstances, having these days marked usually leads to them actually happening. Placing these tasks on the calendar—even if you take blind guesses about when in the year you will facilitate them—will help you structure your year (Figure 12.2).

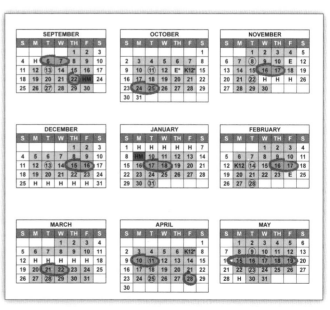

FIGURE 12.2 Putting tasks on the calendar, even far ahead of time, results in better coherence. You'll also thank yourself when you get to that month.

Another benefit of planning tasks well in advance is that it allows us to consider one of our hallmarks of a high-quality task: connecting content. As we've seen, the best tasks reach across mathematical concepts and tie in multiple standards. A bird's-eye view of the year in tasks will encourage you to think about how the mathematical content and practices from September underlie the tasks and topics in February. Identifying these tasks at the beginning of the year and placing them on a calendar can help alleviate some of the problems that understandably arise with the day-to-day approach to lesson planning.

Tending to Effective Facilitation Throughout the Year

Improving one's own facilitation abilities can be a challenge. Most teachers improve their capacity to facilitate effectively through experience. After years of teaching, they have done it enough to know the content and know the lesson well. This accumulation of knowledge helps explain why teacher experience correlates with student achievement (Becoates 2009).

However, there are ways of accelerating one's improvement ahead of schedule, but many of them require an assist from either a colleague or technology.

The teachers at Ridgeland have a commitment to regular peer observations that work to both align their instruction and improve their own via feedback. Teachers sit in on one another's classrooms and provide feedback in a safe, professional, evidence-based manner. This practice is discussed in more detail, including their peer observation form, in Chapter 13.

You can also observe your own lessons: it's never been easier to collect high-quality video of your facilitation. In the time between this book's publication and the moment you're reading this sentence, the quality will have improved even more. The phones we carry around with us at all times capture video and audio better than video cameras of yesteryear, and we can use these tools to record our lessons with the press of a button. For example, every few weeks, or if there's a particular lesson she's interested in (or really just *likes*), Teresa sets up her phone in the back of the room and hits Record. She recently purchased a small, inexpensive tripod to improve the angle and make sure it doesn't flop over. When she gets a moment during planning time or has a check-in with her administrator, she'll view the lesson, fast-forwarding and rewinding to key moments in facilitation.

One specific and helpful form of peer or self-generated video feedback is to monitor who is speaking, and to whom. For how long? Often, teachers don't realize how much they are the ones talking, until they listen to the recording. Also, in Chapter 3 we saw how gender bias reared its head in how infrequently Jamie called on female students. Regular observations can help us monitor for and address our implicit bias. Therefore, we might consider a strategy similar to scheduling the anchor problems throughout the year: plan regular peer or self-observations and put them on your calendar before school starts.

Establishing Routines

In Chapter 6, we saw the importance of establishing structures and routines as part of effective facilitation. Elementary teachers understand that students work better given structures and routines. Elementary teachers have routines for everything from collecting supplies to using the restroom. The structure provided by these routines helps facilitate an environment of high expectations, and the predictability gives students a feeling of safety and security. Secondary teachers would do well to implement structures and routines that do the same.

At Weirmont in Arkansas, students are greeted by Leanne at the door every single period of every single day, and then they grab their math journals and begin working on their warm-ups. They do this routine without thinking and often while talking to their peers. After the bell rings and Leanne has greeted the last students to arrive, she enters the classroom to find students diligently working through the warm-up problem. Leanne doesn't make any introductory statements or tell students to start their work. In her words, "They're already working. Why would I want to interrupt that with my instructions?"

"We practice it all. In the first week we literally practice getting out of our seat and getting calculators."

Across the country in Seattle, Kate's class wraps an assignment by—again, without even thinking about it—placing their groupwork in a folder in the center of their tables. They then place the folders in the appropriate bin for their section, all while Kate circles around the classroom to monitor students' progress and answer questions.

Although these routines relieve relatively small burdens individually, in aggregate they generate hours of additional learning time and a more focused facilitation from the teacher. Actions such as passing out papers, stopping to pass out pencils or calculators, or taking attendance are necessary, but can interrupt both teacher and student thinking and fluidity. These seemingly small routines also help students feel confident in the classroom, empowering them to take action while removing the uncertainty of what's happening in the class period. One student puts it to me this way: "It's just one less thing I have to worry about."

How does a classroom get this way, though?

"We practice it," Kate tells me.

"Practice what?" I ask.

"Everything. We practice it all. In the first week we literally practice getting out of our seat and getting calculators." If I'm being honest, it sounds a little drill sergeant–esque—at least at first. Kate continues, "It's not that students don't know how to get calculators. It's more that it establishes an expectation for how to do it. That first week of school students *generally* don't act out. They're usually more compliant than at any point in the year, if only because they're nervous. So I want them to practice these things now, because it sets the expectation that this is something we do quickly, quietly, and without delay."

Kate's approach suddenly makes total sense. That first week of school is the time kids are most likely to pay attention and listen quietly. Kate takes advantage of this opportunity to make sure actions are done purposefully the first time, and she monitors students throughout the year—reteaching as needed—to make sure students continue meeting her clear expectations.

Here are routines that Kate has students explicitly practice at the beginning of the year:

- ▲ Collecting supplies (calculators, protractors, pencils, etc.)

- ▲ Passing papers forward

- ▲ Trading papers for peer editing (clockwise and counterclockwise around their desks)

- ▲ Exiting the classroom

- ▲ Walking to the computer lab

To practice them, Kate tells students what they are going to do, and she has them do it two or three times. She'll practice a couple of these routines a day for the first five days of school. She's very clear about what she wants out of each procedure, and she maintains these expectations throughout the year.

As you think about your year, think about the most important procedures you want students to undertake first. Consider creating mini-benchmarks for your classes. For example, perhaps by the end of the first week you want students to know where the crucial supplies are and how best to retrieve them. After the second week you want them to be able to log in to their Chromebooks quickly and efficiently. By the end of the third week, you want students to begin working on your warm-ups immediately after you greet them at the door. By Halloween, you'd like students to be able to create a Know/Need-to-Know list on their own. And so on. Make sure you're clear with students about what you want them to do and why each routine is important for their success.

Planning Your First Week

Once we've given thought to the tasks we will be implementing, how we will focus on facilitation, and how we will tend to the social and emotional safety of our students throughout the year, we can plan for a successful first week or so of school. During this fragile and formative time, we want to communicate the importance of content as well as care for each and every one of the students who walk through our doors.

We began this chapter looking at Missy's first-week unit on mathematical smartness. Before Missy even gets to Hotel Snap, she starts her first day with an activity called the Four Directions or Compass Points from the National School Reform Faculty (2014). Although it's intended for adults learning to work with one another, Missy thought it would work well for her students. The protocol involves students self-identifying what kind of team member they are typically: a north (a "go-getter," who likes to try new things), south (socially and emotionally intelligent and responsive), east (needs to see the big picture), or west (detail oriented). After self-identifying their "direction," participants create a poster to address the following questions:

- ▲ What are the strengths of your style?

- ▲ What are the limitations of your style?

- ▲ What style do you find the most difficult to work with, and why?

- ▲ What do people from other "directions" or styles need to know about you, so you can work together effectively?

- ▲ What do you value about the other three styles?

This activity helps establish a safe social environment with positive relationships. It's also instructive. Missy is able to get a sense of how her students work and like to work so she can adjust groups and groupwork accordingly. The responses to the prompts can also foster the rebuilding of trust when groupwork breaks down.

Missy follows the Four Directions activity with Hotel Snap and its debrief. She concludes the week with Broken Circles (discussed in Chapter 6), which is intended to communicate that every member of a group has something to offer and that no one is finished until everyone is finished. Missy makes sure these important ideas come up in the debrief of the task.

In her first week (Figure 12.3), Missy establishes the importance of communication and collaboration in her classroom. This expectation is buttressed by the deep mathematical thinking that occurs throughout the Hotel Snap task. Missy feels if she can achieve these three goals—communication, collaboration, and identifying mathematical dispositions—she'll have a foundation that she can come back to throughout the year.

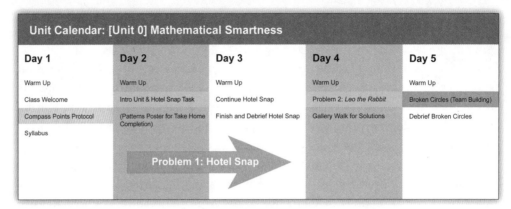

FIGURE 12.3 Missy's first week incorporates lessons and routines that pay dividends for the entire year.

These lofty objectives are often complicated by the reality of a first week of school in which students are swapping classes because of scheduling errors or changing preferences, teachers struggle to recall the names of the hundred-plus students they are meeting, often for the first time, and everyone needs to trade paperwork on everything from grading policies to photography nonpermission forms. How does Missy emphasize care for her students while so much schoolwide logistical information is being disseminated?

"I go into that first week assuming I'll have about fifteen to twenty minutes less class time than I think I will," Missy tells me. "If I have a fifty-minute class period, I assume a good chunk of that will be dealing with paperwork and scheduling issues. I understand that. I accept that. I just want to make sure that the rest of the time I'm able to get across what I want to get across. And that's how the students are smart mathematically."

Missy doesn't attribute her well-running classroom to this, but she also has a policy of assigning seats before the first day of school. As much as we may want to convey our love of mathematics and how much fun students will be having this year, a secondary student's primary concern on the first day of school rests more in the realm of "Where am I going to sit?" and "Is my teacher nice?" Missy has students' names printed and taped to desks where they'll be sitting for the first week or so. She greets every student at her door and asks them to take the seats marked with their names. This routine reassures students and helps Missy learn their names.

Learning students' names quickly is an essential aspect of creating a welcoming environment. Getting to know students will come somewhat naturally when you have a classroom with robust discourse: classrooms where students can stay silent indefinitely can yield anonymity. But we can't just count on picking up students' names as they talk. This method takes too long and favors students who are already comfortable talking in class. If a teacher still doesn't know a student's name a week into school, the implicit message is one of noncaring. Part of a teacher's first week must be dedicated to knowing the names of students (and knowing the proper, culturally responsive pronunciation). The excuse of "I'm not good with names" doesn't fly when it comes to building strong relationships—even if you're not good with names.

Urgent and Important

The biggest barrier to taking a deliberate, yearlong approach to each of our three elements is that, day to day, the Important often gets mothballed for the Urgent (Table 12.2). What are the things that need to be taken care of within the next, say, twenty-four hours (the Urgent) versus within the next couple of weeks (Not as Urgent)? Things like lesson plans, daily grades, or feedback on assignments are Urgent and might require immediate attention, whereas things such as test corrections or progress reports can wait a bit. Similarly, what will significantly move the needle for students' well-being as mathematicians (Important) versus the smaller pieces that may wash out in the long run (Not as Important)? Although everything that happens in a classroom is important to some degree, there are certainly aspects of the math classroom that supersede others. Attending to high-quality tasks, effective facilitation, and the social and emotional safety of the classroom are primary among them.

	Urgent	Not as Urgent
Important	• Identifying a performance task for this unit • Memorizing the names of all students in our class • Grades for progress reports	• Math attitudes surveys • Analysis of student work • Recording and watching video of facilitating • Identifying mathematical "smartnesses" for each student
Not as Important	• Grades for daily assignments • Finding warm-up exercises • Turning in lesson plans to administration	• Grades for test retakes • Ordering additional supplies • Rerview test-proctoring materials

TABLE 12.2

I suggest you and your colleagues make your own Important Versus Urgent grid. The main point of this exercise is to ensure that what is important is made explicit, so that important things don't fall by the wayside. Having this grid posted on the wall or taped to the inside of a grade book will keep bringing these elements to mind and make them more likely to be tended to.

Self-Care and the Call Home

As rewarding as teaching is, it's an emotionally demanding profession. As much as we want to be aware of the well-being of our students, we also want to be mindful of our own well-being, and that of our colleagues. Self-care looks different to different professionals. For some, self-care is a weekend away in a beautiful location. For others, self-care is allowing yourself to sleep in on Sunday, skipping the regular gym routine. It might even mean taking a sub day or half day to enjoy an afternoon with no responsibilities.

Self-care also ought to occur within school walls. During your planning period, you may want to head over to the gym to get in a workout and a shower. One school I work with has one of their yoga-certified teachers conduct a yoga session during her planning period for anyone who wants to come. Listen to music, take a nap, read a book for pleasure, seek out a colleague.

This last recommendation—seek out a colleague—is an act of both self-care and peer-care. Just as this profession is emotionally draining for you, it is for your peers as well. Make it a point to check in with them. Coordinate and invite the people in your department to happy hour one Friday afternoon. If you're going to make it through the year, you need to attend to one another, as you do for yourself and your students.

Speaking of which, I don't want to portray self-care entirely divorced from student interactions. I'll never forget the first time I called Stefon's mother. It was a Friday—you'll understand why I'm sure of that fact in a moment—and relatively early in the year. Stefon was a precocious student. He was quite chatty and quick to socialize. Those were some of the qualities I liked about him, but I'm guessing they didn't serve him well in earlier grades. When I called his mother on that Friday, I was greeted with a curt "What did he do now?" I was taken aback initially, but recovered.

"Some great things!" I responded cheerfully. "Today Stefon helped a fellow student with the warm-up we were working on. He also demonstrated a solution on the board on Wednesday that I hadn't anticipated. I just wanted to let you know that Stefon's a great kid and doing exceptionally well in my class."

Now Stefon's mom was the one taken aback.

I always ended my week that way. Every Friday afternoon I would call the parents of a couple of students and brag on their kid. This was often the first time they had received a call about something positive. Usually calls home are reserved for passing along negative information.

I made calls on Fridays as an act of self-care. Ending the week on a positive experience— even if it had been a brutal week—helped maintain my sanity. On Monday, I knew I'd be greeted by the student with, "Sayyy, Mr. Krall . . . did you call my parents last week?" It consistently made my weekend to make positive calls home. I hope it made theirs as well.

When you can attend to your own emotional needs through student celebrations, do so. When you need to take time for yourself, do so. Give yourself permission to experience satisfaction within the school premises and beyond the school doors.

Conclusion

You've heard the saying "It's a marathon, not a sprint." That's never more true than in teaching. Even the best lessons have a short half-life. It's easy to burn out quickly if you plan with fervent urgency while not taking care of yourself. It's also easy to develop subpar lessons if you're planning for efficiency rather than intentionality. Haste results in poor tasks (or no tasks) and mediocre facilitation, and typically won't attend to academic safety. Teaching such lessons will also fail to communicate the narrative of our year, because lessons will be disconnected from the stories we are trying to tell our students about math and about themselves.

Every new school year brings limitless possibilities and a new opportunity to frame the discipline of math in a positive light. Individual lessons and experiences can have a meaningful effect, but developing a coherent set of tasks, routines, and messages will move the needle significantly over the course of a year.

REVIEW

- Our pedagogy requires a yearlong, consistent approach.
- Prioritize high-leverage content.
- The first week is an opportune time to lay the groundwork to convey to students that they are capable mathematicians.
- The further you can plan ahead, the better off you'll be.
- Make time for yourself throughout the year.

CHAPTER

13

Every system is perfectly designed to get the results it gets.

—PAUL BATALDEN

Aligning the System, Crafting the Story

Weirmont Secondary Academy has earned recognition for its students' performance multiple years in a row, despite having a high population of students in poverty. One of their teachers, Leanne, has featured prominently in this book, but it took a concerted effort by the entire Weirmont secondary math department to achieve these results. To be fair, Weirmont is a small, rural school, so the math department is correspondingly small. Only three math teachers are responsible for students in grades seven through twelve. Practically speaking, it's two-and-a-half teachers, because one of the teachers splits her time between teaching seven through twelve and serving as an instructional coach at the local elementary school.

Although many people praise the school for its test scores, what stands out most to me at Weirmont is the language students use to describe their own learning and the comfort with which they talk about their self-confidence, how they are smart at math, and how their peers are invaluable to their learning. It's clear that this culture wasn't formed in just a single school year but is the result of a sustained approach by dedicated professionals toward shaping these budding mathematicians.

There's an advantage to having such a small, nimble team. There are also advantages to having larger departments, even departments with moderate turnover. New teachers come with different skill sets, interesting ideas, and fresh facilitation moves. Established teachers bring hard-earned wisdom, implementation experience, and skillful facilitation. A larger department can bring the best of all worlds.

It's unfortunate that movies about education tend to focus on the One Dynamic Teacher as the hero. Although it makes for a great narrative—the teacher who just wouldn't give up, the teacher who cared, the teacher who by force of personality changed the lives of his or her students—the truth is it takes a system of alignment and improvement to achieve long-lasting effects. It's one thing for a student to have a great teacher; it's greater still for a student to have a battery of great teachers, all working from the same playbook of academic safety, quality tasks, and effective facilitation.

In the first chapter, we met Damien. At that point he had had three disparate math experiences in high school. His classes were misaligned, with no coherent vision of math. He left his junior year without a proper understanding of the discipline or of himself as a mathematician. Conversely, we've seen examples of math departments that are quite well aligned in their approach. And this sustained approach is more powerful than a single, dynamic classroom (which, mind you, is still tremendously powerful).

In this chapter, we'll think about how to align a department along our framework of tasks, facilitation, and safety to create a coherent, effective experience for students. Typically, *alignment* tends to connote narrowing to a single model of instruction: let's all do it like this. Here, alignment is presented as *improving* along our three pillars of pedagogy, and how colleagues can achieve that system of improvement. Coherence definitely plays a role: a football team needs to operate from the same playbook to get better. Ultimately, that's what alignment is and does: it provides the framework for us to get better at our craft, together.

Aligning and Improving Academic Safety

Creating a cohesive departmental approach to math requires teachers to have a shared understanding of where students are and how they are doing. One of the keys to achieving this is capturing data. Data points that yield insight into students' social-emotional well-being, their mathematical self-identity, and their view of the discipline itself help us create an action plan to improve these very sticky outcomes. It may seem paradoxical, but yes: initially, we treat the most invisible and emotional of our three-legged pedagogy with cold, hard data.

Teachers are awash in data: incoming student proficiency rates, passing rates, previous grades. But these data tell only a portion of the story. Although they may measure students' achievement (typically on standardized tests), they don't measure anything about some of the underlying attitudes and mindsets that may cause low achievement or low engagement. We know from our triad that issues of academic safety are just as important as any other instructional touch point. It is on teachers to develop tools that capture data on academic safety, just as districts may provide data on achievement.

Some teachers implement a beginning-of-the-year survey that asks questions along the lines of *What are your favorite extracurricular activities?* and other getting-to-know-you conversation openers. These surveys can be excellent tools to get to know students, but they don't typically dig deep about underlying attitudes toward math. Nor are they implemented in a routinized manner or analyzed in ways that will help teachers learn from the results. Finally, they are implemented (or not) class by class, so they don't contribute to department-wide conversations or alignment.

Instead, consider developing or adapting a department-wide assessment that achieves the following:

▲ A tool that measures—with some reliability—student attitudes toward math

▲ A schedule to deploy said tool routinely throughout the year

Assessing academic safety via a tool or strategy can be fraught with peril. It's easy and natural for teachers to infer that a class is academically safe (or not) based on anecdotal or biased evidence. For instance, a classroom of traditionally high-achieving students may appear to be an academically safe environment on the surface, but students in the class may actually have fixed-mindset views. A class that appears "out of control" may seem unruly at first glance but may be composed of students who like to work more hands-on problems. Assessing the academic safety of a classroom requires dispassionate evidence collecting, to be analyzed only after the fact. Here are three tools and strategies that may help you collect evidence around academic safety.

Math Attitudes and Mindset Survey

Throughout the year, we want to check in with how our students are experiencing math and how they view themselves as mathematicians. A regularly implemented survey can be an effective tool if it captures student notions about our significant themes of academic safety:

▲ What is mathematics?

▲ Who has access to mathematics?

▲ What does it mean to be a successful mathematician?

▲ Do you see yourself as a mathematician?

▲ Do your peers see you as a successful mathematician?

An effective survey tool need not be overly burdensome. I encourage teachers to have their students write as much as possible, including freewriting or free association. A mix of multiple-choice, agree/disagree statements, and freewriting allows students to express their feelings about math and themselves.

I would encourage you to have any survey around academic safety completed anonymously. Having students put names to their surveys will naturally skew the data. Students may also be worried about teachers being able to identify surveys by the handwriting. Fortunately, free online survey tools (such as Google Forms or SurveyMonkey) allow for anonymous submissions devoid of handwriting. These online survey tools also have some quick data aggregation tools.

In Appendix L and M, I share an online survey I created to gauge students' math attitudes.

Peer Observation Tool

As discussed in Chapter 3, the most telling evidence of the academic safety of a classroom is the discourse. Specifically, who is doing the talking and what are they saying?

In the moment, it can be difficult for teachers to capture this crucial data. After all, we are busy teaching! Therefore, consider inviting a trusted colleague or mentor into your classroom to track the conversation, and offer to observe discourse for others in return. Colleagues need not be from the same department. In fact, if our goal is to collect evidence focused on academic safety, sometimes it's beneficial to *not* have a math teacher observe. A fellow math teacher may get caught up in the content and miss significant student remarks and actions.

Peer observation can stir feelings of vulnerability in teachers, particularly when it's oriented around the academic safety of a classroom. It's important that a peer observation be grounded in an environment of support and trust. It's also important that the observation be entirely evidence based. The observer ought not jump to conclusions. Rather, the observer should collect as much dispassionate evidence as possible:

▲ What specific phrases are the students using?

▲ Who is talking at a given time?

▲ What body language are students and teacher exhibiting?

I have provided a peer observation tool for academic safety in Appendix N. The tool asks the observer to collect evidence around who's talking and when, as well as what they are saying.

Informational/Empathy Interviews: Pizza Is Cheap

Survey data can reveal critical information about a class's attitudes toward math. Informational interviews or focus groups can provide critical information about individual students' math attitudes.

At Bell Academy, teachers schedule regular lunch panels with students to check in and see how well the school or individual classrooms are working for them. "We try to have a small focus panel once a month or so," one of the teachers tells me. "We just order a couple of pizzas and have an informal conversation. Sometimes we have a few questions planned, but more often than not, we just end up talking about how well school is going for them." Sometimes an entire department will invite three or four kids in for a lunch panel. Other times, individual teachers will spring for a pizza and have lunch with two or three students from across the achievement spectrum. "We get good information on where students are being successful and where they're struggling. It also builds rapport. When students know that you're trying to get better at your craft, that goes a long way toward communicating a growth mindset.

"Pizza's cheap too," the teacher adds. "You can get two of them for, like, twelve dollars. Pretty good investment."

Some schools approach student panels or focus groups more formally in the form of *empathy interviews*. These interview sessions are intended to reveal as much about a student's life and schooling experience as possible. The interviewer builds rapport and asks nonjudgmental questions. The questions eventually become more of a conversation exploring emotions with the interviewee. A recorder takes notes to collect evidence teachers can analyze.

Aligning and Improving Tasks

How can we get to alignment and improvement in our tasks? Here are four methods I've seen schools use to get a sense of a task's effectiveness before implementing it on a wide scale. Each is valuable in its own right and will yield better tasks and better alignment, but all are also excellent tools to develop a professional, adult-learning culture. These activities can help a staff create a safe learning atmosphere among teachers and build a common vocabulary about teaching and learning.

Simulate the Problem-Posing Protocol

Because we don't typically have the ability to "beta-test" new tasks with students, testing them with our colleagues is the next best thing. Facilitate a problem-posing protocol such as those discussed in Chapter 7 with fellow teachers. Better yet, facilitate the task (say, using the Notice and Wonder protocol) with *nonmath teachers*. Math teachers tend to rush to figure out what the task is "really" about. If the problem has something to do with projectile motion, for example, math teachers will start sniffing around for variables to plug into a quadratic. Nonmath teachers may not have that inclination, which makes them more representative of secondary math students trying to figure out the relevant information. Nonmath teachers have to make sense of the problem rather than jump at solution methods. Nonmath teachers will also point out issues to address in the way that students might: a confusing term, a poorly scaled diagram, an overly contrived scenario.

After simulating the launch of the problem with teachers (be they math or other content area teachers), you can revisit the initial task: Did teachers identify the information you want students to identify? If not, how can you rework the task? Did they wonder the same things you anticipated they'd wonder? Were they able to identify some concrete next steps when you concluded the problem-posing process? Were they ready to jump into the student work portion of the task?

I think about Dumbledore's Army from time to time. In *Harry Potter and the Order of the Phoenix*, the fifth book of the esteemed series by J. K. Rowling, Harry and his classmates want to learn magic to protect themselves, but the school administration will allow them to learn only from books. So Harry and his fellow agitators form Dumbledore's Army, steal away to a secret room, and practice using magic on each other. Casting and blocking spells, they spend much of that book training as iron sharpens iron. In schools, we teachers rarely get to practice our problems, strategies, and routines. The first time we facilitate a problem is usually with students. I've been in trainings where we've done what I describe above—simulating problem launches or activities with teachers—and it's invariably a valuable experience for the facilitating teacher as well as the participants. In many ways, teaching tasks to one another helps us align and improve both the tasks and our facilitation.

Tuning Protocol: Likes, Wonders, Next Steps

Another technique for aligning systems while improving tasks is the protocol of Likes, Wonders, and Next Steps. Some of the most powerful, culture-building conversations I've been a part of stemmed from a teacher presenting an artifact—be it a fully developed lesson or even just an idea for a task—and colleagues offering feedback using this protocol:

▲ Presenting teacher presents the artifact (2 minutes). If there are any pertinent documents, the presenting teacher may wish to share those as well.

▲ Colleagues ask clarifying questions (2 minutes). These are quickly answerable questions with short answers. (For example, *What grade is this for? How many students do you have in your class?*)

▲ Colleagues share positives using the sentence starter "I like . . ." (5 minutes). Presenting teacher remains silent but is encouraged to take notes.

▲ Colleagues share things they wonder using the sentence starter "I wonder . . ." (5 minutes). Presenting teacher remains silent but is encouraged to take notes—this can be extremely difficult for the presenting teacher! But it's critical to the protocol and to move things along that the teacher *not* answer each and every wonder.

▲ Colleagues share potential next steps using the sentence starter "A potential next step might be . . ." (5 minutes).

▲ Presenting teacher may now speak and reflect on what he or she learned through the conversation (2 minutes). Some facilitators like to encourage the use of the sentence starter "I heard . . ."

Often, as soon as I loosen up after the final phase of the protocol (I adhere to protocols pretty strictly until this point), colleagues exhale and reaffirm how much they appreciate the presenting teacher's lesson, without my prompting. "I hadn't thought about that before," "Thank you for the new ideas," and "This has been so valuable" are common refrains that follow this task-improving, culture-building protocol.

Not only will this strategy yield higher-quality tasks and give teachers a heads-up about how students experience the problem, but it also improves collaboration and professionalism within math departments. Structured discussions help us improve our classrooms by improving collegiality.

Common Planning Forms

Although planning templates may seem like a small, technical detail, using common planning forms can go a long way toward aligning math instruction at your school. I was recently working with a staff on a lesson they were co-developing, but they were all using different documents. Some teachers were scratching it out on paper, and others were using Microsoft Word or a template they had made copies of a decade ago and were still using. Teachers were getting lost on where we were in the lesson-planning process; everyone had differing notes down for various aspects of the facilitation. It was a mess.

I suggested that everyone use the same document to plan the problem. I provided a Google Doc version of the Lesson Plan Template in Appendix G and recommended that we all work from this same document. After some initial grumbling, teachers logged in and began taking notes and sharing ideas. Now, instead of multiple different problem prompts, we had the same wording for our task. We had a more comprehensive list of "anticipated know/notice" elements rather than only the ones teachers had happened to hear. In the end, it probably saved time. Only one person had to type something for everyone to access it (Figure 13.1).

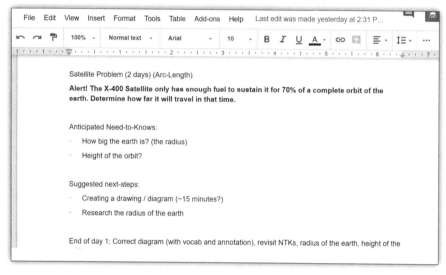

FIGURE 13.1 In this collaborative Google Doc, users can edit a single document simultaneously in real time.

Whether you use the lesson-planning form provided here or your own, make sure the people in your department are using the same or similar templates. Even when teachers aren't pulling from the same lesson or teaching the same content, using the same planning forms helps align language and lessons, making it easier for teachers to learn from each other while subtly aligning lessons better for students.

After a Task: Learning from Student Work

After we've planned and refined a task with colleagues and facilitated it with students, we can continue aligning as a department by analyzing it together. Learning from student work will yield "ahas," similar to how our tuning protocol did about the design of the task, but now our conversation is centered on what students know. In Chapter 10, we saw how Bell Academy teachers use student work to learn what students understand and still struggle with. We can also look at student work to assess the effectiveness of the task itself: What kind of work did it produce? Does the work yield the outcomes we intended?

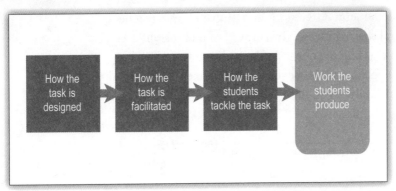

FIGURE 13.2 The journey of a task from the design stage to the resultant student work

Figure 13.2 shows us joints and junctions along the journey from task design to student work. Working backward, student artifacts yield instructive evidence about the quality of our task design, facilitation, and way in which the students worked.

Sometimes, when I work with a math department, I ask teachers to bring a few pieces of student work representing a cross section of the class's work. We use the following See/Think/Wonder protocol:

▲ Describe what you **see**.

▲ What do you **think** about what you see?

▲ What does it make you **wonder**?

After we go through each piece of student work, we have a discussion about the task itself: Was this the right task? Did it achieve what the teacher anticipated?

Admittedly, it's difficult to disentangle the task, its facilitation, and the academic safety that goes into producing each sample of student work (that's essentially the thesis of this book). In particular, some samples of student work display little, if any, work or mathematical thinking. We wonder if the students misunderstood the task or were not engaged by it, but we struggle to determine what's happening from the artifact alone. We'd need to talk to the students. Still, viewing a spectrum of sample work does yield insight into the design of the task. For example, you may discover why students are struggling to apply trig identities or which words in the task were confusing to students. Analyzing student work in a thoughtful way helps teachers move past their own assumptions about how students interpret a problem.

Aligning and Improving Facilitation

It takes practice to become an expert facilitator. Author and speaker Malcolm Gladwell suggests the 10,000-hour rule: it takes 10,000 hours of practice to become an elite performer. Using some back-of-the-envelope math, it would take educators roughly seven years of teaching to achieve 10,000 hours of practice (give or take) based on teaching time alone.

Fortunately, we have more than just our own practice: we have colleagues who are just as dedicated to their craft as we are to ours. By observing one another, we can accelerate the 10,000 hours by witnessing new strategies and giving and obtaining feedback.

It's difficult to build in time in the busy school day for improvement. But it is possible. Here are two strategies that I've seen schools use to improve their facilitation expertise and increase coherence across classes.

Peer Observation: Seven Minutes in Heaven

Kelly is a principal at a school in rural Indiana. She was trying to figure out how to walk that fine line between making time for peer observations and giving teachers enough time to plan and take care of all the obligations that befall a secondary teacher. Kelly and her staff came up with a solution they affectionately call "seven minutes in heaven" (younger readers will do well *not* to search for the meaning of that phrase).

Teachers at the school had one planning period a day. They used block scheduling, with about ninety minutes per block. As a staff, they agreed to spend the first seven minutes of their planning period observing another teacher. They didn't have a particularly rigid format for which teachers they were to observe; they would just find somewhere to go, and they'd switch every day. Because a limited number of them were teaching at any given time, teachers would often see other teachers multiple times over the course of a month.

The "seven minutes" construct allowed teachers just enough time to see how their colleagues greeted students and opened a lesson. Although there's clearly a lot more that goes into teaching, they thought that watching the opener could be particularly insightful.

I should note that seven minutes in heaven did *not* just include math teachers; rather, this was a peer-observation commitment from the entire staff. A math teacher might observe a social studies teacher. A science teacher might spend his or her seven minutes in an agriculture class. As we saw earlier in this chapter (under "Aligning and Improving Academic Safety"), being observed by teachers from another content area is sometimes preferable. However, when the focus is improving facilitation and getting deeper into mathematical content with students, a colleague with a keen mathematical ear might be the best observer.

Staff meetings at this school consisted largely of debriefing the previous month's "seven minutes in heaven" experiences. Teachers volunteered what they saw and learned from their observations. Not only did this structure allow for teachers to learn from their peers, but the staff meetings afforded an opportunity for teachers to celebrate the craft of their colleagues. Few things start a staff meeting off better than colleagues publicly praising each other for their professionalism. And, thinking back to Chapter 3 and assigning academic status, we can safely say that teachers and students aren't so different in that respect.

Taking Videos of Instruction

Not even ten years ago it was an ordeal to videotape a teacher. It often required large, thousand-dollar camcorders that interfered with instruction as much as garnered evidence of it. Even five years ago, we had the technology to collect high-quality video seamlessly with flip cams or even mobile phones, but the audio was lacking. It was difficult to make out what the teacher or students were saying. Or the memory in our mobile device was relatively limited and we'd run out of space just a few minutes into a lesson.

At the time of this writing, our mobile phones can collect high-quality video and discernible audio with memory to spare. We also have free online video platforms to archive and share the videos we create. In an age when football players are using tablets to examine plays that just occurred, teachers have the ability to watch an "instant replay" of their own facilitation to look for successes and missed opportunities.

"I talk way, *way* too fast," a teacher shares with me as we're watching a video of a recent lesson. I had recorded his warm-up, which lasted about five minutes. Even in that five-minute rewatching, he's able to identify things that went well and things he needs to work on. Teachers are adept at identifying flaws in their facilitation when watching it through a camera lens. It's my job to make sure he's also focusing on the positive.

"What do you see the students doing?" I ask.

"It looks like every student is working on the problem. These students appear to be consulting one another to see if they got the same answer."

In addition to quick, informal recording and rewatching of short bits of instruction for self-assessment, we can use video to anchor conversations and professional development as a larger department or staff, which can help us create a shared vision for math teaching and learning. For such occasions, I'd recommend using a structured lesson study protocol. Protocols are necessary to ensure that criticism and praise can take place among colleagues in a nonthreatening way. There is an example lesson study protocol in Appendix O to help facilitate these conversations and increase collaboration and coherence.

On the more technical side, here are a few tips to obtain the highest-quality video using a mobile device.

▲ **Orient your phone so it's in landscape mode.** We typically hold our phones vertically (in "portrait" mode) but turn it sideways to give the viewer a broader sense of what's going on in the classroom. It also makes the viewing experience more pleasurable, because the video will presumably be viewed on a rectangular screen that is wider than it is high.

▲ **Purchase a tripod for your (and others') phone(s).** Companies manufacture inexpensive tripods specifically for phones. They take almost no time to set up and typically have the ability to bend and twist to ensure the best possible angle for your recording. Figure 13.3 shows a tripod that I use frequently and cost me about fifteen dollars.

▲ **Archive the videos soon after recording.** As soon as you're finishing taking videos, either begin uploading them to the Web or connect your phone to your computer and import them, and then delete them from your phone. Otherwise, they may languish on your phone until the day you need the space for other media.

FIGURE 13.3 A tripod is useful for taking videos of instruction.

Uploading videos of your facilitation to free, online video platforms such as YouTube or Vimeo allows you to free up space on your computer for other media, and also ensures that you'll have the videos at your disposal on all your devices. Be sure to take note of the privacy settings for your videos, however. Make sure they're set to "private" so that only you may see them. Districts and schools often have strict laws protecting students' privacy, which a publicly shared video would violate.

Supporting New Teachers: Observational Planning Periods

Sadly, teacher turnover rates have grown so high that schools are continually bringing new teachers on board, whether they are new to the school, new to the content area, or new to the profession entirely. The current mode number of years of teacher experience in the United States (the number that appears most often) is *one*. That is, there is a plurality of teaching professionals who are in their first year of teaching (Headden 2014). A school system or department that does not acknowledge this issue will get the predictable results of unsteady instruction. Because teaching math requires so much new learning (and unlearning), a teacher new to the profession requires additional support. Many schools do not have a systematized means of hiring, training, or acclimatizing new teachers. Especially when departments have worked together to align goals and pedagogy, new teachers need to be brought up to speed on building culture, which takes significant time and work.

At Ridgeland High School, teachers and administrators have developed a system that ensures new hires have an appropriate "apprenticeship" as they learn throughout their first year of teaching at the school. One strategy they use is to lag the new teacher's schedule by one day. If the veteran geometry teacher is teaching a lesson on Wednesday, the new-to-Ridgeland teacher will facilitate that lesson on Thursday. On Wednesday, the new teacher will spend his or her planning time in the classroom of the veteran teacher. I can't say it's a formal observation, because it isn't; it's more like *osmosis*. Ridgeland administrators understand that new teachers need that time for actual planning and other to-dos, and losing a planning period for the sake of observation is more detrimental than helpful. Therefore, rookie teachers are encouraged to bring their planning materials, their grade books, and whatever else they need to prepare for the rest of the day. The hope is that, by working in the room of a veteran teacher, new teachers will pick up techniques for math instruction. They will adopt common language. They will assume similar levels of respect for students. Occasionally, they might look up from their grade book to hear how the veteran teacher asks certain questions that get kids to think more deeply, or how the veteran teacher assigns status to certain students.

It's important to note, too, that the school tries desperately to avoid making this structure a power dynamic. Rookie teachers are given just as much agency and power in the lesson-design process as veterans. Veteran teachers are quick to point out when a rookie teacher has spurred new learning or new thinking in *them*. This mutuality is essential. Otherwise it could become a prescriptive model, where the veteran teachers are the only ones with worthwhile ideas or teaching moves. Ridgeland establishes this apprenticeship-by-osmosis while soliciting and valuing new, fresh ideas from first-year teachers.

Now What? Developing Next Steps for Continued Improvement

If you've designed and implemented tools to collect evidence around teaching and learning as recommended in this chapter, you'll have mostly first-order data. That is, these tools and strategies are intended to help you collect evidence, not insinuations. You have the raw, unprocessed goods, either in the form of quantitative survey data, qualitative observation data, student work, or (most likely) a mix. Once we have gathered these data, we want to identify patterns and develop appropriate strategies.

As you lay out your data in front of you (in whatever form it takes), consider the following questions:

▲ What patterns do I see emerging?

▲ What data do I find surprising?

▲ What data do I find unsurprising?

▲ Do these data match with my perception of my classroom environment?

▲ What successes do I see in the data?

▲ What areas of growth do I see?

▲ Do the data suggest a specific area of focus?

That last question about focus will yield your immediate next steps. Are students exhibiting misinformed assumptions about the discipline of math? You may want to spend some time providing opportunities to do math as described in Chapter 2. Are students displaying boredom? You may want to revisit task design, as discussed in Chapter 4.

Here are some common symptoms and potential next steps to employ (Table 13.1).

Common issues of academic safety	Potential next steps
Students don't understand or misunderstand the discipline of math.	Provide tasks that embody the spirit of mathematics: problem solving, open-ended and open "middle" work. Evaluate your tasks for quality, access, and openness.
Students are exhibiting or reporting boredom.	Conduct an audit of tasks to make sure they are relevant and curiosity inducing.
Students are exhibiting or reporting poor groupwork dynamics.	Employ protocols to better structure collaboration and groupwork. Check for academic safety.
Students don't feel like they are capable mathematicians.	Commit to assigning academic status to each and every student. Check your assessment practices; employ high-quality rubrics with common and specific indicators.
There is a lack of academic engagement or participation.	Videotape instruction and/or invite an observer to check your facilitation.

TABLE 13.1

Be sure to celebrate where the data show positive indicators of an academically safe classroom. Where are the bright spots? Are students showing positive attitudes toward collaboration? Do they see the value in completing a challenging problem? Are they suggesting they have positive views of your classroom? It's easy for teachers to get bogged down in deficit thinking. Make sure to take time to celebrate the bright spots.

Routinized Deployment

When I've encouraged teachers to employ one of these data collection tools, more often than not they've done so once, with great enthusiasm. It's much more difficult to make meaningful data collection a regular, routinized part of their practice. It takes concerted, scheduled effort. But we don't want it to be such a heavy lift or so cumbersome that it feels like yet another add-on to teachers' already overfilled schedules. Three or four times a year is enough for a good measure of academic safety. It's enough to give you solid trend information, but not so burdensome that it eats up a significant portion of your planning time.

In a ten-month school year, three times a year could equate to the fall, winter, and spring. A teacher may start with an initial data collection toward the start of the year, one about halfway through, and one toward the end of the year, perhaps September, December, and April. I encourage teachers to put a window for such data collection on their calendar at the beginning of the year, lest they get lost in the hustle and bustle of the school year. It doesn't have to be a specific date, just a sort of "window" during which they can deploy the relevant data collection tool.

It also reduces the lift if you're using the same or similar data collection tools each time, whether it's the same survey, the same observation tool, or similar interview questions. You'll be able to compare like data sets as well as get better at asking interview questions or noticing interactions while observing a peer.

Listen: The Words Tell the Story

I'm visiting a seventh-grade classroom in a charter school in Denver when one of my colleagues notes that the classrooms have a sense of "peace." He's quick to clarify that he doesn't mean *peace* in the sense of absence of volume. The classrooms aren't quiet per se. Rather, he sees peace in the *way* students are talking to one another. They're using words such as *persistence*: "You really *persisted* through this problem," I hear one student say to another. "Are you going to include this problem in your *presentation of learning* at the end of the semester?"

We enter an eighth-grade classroom, and sure enough, I hear the same words: "persistence, presentation of learning." I hear similar words in a sixth-grade classroom, even in a fourth, and eventually a second-grade classroom.

I wonder if you've noticed something about many of the schools profiled in this book. It's a subtle yet crucial undercurrent of what allows them to be successful. The most successful schools I've visited have a *common vocabulary*. Whether it's the way teachers talk about students (both in front of them and behind closed doors), the protocols they run, or the sentence starters they provide, they talk similarly. You hear it when students start sentences about peer work with "I like . . ." or "I wonder. . . ." You hear it when students discuss "revisiting initial estimates" or use words such as "agency" or "growth mindset." You hear it in the cadence with which students describe their Need-to-Knows. The faculty of these schools provide a vernacular that enables staff and students to communicate effectively. This common vocabulary also tells a story.

I'd suggest that it's not even entirely crucial *what* this vocabulary entails, just that schools have it. I've been in schools where students and staff celebrate and assess the "schoolwide learning outcomes" (Chapter 10), and in others where "mathematical smartness" is routinely referenced. Some schools use the language of "college readiness," and others discuss elements of a successful student portfolio. Regardless of what that *thing* is that they're calibrated around, they have that *shared thing*.

In the most successful schools, you hear the story of the school in the words students use. No, you don't get the history of the land acquisition that allowed the school to be built, or the Great Power Outage of 2005. Those stories are told as well. I'm referring to the story of what the school is about, what the discipline of mathematics is about. When you listen to students in successful schools, you hear what makes them successful.

In Chapters 2 and 3, we learned about the teachers at Ridgeland, who had to take a step back and rediscover the very discipline of mathematics itself. From here they began to communicate the story of math to their students. And they made their students part of the story.

In Chapters 4 and 5, we heard the story of how Leanne was excited to be present for her students' mathematical insights. We heard how Christine made mathematics relevant to students through project-based learning. Students talked excitedly about being able to use math to influence their school and community. It was meaningful to them.

In Chapters 6 and 7, we read the story of math as a collaborative discipline. We heard students discussing what mathematical collaboration looks like, thanks to Kate's adept facilitation and public acknowledgment of positive group norms. Students used the same language Kate did when describing how they worked with one another. We heard how Sarah's students "always talk like that," because of their teacher's intentional rolling out of sentence starters and prescribed questions.

As Roger Schank, founder of the Institute for Learning Sciences at Northwest University, puts it, "Humans are not ideally set up to understand logic; they are ideally set up to understand stories." In successful classrooms, students can convey a story about math, and about themselves as mathematicians. Sometimes the story is one of conflict and triumph. In all stories, the teacher plays a key part, a crucial part. Then the school year ends, summer vacation goes by, and we start with the next chapter of the story. Is it a sequel? Or is it written by a different author? Does it tell a different story? Can students describe their story with confidence and clarity? If you're not sure what the story is, listen to your students tell it. They have much to tell.

Keep Your Math Everywhere

Many districts attempt to treat issues in mathematics education in isolation. That's why many schools suffer from initiative fatigue. Every couple of years, a new initiative comes through, sometimes in the form of a new curriculum, sometimes in the form of a new teaching strategy. In fact, you may even recognize some of the content of this book as echoes of an ephemeral initiative from years ago. The problem with these initiatives is their myopic view of the issue: *Students just need to work harder*, or, *We need to improve the rigor*, or, *We need to enhance relevance to our students*, or, *We need to try this new teaching strategy*. These are the echoes of failed initiatives. They don't treat math holistically, and they don't treat students holistically.

Initiatives aren't pedagogy. Textbooks aren't pedagogy. Even taking individual sections within this book (such as the one on project-based learning) is insufficient pedagogy. Put it all together, though? Now, *that's* pedagogy.

I've proposed a pedagogical framework of tasks, facilitation, and academic safety. But this framework describes the same threefold way students experience math, which is through

▲ the task they're working on,

▲ the facilitation provided by their instructor, and

▲ the academic safety of the classroom, including their own self-image as mathematicians.

Students come to you as the accumulation of years of instruction and messaging that permeate their identity as mathematicians. We must be responsive to their reality. Whether they know it or not, students keep their math everywhere: at the bottom of their backpacks, in the front of the class, on the city bus on the ride home. They also keep it in their hearts and seared into their memories and sense of self.

One of the things I love about this subject that we hold dear is just how challenging it is to learn and teach. We're still figuring it out. The best teachers I know have spent their careers refining their practice and getting better each year. They try new things and are hungry to know what cool stuff is on the horizon. They are reflective and experimental.

When you look at your craft—and because you've made it to the end of the book, I assume you're the introspective type—take a look at *your* math. Personally, I enjoy teaching and learning about math because it continues to feel so new and fresh. Every lesson is a new opportunity to see through the eyes of a student approaching a task in a novel way. Every assignment is an opportunity to celebrate how a budding mathematician has grown. There's never been a more exciting time to be a math teacher. We're no longer handcuffed to a single textbook. We can push the boundaries of the types of mathematical experiences and puzzles we can pose to our students. There's no limit to the amount of deep contemplation we can ask of our students. And we can continue to learn from one another, sharing lessons across geography via social media, email, and blogs. Ten years ago, we had no access to the concept of growth mindset. Fifteen years ago, posing a problem with a picture or video was unheard of. Twenty years ago, using a lesson designed by a teacher from another state was unthinkable. In many ways it feels like we're just on the cusp of a whole new world of math instruction.

Still, the same three elements appear over and over again: quality tasks, effective facilitation, and academic safety. Whether a teacher is in inner-city Seattle or rural Arkansas, these are the central elements in their dynamic classrooms. Their classrooms and students look very different but feel the same.

So what is it you love about teaching and learning math? What is it you love about teaching mathematicians? Where does this love show up? Where is it in the tasks you're giving? Where is it in your facilitation? Where is it in the academic safety you provide? We know that students keep their math everywhere. I hope you'll keep your math everywhere, too.

APPENDICES

Suggested Math Reading/ Viewing/Listening

Teachers and students have greater access to the work of mathematicians than ever before. Readily accessible books, videos, podcasts, and articles can allow authentic mathematical work into your school. Should you choose to steep yourself in the work of mathematicians, you'll find that these artifacts are approachable and delightful. You may want to use them to rethink your classroom or simply to satisfy your own curiosity.

Consider this a starter list of potential artifacts to read, watch, or listen to.

Books

How Not to Be Wrong: The Power of Mathematical Thinking by Jordan Ellenberg

The Joy of x: A Guided Tour of Math, from One to Infinity by Steven Strogatz

Thinking Statistically by Uri Bram

Women in Mathematics by Lynn Osen

Measurement by Paul Lockhart

Articles

"A Mathematician's Lament" by Paul Lockhart, Mathematical Association of America

"No Such Thing as a Math Person" by Perri Klass, MD, *New York Times*

"The Unforgiving Math That Stops Epidemics" by Tara Smith, *Scientific American*

"How Animals Got Their Spots and Stripes—According to Math" by Thomas Woolley, *Scientific American*

"The Pursuit of Beauty" by Alec Wilkinson, *New Yorker*

Videos

"Steven Strogatz and Hilbert's Infinite Hotel"

"Navajo Math Circles," PBS

"The Mathematics of Love," Hannah Fry

"The Magic of Fibonacci Numbers," Arthur Benjamin

"Why I Fell in Love with Monster Prime Numbers," Adam Spencer

"The Beautiful Minds," Cedric Villani

Audio

"Remembering Maryam Mirzakhani," NPR

"Mathematics' Unintended Consequences," *In Our Time*

"How Much Brain Damage Do I Have?" *Freakonomics*

"Henri Poincaré," *A Brief History of Mathematics*

"On Average," *99% Invisible*

Necessary Conditions: Teaching Secondary Math with Academic Safety, Quality Tasks, and Effective Facilitation by Geoff Krall. Copyright © 2018. Stenhouse Publishers.

Profiles of Notable Mathematicians

Throughout this book, we've gotten glimpses into the vast, varying world of mathematicians' work and personalities. Authentic mathematical work and the dispositions of mathematicians have influenced educators as they've rethought their approach to math. In this appendix are brief profiles of a few of my favorite mathematicians, from the eighth century to the present day.

When students think of mathematicians, they typically think of white men working in isolation on indecipherable problems. Be sure to provide models of mathematicians who represent the diversity of those in the field by race, gender, sexual orientation, personality, and ways of working.

Going forward, I hope you'll create your own list of all-star mathematicians for your students. Annie Perkins has created a more comprehensive database of mathematicians at her website arbitrarilyclose.com.

Maryam Mirzakhani (1977–2017)

Maryam Mirzakhani was born in Tehran, Iran, where she attended Sharif University. While there, she won gold medals in the International Mathematical Olympiad after being the first woman on the Iranian team. After earning her degree, she moved to the United States to attend graduate school at Harvard. Later, she became a professor at Stanford University.

In 2013, Mirzakhani coauthored a paper in which she and peer Alix Eskin analyzed the path of a pool ball around a polygonal pool table. In 2014, she became the first woman to win the prestigious Fields Medal, the equivalent of a Nobel Prize in Mathematics, for her "striking and highly original contributions to geometry and dynamical systems" (Math Union 2014). Her work was as delightful as it was insightful. Her daughter once referred to Mirzakhani's mathematical work as "painting."

Martha Euphemia Lofton Haynes (1890–1980)

Martha Euphemia Lofton Haynes was born and lived her entire life in Washington, DC, and was given numerous awards for her contribution to the betterment of her community. In 1943, she became the first African American woman to obtain a PhD in mathematics, achieving this distinction with the successful dissertation at Catholic University of America titled "The Determination of Sets of Independent Conditions Characterizing Certain Special Cases of Symmetric Correspondences."

Necessary Conditions: Teaching Secondary Math with Academic Safety, Quality Tasks, and Effective Facilitation by Geoff Krall. Copyright © 2018. Stenhouse Publishers.

Dr. Haynes taught first grade through high school in the DC public school system for forty-seven years. After her public teaching career, she became a professor and established the mathematics department at Miner Teachers College.

Nancy Grace Roman (1925–)

Nancy Grace Roman is known colloquially as the Mother of Hubble because of her work with NASA, planning the Hubble Space Telescope. Early in her life, she was discouraged from going into astronomy. Her high school guidance counselor tried to persuade her to take Latin rather than a second year of algebra.

Roman helped found NASA and pioneered several projects, including the launching of twenty satellites, the most famous of which is the Hubble Space Telescope. She not only planned the launch of the telescope, but she also secured funding and built a team that enabled the construction and successful launch of the satellite, which has told us more about the universe than perhaps any other.

Hee Oh (1969–)

Hee Oh is a South Korean mathematician who specializes in dynamic systems, specifically the dynamics of homogeneous spaces. She took a break from mathematics during her junior year at Seoul University in South Korea to focus on social activism, advocating for the underprivileged. When she returned to math full-time, she became the first tenured female professor of mathematics at Yale University.

Vivienne Malone-Mayes (1932–1995)

Vivienne Malone-Mayes grew up in Waco, Texas, a highly segregated community in a highly segregated state. She attended a segregated high school, from which she graduated two years early at the age of sixteen. Malone-Mayes pursued mathematics at Fisk University, where she graduated in four years with a bachelor's degree and earned a master's two years later. She worked as a professor at Paul Quinn College and Bishop College.

In 1961, Malone-Mayes applied to take additional courses to begin her PhD work at Baylor University but was rejected explicitly because of her race. Required to do so by federal law, the University of Texas admitted her (Baylor is a private university). Though she was admitted, she was not welcomed. "My mathematical isolation was complete," she noted (Case and Leggett 2016), as she described her experience of being the only woman and the only African American in many of her classes.

Necessary Conditions: Teaching Secondary Math with Academic Safety, Quality Tasks, and Effective Facilitation by Geoff Krall. Copyright © 2018. Stenhouse Publishers.

Despite these challenges, Malone-Mayes obtained her PhD in 1966 with her dissertation "A Structure Problem in Asymptotic Analysis." Throughout her education she took part in civil rights demonstrations.

After she earned her doctorate, she became the first full-time African American professor at Baylor University, the institution that had refused to let her take courses just a few years earlier. There she was voted the most outstanding faculty member by the student congress in 1971.

Alan Turing (1912–1954)

Alan Turing is a pillar in the fields of mathematics, cryptology, and computer science. He put each of those disciplines to work during World War II, when he and his team secretly developed a machine that cracked German codes. The Germans would consistently change their code keys, making it impossible for Allied forces to decipher the messages they intercepted. That changed when Turing and his team built a machine called *Bombe* that could quickly and automatically determine the code keys the Germans were using and altering.

So influential was Turing's work on early computing that he has a test named after him. The Turing Test is referenced even today when determining the capacity for a computer to act as artificial intelligence.

In 1952, after having been discovered to be in a sexual relationship with another man, Turing stood trial for "indecency." As part of a plea bargain, he agreed to undergo "treatment" intended to reduce his libido. Doctors injected him with hormones that eventually caused significant health and cognitive degeneration, and in 1954, he was found dead in his apartment from apparent cyanide poisoning.

Hannah Fry (1984–)

Hannah Fry is a British mathematician specializing in the intersection between mathematics and human behavior. After obtaining a PhD in fluid dynamics, she began to apply her math knowledge to social systems, such as trade, migration, and security. She uses math to develop models that represent human interactions and incentives.

Her TED Talk "The Mathematics of Love" has been viewed millions of times. In it she delightfully provides data, combinatorics, and stories to help make sense of a chaotic system: the dating scene. She's also written two books playfully integrating math and social science: *The Mathematics of Love: Patterns, Proofs, and the Search for the Ultimate Equation* and *The Indisputable Existence of Santa Claus*. Fry provides an example of the wide variety of fields mathematicians may find themselves in.

Necessary Conditions: Teaching Secondary Math with Academic Safety, Quality Tasks, and Effective Facilitation by Geoff Krall. Copyright © 2018. Stenhouse Publishers.

Ada Lovelace (1815–1852)

Ada King-Noel, Countess of Lovelace is known as perhaps the world's first computer programmer. In 1833, she met Charles Babbage, who had developed a Difference Engine, which was essentially a calculator. Working with Babbage, she was the first to see the potential for using machines to develop complex algorithms rather than simple computation. The engines that Lovelace and Babbage worked on are recognized as early computer models.

Srinivasa Ramanujan (1887–1920)

Srinivasa Ramanujan was an Indian mathematician who pioneered work in analysis and number theory and solved problems that were thought to be unsolvable—despite having no formal training in mathematics. He worked on mathematical problems for years in isolation before reaching out to British mathematicians by mail correspondence. His work proved so astounding that he was invited to study at Cambridge, where he eventually earned a PhD in 1916.

His work was often criticized for its meandering quality. What should have taken a few pages took dozens. But as difficult as his papers were to read, they were equally as innovative. Throughout his short life, Ramanujan developed several conjectures and unique solutions, and he even has a number co-named for him, 1729, the Hardy-Ramanujan number: the smallest number that can be expressed as the sum of two cubes in two different ways.

$$1729 = 1^3 + 12^3 = 9^3 + 10^3$$

Emmy Noether (1882–1935)

Emmy Noether spent much of her mathematical career learning, working, and collaborating, with little or no public acknowledgment. Rather than enroll in Germany's University of Erlangen, where her father was a professor, she audited math courses, not officially obtaining credit. Then she audited again at University of Göttingen the following year. When Erlangen allowed women to officially enroll in 1904, she promptly did so, receiving her PhD in 1907.

She continued to work as a mathematician at the university without pay or title for the next seven years, collaborating with many prominent mathematicians. In 1915, she returned to Göttingen, but could not be a professor because of her gender. She lectured as an assistant to David Hilbert, though she was more of an equal partner

Necessary Conditions: Teaching Secondary Math with Academic Safety, Quality Tasks, and Effective Facilitation by Geoff Krall. Copyright © 2018. Stenhouse Publishers.

in his work. Eventually Hilbert and Albert Einstein advocated for Noether and she was allowed to lecture under her own name, but without salary until three years later. Still, she faced discrimination as a woman, a Jew, and a pacifist.

In 1933, she was barred from teaching and eventually fled Nazi Germany. She became a professor at Bryn Mawr College in the United States. Noether died two years later from complications from surgery.

Katherine Johnson (1918–)

Katherine Johnson was one of many female African American mathematicians who pioneered the first shuttle launches for NASA. Not only did she pioneer the United States' space race efforts, but she was a trailblazer her whole life. She graduated high school at age fourteen. In college, Johnson took so many math courses and completed them with such virtuosity that they had to invent new courses just for her. At age eighteen, she graduated summa cum laude with degrees in math and French. After marrying and starting a family, she became the first African American woman to attend graduate school at West Virginia University (Morgantown).

In 1953, Johnson accepted a job at NASA, where she worked in a "pool" of women dedicated to performing math calculations. Essentially, they were human calculators. Johnson's expertise, along with her assertiveness, eventually led to her recognition as one of the most talented and trusted "computers" at NASA. Astronaut John Glenn refused to fly his orbit around Earth until Johnson herself verified the calculations of the new digital computers. Johnson calculated 1969's Apollo 11 mission to the moon. She helped bring the Apollo 13 astronauts back to earth safely when that mission went awry.

Katherine Johnson, along with Mary Jackson, Dorothy Vaughn, Annie Easley, and others, helped make NASA into the scientific and cultural institution it is today, starting long before the Civil Rights Act of 1964.

Muhammad ibn Mūsā al-Khwārizmī (c. 780–c. 850)

Mūsā al-Khwārizmī is known as the "father of algebra." Around the year 820, he wrote a book titled *The Compendious Book on Calculation by Completion and Balancing* in which he described methods to create and solve equations. The method of isolating variables by canceling like terms from both sides of an equation? That came from this seminal tome. Parent functions are also included in *Completion and Balancing*.

There were no mathematical notations or symbols at the time to aid al-Khwārizmī's communication. He had to make do with words. He described variables as "things" to multiply or divide. However, he did make use of diagrams to aid his discussions. With the publication of *Completion and Balancing*, Al-Khwārizmī created an entire field of mathematics, one we take for granted today.

Blaise Pascal (1623–1662)

Blaise Pascal was a French mathematician and theologian, among other things. He's perhaps best known for Pascal's Triangle. Beginning with one, each number below is the sum of the two above it:

$$
\begin{array}{c}
1 \\
1 \quad 1 \\
1 \quad 2 \quad 1 \\
1 \quad 3 \quad 3 \quad 1 \\
1 \quad 4 \quad 6 \quad 4 \quad 1
\end{array}
$$

This pattern, although delightful in and of itself, contains hidden mysteries that hold a surprising number of applications.

Pascal was as respected a mathematician as he was a theologian, and his work culminated in what was posthumously titled *Pensées* (Thoughts), where he examined and defended the Christian faith, which he held dear.

René Descartes (1596–1648)

Like many mathematicians, René Descartes was a polymath, also interested in theology, science, and philosophy. While an officer in the military, he spent the night in a room with an oven to escape the cold. There in the room, he had a series of visions that instructed him to pursue science and math. In these visions, he saw the unity of philosophy and math, truth and logic. In 1637, in *Discourse on the Method*, he published his most famous words and perhaps one of the most famous phrases in Western civilization: "*Je pense, donc je suis*" or "I think, therefore I am."

Descartes's biggest contribution to math hides in plain sight. All secondary math students are familiar with the Cartesian coordinate plane. This was Descartes's invention. He is credited with being the first to recognize the relationship between algebra and geometry, creating a convention of *x*- and *y*-axes. He also created the superscript as a representation of powers. His work and conventions developing the field of analytical geometry paved the way for Isaac Newton's foray into calculus.

Necessary Conditions: Teaching Secondary Math with Academic Safety, Quality Tasks, and Effective Facilitation by Geoff Krall. Copyright © 2018. Stenhouse Publishers.

Paul Erdős (1913–1996)

Paul Erdős was as eccentric as he was brilliant. Born in Hungary, Erdős worked tirelessly on math problems, perhaps more than any mathematician in history, devoting almost his entire waking life to the discipline. He traveled from town to town, country to country, to work with different mathematicians. Believing math to be a social activity, Erdős would show up on the doorsteps of renowned mathematicians to write papers, only sometimes announced. He had few possessions: he was a mathematical nomad of sorts.

So prolific was Erdős's output that the discipline of mathematics plays a game in which everyone has an Erdős number. Much like the six degrees of separation/Kevin Bacon phenomenon, a person's Erdős number is the number of publications and collaborators between the person and Erdős. Immediate collaborators with Erdős have an Erdős number of one. Collaborators with them have an Erdős number of two, their collaborators have a number of three, and so on.

David Hilbert (1862–1943)

David Hilbert was a German mathematician best known for two significant contributions to the field of mathematics. First, Hilbert spaces allow us to extend our understanding of three-dimensional space to any number of dimensional space. Hilbert spaces are a generalization of Euclidean space.

Hilbert's second (but not final) major contribution to the field occurred at the turn of the last century, when he gave a talk titled "The Problems of Mathematics." In it, he posed several open-ended problems to frame the next century of mathematics. Through subsequent talks and papers, Hilbert eventually landed on twenty-three problems that would help "lift the veil behind which the future lies hidden." Some of these problems were solved soon afterward, whereas others have been deemed unsolvable. To this day, mathematicians continue to work on problems that Hilbert posed more than a century ago.

Necessary Conditions: Teaching Secondary Math with Academic Safety, Quality Tasks, and Effective Facilitation by Geoff Krall. Copyright © 2018. Stenhouse Publishers.

Consultancy Protocol for Discussing a Dilemma

Prework

The presenter of the dilemma writes about it, using full paragraphs and complete sentences. The presenter should give the audience as much context as possible and craft a guiding question. Examples of a guiding question:

▲ How do I reach a student who is succeeding in other classes but not mine?

▲ Why aren't my students explaining their work sufficiently?

▲ What can I do to make sure I'm challenging a particular group of students?

The Protocol

▲ *Presenting the dilemma*. The presenter describes the dilemma, giving as much context as possible. You may want to have participants read the prewriting. (5 minutes)

▲ *Clarifying questions*. Participants ask the presenter quick, clarifying questions to gain a better understanding of the context. (5 minutes)

▲ *Probing questions*. Participants ask more in-depth questions about the dilemma that help clarify the underlying issues for the presenter and participants. The presenter is encouraged to respond to the questions with as much detail as necessary. (5 minutes)

▲ *Discussion*. At this point, the presenter is silent while the participants discuss what they heard. Participants may discuss similar dilemmas they've had in the past, express empathy for the presenter, offer potential next steps, and build off one another's comments. The presenter listens and takes notes. (10 minutes)

▲ *Presenter responds*. The presenter is invited back into the conversation to reflect on what he or she heard during the discussion section and what he or she will take away from the protocol. (5 minutes)

Necessary Conditions: Teaching Secondary Math with Academic Safety, Quality Tasks, and Effective Facilitation by Geoff Krall. Copyright © 2018. Stenhouse Publishers.

Task-Quality Checklist

Hallmarks of a Quality Task	Quality Assessment
Quality tasks do the following: • Spark curiosity and foster engagement • Yield creativity and lead to new ideas • Promote access for all students in the classroom • Require and convey deep, crucial mathematical content • Connect and extend content	Here are a few potential indicators for each hallmark of a quality task. Although it isn't necessary for a task to contain all hallmarks or all indicators, consider modifying them to maximize the number of each. **Spark curiosity and foster engagement** ☐ Task stirs curiosity in the teacher. ☐ Task elicits student questions and questioning. ☐ Task contains just-out-of-reach information. ☐ Task elicits a student prediction. ☐ Task breaks expectations in some way. **Yield creativity and lead to new ideas** ☐ Task invites new definitions from students. ☐ Task has multiple solution paths. ☐ Task has multiple solutions. **Promote access for all students** ☐ Task is clear and to the point. ☐ Task includes or necessitates a diagram. ☐ Task ensures all students can get started. ☐ Task includes multimedia. **Require and convey deep, crucial mathematical content** ☐ Task is aligned to important standards. ☐ Task results in long-term conceptual understanding. ☐ Prompt contains qualifying words such as most, least, highest, lowest, closest, etc. ☐ Task involves a comparison. **Connect and Extend Content** ☐ Task uses know-how from previous lessons. ☐ Task hints at future lessons. ☐ Task contains concepts from other content areas (math or otherwise).

Sample Norms

Below is a list of various norms I've seen in effective classrooms across the country. Some are more technical in nature; others are aspirational. People's definition of what makes a norm may differ, but the classrooms from which I copied these were all successful classrooms. So, feel free to mix and match as well as develop your own. I recommend no more than five or six. Below, you'll also find some potential prompts to debrief the norms, a practice I recommend doing regularly.

Norms to Streamline Work and Procedures

Write in pen: each team member should use a different color.	Use a single sheet of paper for your calculations and diagrams.	Check in with your partner before asking the teacher.	Be respectful of the learning environment.

Norms to Promote Positivity

Trust, Respect, Responsibility.	Say a kind word to one another.	Keep discussions and feedback constructive. (Use "I like," "I wonder," and "next steps.")	Listen actively and respect the ideas of others.

Norms for Equitable Groupwork

Share the airtime.	Same problem, same time.	We are better when we work together.	Everyone must contribute.
All heads in, all feet in.	Don't give the answer; guide the process.	We are each a capable mathematician.	Ask the group for help and clarification when needed.

Necessary Conditions: Teaching Secondary Math with Academic Safety, Quality Tasks, and Effective Facilitation by Geoff Krall. Copyright © 2018. Stenhouse Publishers.

Norms to Promote Academic Safety

Speed isn't important.	Everyone can learn math.	Be present.	Take agency over your needs and advocate for yourself.

Norms to Produce Quality Work

Explain and record your thinking.	A written explanation must accompany calculations and diagrams.	Revisions are always accepted and encouraged.	Go back and check your answers for reasonableness.

Norms to Promote Risk Taking

Mistakes are accepted, inspected, and respected.	Disagree with ideas, not people.	Mistakes may be crossed off, but do so minimally.	Don't be afraid to try out an idea.

Norm Reflection Prompts

▲ Which of our norms did we embody well today? How do you know?

▲ Which of our norms do we need to work on? How do you know?

▲ As a group and personally, which norm are you exhibiting well?

▲ What norm did a classmate of yours embody well today? Cite a specific example.

▲ Should we add to our norms or revise one of them?

Necessary Conditions: Teaching Secondary Math with Academic Safety, Quality Tasks, and Effective Facilitation by Geoff Krall. Copyright © 2018. Stenhouse Publishers.

Effective Facilitation Guide

This guide identifies various moments of facilitation and provides a menu of strategies.

Structures and Routines

Establishing and Defining Norms	• What norms do you want for your class? How will you decide on them?
	  • Consider using some of the sample norms provided in Appendix E.
	  • Will you have students help decide on your class norms?
	  • Will you have department-wide norms (for teachers and students)?

Teaching and Reinforcing Norms	• How will you teach the norms?
	  • Public display of the norms and what they look/sound like
	  • Reflecting on and debriefing the norms
	  • Public monitoring of norms

Routines	• How will students enter the room? • How will students obtain supplies? • How will students turn in work? • Where will students sit?

Groupwork	• Teaching ways of groupwork
	• Establishing groups
	• Establishing group roles
	  • norms manager
	  • task manager
	  • resource manager
	  • communication manager
	• Maintaining groupwork

Solo Work	• Structures for solo work • How will you ensure that students can think and concentrate deeply while working individually?

Necessary Conditions: Teaching Secondary Math with Academic Safety, Quality Tasks, and Effective Facilitation by Geoff Krall. Copyright © 2018. Stenhouse Publishers.

Within the Task

Posing the Task	• Know/Need to Know • Notice and Wonder • Estimation

Workshops	• What kind of workshop is needed?
	  • Concept development versus product refinement versus getting unstuck
	• Who needs to attend the workshop?
	  • Sign-up sheets
	  • Self-assignment
	  • All groups versus some groups

Visual/Visible Learning	• Concept mapping • Student demos and drawings
Solution Sharing	• Gallery walk: Likes and Wonders • Formal presentation • Informal presentation • Sixty-second video shorts
Revision	• Peer editing • Self-check against rubric
Quick Moves	• Listening and exploring • "Permission to be inarticulate?" • "Turn and talk." • "Say more about . . ." • "Explain her answer."

Necessary Conditions: Teaching Secondary Math with Academic Safety, Quality Tasks, and Effective Facilitation by Geoff Krall. Copyright © 2018. Stenhouse Publishers.

Lesson Plan Template

Lesson Title:	Content and Practice Standards:
Topic:	

Agenda	Planning for Academic Safety

Warm-Up

How will you engage students' minds to prepare them for math for the day?

Posing the Task

How will you spark curiosity, highlight essential questions, and ensure understanding of the task?

Student Work Time

How will you use this time to assign academic status and listen for student understanding?

Planned Workshops

How will you structure and facilitate workshops?

Solution Sharing

Why and how will you have students present their ideas and solutions?

Debrief/Exit Ticket

What concepts or understandings do you want students to reflect on?

Planning for Academic Safety

Mathematical habits you want to highlight and amplify during the lesson:

Students to assign academic status:

Planning Effective Facilitation	Planning a Quality Task
Structures and Routines:	Task Type and Description:
Workshops:	Student Work to Collect:

Necessary Conditions: Teaching Secondary Math with Academic Safety, Quality Tasks, and Effective Facilitation by Geoff Krall. Copyright © 2018. Stenhouse Publishers.

Energy Efficiency

Lesson Title

Energy Efficiency

Topic

Finding the solution for a system of equations.

Content and Practice Standards

A-CED.3. Represent constraints by equations or inequalities, and by systems of equations and/or inequalities, and interpret solutions as viable or nonviable options in a modeling context.

F-LE.2. Construct linear and exponential functions, including arithmetic and geometric sequences, given a graph, a description of a relationship, or two input-output pairs (include reading these from a table).

F-LE.3. Observe using graphs and tables that a quantity increasing exponentially eventually exceeds a quantity increasing linearly, quadratically, or (more generally) as a polynomial function.

Agenda (2 days)
Day 1

Warm Up (15 minutes)
Math Talk: Visual Pattern

Posing the Task
Show students the picture of the energy-efficient light bulb with its claims (Figure 5.12)

Ask: What do you notice? What do you wonder?

Student Work Time (35 minutes)
Make sure every group has a good start on the task. Meanwhile, consider offering the following optional/as-needed workshops:

- Workshop on writing equations from given information
- Workshop on graphing linear equations

Exit Ticket (Day 1)
Quadrant formative assessment grid (Figure 8.5)

Planning for Academic Safety

Mathematical Habits you want to highlight and amplify during the lesson:
Organizing information, visual representation, skepticism about claims, using technology effectively

Students to assign academic status: Redd, Misha, Aldon, Vega, Yvonne, Sam

Planning Effective Facilitation

Structures and Routines:
Notice and Wonder, groupwork behavior elevation

Workshops:
Writing equations from given information (assign for struggling groups/students).

Workshop on graphing linear equations (student-led workshop, provide sample problems).

Finding the intersection of two simultaneous equations (whole-class lecture).

Planning a Quality Task

Task Type and Description:
Problem-based learning task in which students must validate or refute claims made on the box of an energy-efficient light bulb.

Student Work to Collect:
Video shorts and problem solutions (poster paper)

Necessary Conditions: Teaching Secondary Math with Academic Safety, Quality Tasks, and Effective Facilitation by Geoff Krall. Copyright © 2018. Stenhouse Publishers.

Day 2

Planned workshops
(15 minutes)

Whole-class workshop: how to find the intersection coordinates of two simultaneous equations.

Solution Sharing
(10 minutes)

Video shorts. Groups will submit their solutions on poster paper and record themselves discussing their models and how they arrived at the solution.

Debrief/Exit Ticket

Agenda Aha's. Display the agenda from the past two days and ask students to post stickies of when they had a specific "aha" moment.

Also ask students to share when they struggled. What was difficult about this task?

Necessary Conditions: Teaching Secondary Math with Academic Safety, Quality Tasks, and Effective Facilitation by Geoff Krall. Copyright © 2018. Stenhouse Publishers.

Hot Rod Quadratics

Lesson Title	Content and Practice Standards	
Hot Rod Quadratics	CCSS.MATH.CONTENT.HSF.IF.C.7 Graph functions expressed symbolically and show key features of the graph, by hand in simple cases and using technology for more complicated cases.	CCSS.MATH.CONTENT.HSF. IF.C.7.A Graph linear and quadratic functions and show intercepts, maxima, and minima.
Topic		
Quadratics • Creating a quadratic function based on coordinates • Finding the zeros of a quadratic		

Agenda

Warm Up (5 minutes)

Which One Doesn't Belong? quadratics

Posing the Task (15 minutes)

Play Act 1 of the video for clarity.

Ask, "After watching Act 1, what are you left wondering about?"

Potential questions to co-develop:

- Will he make it to the other side?

- What shape is the trajectory of the cycle?

Student Work Time (15 minutes)

Share Act 2 materials.

Check in with each group. Make sure they've identified three coordinate pairs before hosting a workshop.

Look for groups creating their parabola carefully.

Planning for Academic Safety

Mathematical Habits you want to highlight and amplify during the lesson:

Organizing information

Using technology as a mathematical tool

Encouragement of peers

Seeking help and understanding

Students to assign academic status:

Mina, Rafael, Oscar, Niel

Planning Effective Facilitation

Structures and Routines:

Reviewing and debriefing classroom norms

Groupwork structures & roles

Workshops:

Creating a quadratic (optional)

Finding roots (Jigsaw — one participant per group)

Planning a Quality Task

Task Type and Description:

3-Act Task: Hot Rod Quadratics

Will Andy Samberg make his jump over 15 school busses?

https://emergentmath.com /2013/04/23/hot-rod-quadratics -lets-jump-this-jump/

Student Work to Collect:

Poster paper, after feedback has been utilized to improve groups' work

Planned Workshops

(20 minutes)

Optional workshop: Creating a quadratic based on three points

Jigsaw workshop: Finding the roots of a quadratic

Solution Sharing

(20 minutes)

Gallery walk—Students will post their solutions on poster paper. Each group will spend five minutes at a poster and leave feedback on sticky notes.

Debrief/Exit Ticket

Play the final video, Act 3

- What feedback did you find useful?

- What questions do you still have about the content?

- How did we do with our norms today? Are there any we need to think about for tomorrow?

Necessary Conditions: Teaching Secondary Math with Academic Safety, Quality Tasks, and Effective Facilitation by Geoff Krall. Copyright © 2018. Stenhouse Publishers.

Problem-Solving Framework

Define the Problem

What is the problem about? What is it asking you to do?

Analyze the Problem

What do you **know** from the problem scenario or lessons that can help solve the problem?	What concepts or information do you **need to know** to solve the problem?

Brainstorm Strategies for Solving the Problem

What strategies might you use to solve the problem? How will you start the problem?

Your Work

Necessary Conditions: Teaching Secondary Math with Academic Safety, Quality Tasks, and Effective Facilitation by Geoff Krall. Copyright © 2018. Stenhouse Publishers.

RUBRIC EXAMPLES WITH SPECIFIC AND COMMON INDICATORS

Problem-Specific Rubric Indicators

	EMERGING	E/D	DEVELOPING	D/P	PROFICIENT	P/A	ADVANCED
Identify the speed of each runner.	Doesn't accurately identify the speed of either runner.		Accurately identifies the speed of one runner.		Accurately identifies the speed of each runner: 20 ft/s 28 ft/s		In addition, all work is shown and proper units are used throughout.
Create an equation for each runner.	No equations are present or accurate.		Accurately creates one of the equations.		Accurately creates the equation for each runner: $d(t) = 20t + 68.6$ $d(t) = 28t$		In addition, all work is shown and proper mathematical notation is used throughout, including identifying the y-intercept as the head start.
Graph the equations for each runner.	No graph accompanies the work.		Graph is inaccurate or incomplete.		Accurately creates a graph showing the simultaneous equations.		In addition, the graph includes labels and key points, and is drawn with precision.
Points	Redo/attend a workshop		6———7		8———9		10

Necessary Conditions: Teaching Secondary Math with Academic Safety, Quality Tasks, and Effective Facilitation by Geoff Krall. Copyright © 2018. Stenhouse Publishers.

"Common Indicators" for Squirrel Guy Race

	EMERGING	E/D	DEVELOPING	D/P	PROFICIENT	P/A	ADVANCED
Problem Solving	Identifies and uses very few important quantities and variables in a practical situation.		Identifies and uses important quantities and variables in a practical situation in a limited way.		Identifies and uses important quantities and variables in a practical situation.		Creates a model to simplify a complicated situation.
Reasoning and Proof	Provides partially correct or incorrect solutions without justifications.		Provides partially correct solutions with justification or correct solutions without logic or justification.		Explains logical, correct, complete solutions with justifications.		Explains logical, correct, complete solutions with justifications and identifies any sources of error.
Communication and Representation	Uses incorrect definitions or mathematical notation (units of measure, labeled diagrams and axes, equation formats, etc.).		Uses imprecise definitions or incomplete mathematical notation (units of measure, labeled diagrams and axes, equation formats, etc.).		With few exceptions, uses accurate definitions and accurate mathematical notation (units of measure, labeled diagrams and axes, etc.).		With few exceptions, uses precise definitions and accurate mathematical notation (units of measure, labeled axes, equation formats, etc.).

Necessary Conditions: Teaching Secondary Math with Academic Safety, Quality Tasks, and Effective Facilitation by Geoff Krall. Copyright © 2018. Stenhouse Publishers.

Agency (Self-Reflection, Exit Ticket, or After the Problem)

Prompt: Throughout the Squirrel Guy Race problem, you were asked to **actively participate** and **seek feedback.** With that in mind, assign yourself a score based on your work during the problem, followed by specific examples and evidence for why you chose that score.

	EMERGING	E/D	DEVELOPING	D/P	PROFICIENT	P/A	ADVANCED
Actively Participate	Stays focused for part of the activity/discussion, team meeting, or independent time but often cannot resist distraction or does not notice when or why a loss of focus happens.		Mostly stays focused on the activity/discussion, team meeting, or independent time, and knows when and why disengagement or distraction happens.		Actively participates in the activity/discussion, team meeting, or independent time and has strategies for staying focused and resisting most distraction.		Actively participates and takes initiative on the activity/discussion, team meeting, or independent time and has strategies for staying focused.
Seek Feedback	Rejects feedback and/or does not revise work.		Sometimes shows evidence of accepting feedback to revise work, but at times may resist when it's difficult.		Consistently shows evidence of accepting and using feedback to revise work to high quality.		Consistently shows evidence of actively seeking, identifying, and using feedback to revise work to high quality.

Necessary Conditions: Teaching Secondary Math with Academic Safety, Quality Tasks, and Effective Facilitation by Geoff Krall. Copyright © 2018. Stenhouse Publishers.

Student Work Analysis Protocol

Prework

The presenting teacher selects an artifact of student work* based on a rich task and brings it to the session. How the artifact is selected is up to the teacher. Perhaps it is representative of the class's work; it could also be from a student that you are interested in learning more about. The group just needs enough work to be able to learn something about what the student knows and can do.

Protocol

▲ Presenting teacher describes the task the student work came from. (2 minutes)

▲ Participants analyze and annotate the work silently. (5–10 minutes)

▲ Facilitator asks, "What did you see in the student work?" Participants describe what they noticed about the work. (5–10 minutes)

▲ Facilitator asks, "What do you think the student thought he or she was working on, based on the evidence we see?" Participants talk about the work from the student's perspective. (5–10 minutes)

▲ Facilitator asks, "What questions are you left with after this discussion?" Participants share questions they have for the student and/or presenting teacher. (5–10 minutes)

▲ Presenting teacher reflects aloud on the conversation. (5 minutes)

* Variations of this protocol could be used for multiple samples of student work. In such instances a teacher ought to bring two or three samples of student work that well represent the work his or her students produced.

An Inservice Agenda: Task Selection (3 hours)

Objective: Identify ten high-quality tasks to implement during the year that will yield crucial content knowledge and/or reinforce messaging around mathematics.

▲ With the entire department: Introduce the objective and discuss. (15 minutes)

▲ Share favorite curriculum resources, websites, books, textbooks, tasks on hand. (15 minutes)

▲ Alone or with people from like-content areas: Identify units of instruction and find one or two tasks per unit. (60 minutes)

▲ Identify roughly where in the year or scope and sequence these tasks belong. (30 minutes)

▲ Peer review: Staff from content areas trade task documents. (30 minutes)

▲ Revise: Identify more precise dates for implementation and place on calendar (such as a shared Google calendar). (30 minutes)

Task Document

Task	Where located	What general content	When in the year?

Necessary Conditions: Teaching Secondary Math with Academic Safety, Quality Tasks, and Effective Facilitation by Geoff Krall. Copyright © 2018. Stenhouse Publishers.

Math Mindsets and Attitudes Student Survey

Section 1

Free association: When you hear the word *math*, what words pop into your head? (2 minutes)

Section 2

Freewrite: What kinds of things do you do in your math classes? (2 minutes)

Section 3

Freewrite: What would you like to do more of in math class? What would you like to do less of in math class? (2 minutes each; 4 minutes total)

    More of:

    Less of:

Section 4

Prompt: Do you think you are smart in math? Why or why not? (2 minutes)

Necessary Conditions: Teaching Secondary Math with Academic Safety, Quality Tasks, and Effective Facilitation by Geoff Krall. Copyright © 2018. Stenhouse Publishers.

Section 5

Freewrite: In your best estimation, what do mathematicians do? (2 minutes)

Section 6

Agree/Disagree statements (3 minutes for all)

Statement	Agree	Disagree	Neutral/Not Sure
I get to share my ideas in math.			
I value the input of my peers when I'm working on a math problem.			
Math is about using the right formula.			
I think I am good at math.			
My peers think I am good at math.			
Math is about discovering new ideas.			
In math, it's okay if I get an answer wrong.			
I am allowed to learn at my own pace and do not feel ashamed if I'm slower than my peers.			
I see mathematics as a subject I will use often throughout life.			
Math is fun.			

Necessary Conditions: Teaching Secondary Math with Academic Safety, Quality Tasks, and Effective Facilitation by Geoff Krall. Copyright © 2018. Stenhouse Publishers.

Math Mindsets and Attitudes Student Survey Facilitation Guide

The survey is split into six sections. The first five are freewriting exercises. The final section is a series of ten *agree/disagree/neutral or not sure* questions, followed by a question about grade level. The survey is provided in Appendix L, but I recommend creating an online, digital version using a platform such as Google Forms or SurveyMonkey.

The survey requires some light facilitation: when giving the freewriting exercises (Sections 1–5) please ensure that you give students two full minutes per question. Even if they stop typing/writing for a period of time, please wait the full two minutes so that they have time to respond to the prompt completely. Also, single-word answers are acceptable. Students may choose how to separate their responses, whether by commas, spaces, or new lines.

Overall, the survey should take about fifteen minutes of class time.

Here are the questions/sections to read aloud.

Section 1

Free association: When you hear the word *math*, what words pop into your head? (2 minutes)

Section 2

Freewrite: What kinds of things do you do in your math classes? (2 minutes)

Section 3

Freewrite: What would you like to do more of in math class? What would you like to do less of in math class? (2 minutes each; 4 minutes total)

Section 4

Prompt: Do you think you are smart in math? Why or why not? (2 minutes)

Necessary Conditions: Teaching Secondary Math with Academic Safety, Quality Tasks, and Effective Facilitation by Geoff Krall. Copyright © 2018. Stenhouse Publishers.

Section 5

Freewrite: In your best estimation, what do mathematicians do? (2 minutes)

Section 6

Agree/Disagree statements (3 minutes for all, estimated)

- ▲ I get to share my ideas in math.
- ▲ I value the input of my peers when I'm working on a math problem.
- ▲ Math is about using the right formula.
- ▲ I think I am good at math.
- ▲ My peers think I am good at math.
- ▲ Math is about discovering new ideas.
- ▲ In math, it's okay if I get an answer wrong.
- ▲ I am allowed to learn at my own pace and do not feel ashamed if I'm slower than my peers.
- ▲ I see mathematics as a subject I will use often throughout life.
- ▲ Math is fun.

Necessary Conditions: Teaching Secondary Math with Academic Safety, Quality Tasks, and Effective Facilitation by Geoff Krall. Copyright © 2018. Stenhouse Publishers.

Check for Academic Safety

When assessing for academic safety in a classroom, the first things to look for are who is talking and what they are saying. You can use this template to collect such evidence.

Who Is Talking?

Teacher talking to class	Student talking to class	Teacher talking to student	Student talking to teacher	Student talking to student
Tally	Tally	Tally	Tally	Tally
Comments	Comments	Comments	Comments	Comments

What Is the Teacher Saying?

Asking a question about math	Checking in with a student personally	Giving instructions
Tally	Tally	Tally
Comments/phrases used	Comments/phrases used	Comments/phrases used

What Are the Students Saying?

A question about math	An idea about math	A word of encouragement
Tally	Tally	Tally
Comments/phrases used	Comments/phrases used	Comments/phrases used

Necessary Conditions: Teaching Secondary Math with Academic Safety, Quality Tasks, and Effective Facilitation by Geoff Krall. Copyright © 2018. Stenhouse Publishers.

Survey/Interview/Questions for Students

Consider asking your students these questions to determine issues of status and mindset. They could be asked via a formal survey or in small focus groups.

Freewriting/Journaling/Conversation

▲ Free association: When you hear the word *math*, what words pop into your head?

▲ Freewrite: What kinds of things do you do in your math classes?

▲ Freewrite: In your best estimation, what do mathematicians do?

▲ Do you think you are smart in math? Why or why not?

Agree/Disagree

▲ I get to share my ideas in math.

▲ I value the input of my peers when I'm working on a math problem.

▲ Math is about using the right formula.

▲ I think I am good at math.

▲ My peers think I am good at math.

▲ In math, it's okay if I get an answer wrong.

▲ I am allowed to learn at my own pace and not feel ashamed if I'm slower than my peers.

▲ What I am learning in math is helping me right now.

▲ What I am learning in math will help me in the future.

Necessary Conditions: Teaching Secondary Math with Academic Safety, Quality Tasks, and Effective Facilitation by Geoff Krall. Copyright © 2018. Stenhouse Publishers.

Video Lesson Study Protocol

Prework

▲ The presenting teacher records a video of him- or herself teaching. Some best practices around recording instruction include the following:

    ▲ Make sure you are within five feet of the recording device most of the time. This will allow the audio to come through better.

    ▲ If you are using a mobile device to record, such as a phone, be sure to record in landscape mode (i.e., turn the phone sideways) rather than portrait mode.

    ▲ Trim the video to ten to fifteen minutes for viewing.

▲ (Optional) The presenting teacher may wish to print the lesson plan for the recorded lesson.

▲ (Optional) The presenting teacher crafts a focus question. This will help peers identify what they ought to be looking and listening for while watching.

Protocol

▲ The presenting teacher introduces the lesson we are about to view. This could include key learning objectives, what prior knowledge students have, and so on. If the teacher has crafted a focus question, he or she should share that here. (5 minutes)

▲ Peers may ask clarifying questions. These questions ought to be technical and logistical in nature, rather than probing. These are questions that have an easy answer, such as "How many students are in the class?" or "How often do students typically work in groups in your class?" (2 minutes)

▲ Watch the video, taking note of as much evidence as possible. To ensure these notes are evidence based, consider the sentence starters "I see . . ." and "I hear . . ." while note-taking. (10 to 15 minutes)

▲ Peers may ask additional clarifying questions. Again, keep these short and technical in nature. (2 minutes)

Necessary Conditions: Teaching Secondary Math with Academic Safety, Quality Tasks, and Effective Facilitation by Geoff Krall. Copyright © 2018. Stenhouse Publishers.

▲ Watch the video again. This time, add notes that are more probing in nature. Consider the sentence starters "I wonder . . ." and "I think. . . ." When you can, map these probing notes onto the more evidence-based notes. For example, "I *noticed* one student didn't have his supplies. I *wonder* if he knows where those supplies are in the room or if you have them." (10 to 15 minutes)

▲ Peers have a discussion about what they saw and heard in the video. During this time the presenting teacher is *not* part of the discussion but should take notes. Be sure to stay in "evidence mode" ("I noticed . . .") and "curiosity mode" ("I wonder . . ."). While the discussion is intended to be free flowing, be sure to point out positive things you noticed in the classroom. Also be sure to cite evidence around the presenting teacher's focus question if he or she provided one. (15 minutes)

▲ The presenting teacher reflects on what he or she heard during the peer discussion. This could include new insights into the focus question, next steps based on the discussion, or other reflections. (3 minutes)

▲ Peer teachers thank the presenting teacher. (1 minute)

Necessary Conditions: Teaching Secondary Math with Academic Safety, Quality Tasks, and Effective Facilitation by Geoff Krall. Copyright © 2018. Stenhouse Publishers.

TASK LIBRARIES

Task Models and Content Clusters

Task Type	Natural Alignment: Common Core Standards for Mathematical Practice and Content Standards
Number Talks	Practice arithmetic, ratios and proportion, percents, fractions, decimals. Apply and extend understanding of fractions. Recognize the relationship between visual patterns and algebraic expressions. SMPs 3, 5, 6, 7, 8
Estimation	Hone number sense. Understand measurement and units. Collect and analyze data and statistics. SMPs 1, 2, 3, 6, 7
Always/ Sometimes/ Never	Evaluate geometric conjectures, geometric constructions, reasoning. Draw, construct, and describe geometric figures and describe the relationships between them. Interpret the structure of expressions, including algebraic properties. Prove and apply trigonometric identities. SMPs 2, 3, 6, 7
Which One Doesn't Belong?	Build or learn vocabulary. Classify or describe geometric objects based on their attributes. Understand the concept of functions and how they appear graphically. Experiment with transformations in the plane. Visualize relationships between two-dimensional and three-dimensional objects. SMPs 2, 3, 6, 7
Polygraph or Guess Who?	Build or learn vocabulary. Interpret functions that arise in applications in terms of the context. Analyze functions using different representations. SMPs 3, 6

Necessary Conditions: Teaching Secondary Math with Academic Safety, Quality Tasks, and Effective Facilitation by Geoff Krall. Copyright © 2018. Stenhouse Publishers.

Task Type	Natural Alignment: Common Core Standards for Mathematical Practice and Content Standards
Card Sorts and Dominoes	Evaluate algebraic expressions, proofs. Use properties of operations to generate equivalent expressions. Write expressions in equivalent forms to solve problems. Model periodic phenomena with trigonometric functions. Prove geometric and algebraic theorems. SMPs 7, 8
Would You Rather . . .	Investigate chance processes and develop, use, and evaluate probability models. Understand the connections among proportional relationships, lines, and linear equations. Reason quantitatively and use units to solve problems. Use probability to evaluate outcomes of decisions. SMPs 1, 2, 3, 4
Three-Act Math	Write equations from scenarios. Solve real-life and mathematical problems using numerical and algebraic expressions and equations. Use functions to model relationships between quantities. Create equations that describe numbers or relationships. SMPs 1, 2, 4, 5
Problem-Based Learning	Solve real-life and mathematical problems involving angle measure, area, surface area, and volume. Analyze and solve linear equations and pairs of simultaneous linear equations. Understand and apply the Pythagorean theorem. Represent and solve equations and inequalities graphically. Build a function that models a relationship between two quantities. SMPs 1, 4
Project-Based Learning	Collect data and conduct appropriate analyses to interpret the significance of an event. See connections between math in the classroom and math outside of the classroom. Use mathematical tools to take measurements for the purposes of application. SMPs 1, 2, 4, 5

Necessary Conditions: Teaching Secondary Math with Academic Safety, Quality Tasks, and Effective Facilitation by Geoff Krall. Copyright © 2018. Stenhouse Publishers.

Always/Sometimes/Never

The morning is the coldest part of the day.	The temperature is higher in Fahrenheit than it is in Celsius.	Computers keep getting better.
A triangle with the same height and the same base as the bottom of a trapezoid has a smaller area.	The circumference of a circle is a smaller value than the area.	If you cut a shape in half, you are reducing the area and perimeter of the shape.
A fraction with a larger numerator and a larger denominator will be greater than the other fraction OR If $a > b$ and $c > d$, then $\frac{a}{c} > \frac{b}{d}$.	A number squared is always bigger than the original number OR $a^2 > a$	$x + 5 < x$
Two complementary angles are greater than one supplementary angle.	For triangle ABC and triangle DEF, if angle $B >$ angle E, then $AC > DF$.	If $\triangle ABC \sim \triangle DEF$ then $\frac{AB}{DE} = \frac{BC}{EF}$.
$4(x + 2) = 4x + 8$	$(x + 4)^2 = x^2 + 16$	$\sqrt{x^2} = x$
$tan\theta = \frac{\cos\theta}{\sin\theta}$	$\log_x z > \log_z x$	$\tan x \neq \tan^2 x$

Necessary Conditions: Teaching Secondary Math with Academic Safety, Quality Tasks, and Effective Facilitation by Geoff Krall. Copyright © 2018. Stenhouse Publishers.

Which One Doesn't Belong?

Suggested protocol:

1. Prompt: Have students take sixty seconds and silently decide which one of these doesn't belong with the other three, and why.

2. Prompt: Have them turn and talk to a neighbor and share which one they selected that doesn't belong, and why.

3. Call on students to solicit their selections and reasons. Try to get two or three reasons for each item.

Numbers

24	81
1	-36

Necessary Conditions: Teaching Secondary Math with Academic Safety, Quality Tasks, and Effective Facilitation by Geoff Krall. Copyright © 2018. Stenhouse Publishers.

Graphs—Linear

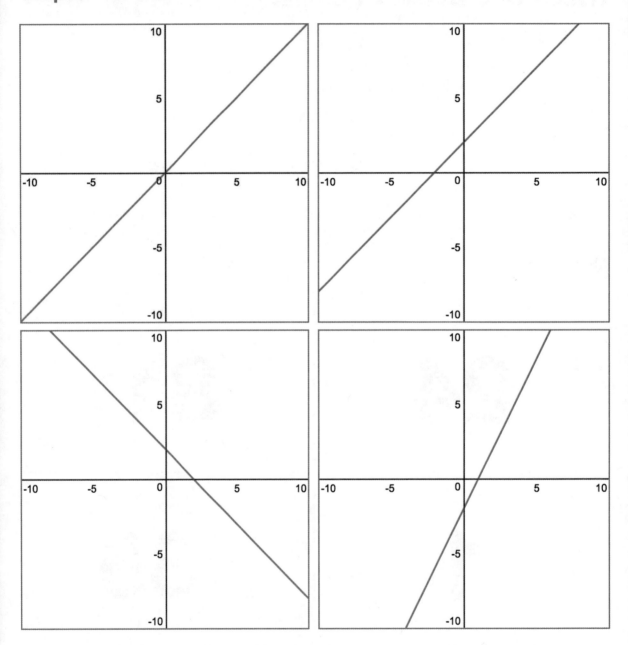

Necessary Conditions: Teaching Secondary Math with Academic Safety, Quality Tasks, and Effective Facilitation by Geoff Krall. Copyright © 2018. Stenhouse Publishers.

Special Functions

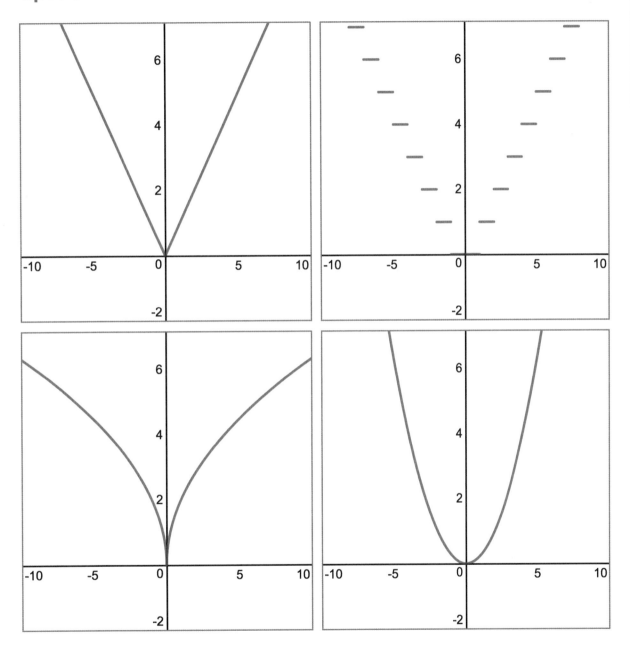

Necessary Conditions: Teaching Secondary Math with Academic Safety, Quality Tasks, and Effective Facilitation by Geoff Krall. Copyright © 2018. Stenhouse Publishers.

Graphs—Periodic Functions

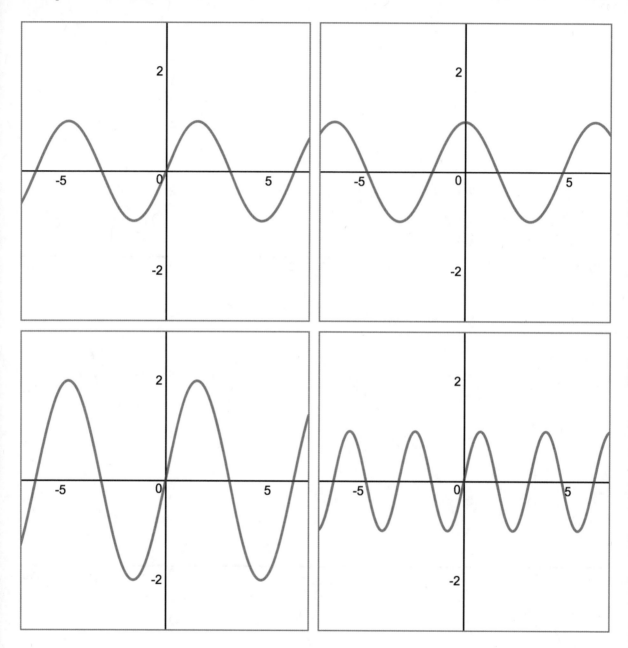

Necessary Conditions: Teaching Secondary Math with Academic Safety, Quality Tasks, and Effective Facilitation by Geoff Krall. Copyright © 2018. Stenhouse Publishers.

Equations

$x^2 + 8x + 16$	$16 - 8x + x^2$
$x^2 - 16$	$x^2 - 4$

Necessary Conditions: Teaching Secondary Math with Academic Safety, Quality Tasks, and Effective Facilitation by Geoff Krall. Copyright © 2018. Stenhouse Publishers.

Triangle Congruency

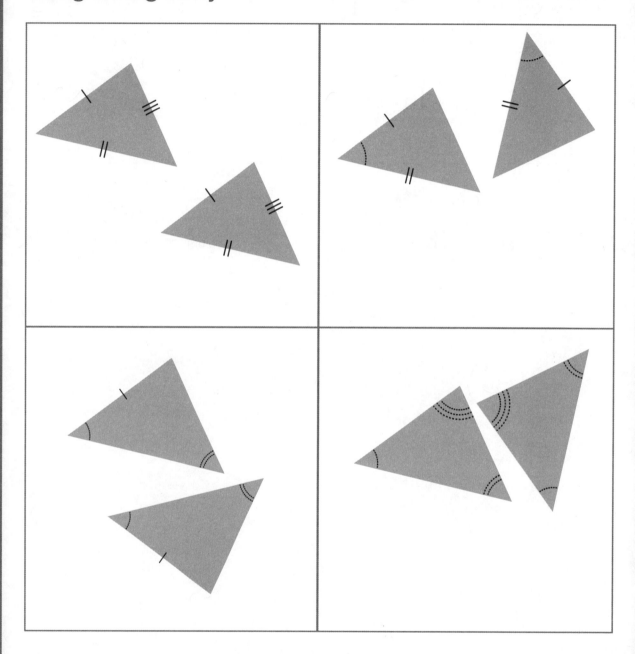

Necessary Conditions: Teaching Secondary Math with Academic Safety, Quality Tasks, and Effective Facilitation by Geoff Krall. Copyright © 2018. Stenhouse Publishers.

Integrals/Area Under a Curve

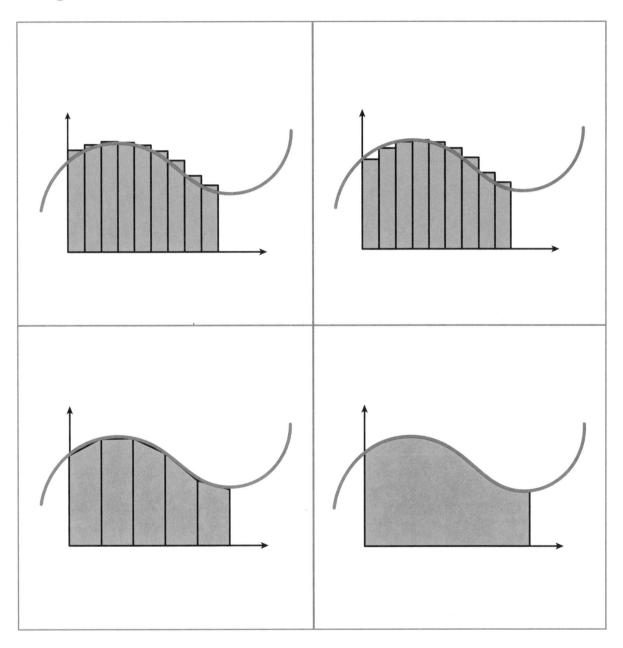

Necessary Conditions: Teaching Secondary Math with Academic Safety, Quality Tasks, and Effective Facilitation by Geoff Krall. Copyright © 2018. Stenhouse Publishers.

Card Set A

Necessary Conditions: Teaching Secondary Math with Academic Safety, Quality Tasks, and Effective Facilitation by Geoff Krall. Copyright © 2018. Stenhouse Publishers.

Card Set B

Necessary Conditions: Teaching Secondary Math with Academic Safety, Quality Tasks, and Effective Facilitation by Geoff Krall. Copyright © 2018. Stenhouse Publishers.

Card Set C

Necessary Conditions: Teaching Secondary Math with Academic Safety, Quality Tasks, and Effective Facilitation by Geoff Krall. Copyright © 2018. Stenhouse Publishers.

Card Set D

Necessary Conditions: Teaching Secondary Math with Academic Safety, Quality Tasks, and Effective Facilitation by Geoff Krall. Copyright © 2018. Stenhouse Publishers.

Dominoes—Linear Functions

Directions: Match the left and right element on each domino to the corresponding equation/graph on another domino. When you're finished, the dominoes should make a complete loop.

$y = 2x - 1$	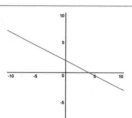
$y = \dfrac{1}{2}x + 2$	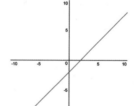
$x - 2 = y$	
$y - 2 = \dfrac{1}{4}x + 1$	
$y = x - 2$	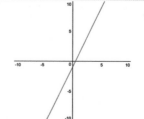

Necessary Conditions: Teaching Secondary Math with Academic Safety, Quality Tasks, and Effective Facilitation by Geoff Krall. Copyright © 2018. Stenhouse Publishers.

Problem-Based Learning

Goats

A group of students suspect that farm animals eat less when the weather is warm. They asked the farm staff to record how much food an adult goat ate on days with different average temperatures.

Food Consumption of a Goat

Average daily temperature (F)	30	40	45	55	60	75	85	90
Food eaten (kg)	3.9	3.6	3.4	3.0	2.7	2.5	2.2	1.9

After analyzing the data, create a model to predict how much a goat would eat based on a given average temperature. Be sure to communicate and defend your model using scatter plots, equations, complete sentences, and proper mathematical notation.

Scaffolds or hint cards:

- Make a graph of the data.

- Draw a line that fits the data.

- Find a linear equation in the form of $y = mx + b$.

- What do the values of m and b in your equation tell you about the relationship between daily average temperature and the goat's food consumption?

- How much could we expect a goat to eat on a 50-degree day?

Necessary Conditions: Teaching Secondary Math with Academic Safety, Quality Tasks, and Effective Facilitation by Geoff Krall. Copyright © 2018. Stenhouse Publishers.

Hotel Snap

Entry Document

Greetings, Math Students!

The Unit

During this unit, we'll be learning and relearning what it means to be "mathematically smart." Many of you have probably experienced mathematics in a black-and-white, fixed-mindset, "you're good at math or you're not good at math" sort of way. I want to take some time at the beginning of this year to explode that myth and explore ways that you can be mathematically smart, which will then propel us for the rest of the year.

The Task

For the first task of the unit, we'll be doing some hotel modeling using Snap Cubes.

The Challenge

In your teams, try to maximize the amount of profit your "hotel" generates.

Different room orientations are worth different profit totals. Please refer to the Project Briefcase to identify the requirements and restrictions for your team's hotel model.

Good luck!

Necessary Conditions: Teaching Secondary Math with Academic Safety, Quality Tasks, and Effective Facilitation by Geoff Krall. Copyright © 2018. Stenhouse Publishers.

Hotel Snap

Daily COSTS of building		
	Each square unit of land	$400
	Each roof	$10
	Each window	$5

Multiply the percent by total **land** cost

Daily TAX based on land		
	1–10 floors	50%
	11–20 floors	1,000%
	21–30 floors	2,000%
	31–40 floors	3,000%
	41–50 floors	5,000%

More windows, more income

INCOME from each type of room		
	4 windows, 1 roof	$600
	4 windows, 0 roof	$500
	3 windows, 1 roof	$300
	3 windows, 0 roof	$250
	2 windows, 1 roof	$200
	2 windows, 0 roof	$175
	1 window, 1 roof	$150
	1 window, 0 roof	$125

This task is courtesy of Fawn Nguyen: http://fawnnguyen.com/hotel-snap/.

Rubric—Hotel Snap

Collaboration: the ability to be a productive member of diverse teams through strong interpersonal communication, a commitment to shared success, leadership, and initiative.

	EMERGING	E/D	DEVELOPING	D/P	PROFICIENT	P/A	ADVANCED
INTERPERSONAL COMMUNICATION	Distracts conversations by expressing ideas that are off topic, undeveloped, or based on limited understanding of the topic. Shows little interest in the ideas of others.		Sometimes is awkward or has difficulty expressing ideas, but conversations are relevant to the topic and based on facts or evidence. Listens with partial interest in the speaker's message, providing sporadic verbal/nonverbal feedback to indicate some understanding or agreement.		Listens with interest to the ideas of others, providing verbal or nonverbal feedback to signal understanding or agreement. Acknowledges and helps clarify others' ideas by asking probing questions.		Thoroughly prepares for conversations by reading about and researching the topic. Invites and encourages other speakers to contribute.

Agency: the ability to develop and reflect on growth mindset as well as demonstrate ownership over one's learning.

	EMERGING	E/D	DEVELOPING	D/P	PROFICIENT	P/A	ADVANCED
ACTIVELY COMMUNICATION	Stays focused for part of the activity/ discussion, team meeting, or independent time but often cannot resist distraction .		Mostly stays focused on the activity/ discussion, team meeting, or independent time and knows when and why disengagement or distraction happens.		Actively participates in the activity/ discussion, team meeting, or independent time and has strategies for staying focused and resisting most distraction.		Actively participates in and takes initiative on the activity/ discussion, team meeting, or independent time and has strategies for staying focused.

Necessary Conditions: Teaching Secondary Math with Academic Safety, Quality Tasks, and Effective Facilitation by Geoff Krall. Copyright © 2018. Stenhouse Publishers.

Math Knowledge and Thinking: habits and ways of thinking that represent the discipline of mathematics.

	EMERGING	E/D	DEVELOPING	D/P	PROFICIENT	P/A	ADVANCED
PROBLEM SOLVING	Does not provide a model. Ignores given constraints. Uses few, if any, problem-solving strategies and tools.		Creates a limited model to simplify a complicated situation. Attends to some of the given constraints. Uses inappropriate or inefficient problem-solving strategies and tools.		Creates a model to simplify a complicated situation. Analyzes all given constraints, goals, and definitions. Uses appropriate problem-solving strategies and tools.		Creates a model to simplify a complicated situation and identifies limitations of model. Analyzes all given constraints, goals, definitions, and implied assumptions. Uses novel problem-solving strategies and tools and/or extends previous knowledge correctly to a given problem.

Necessary Conditions: Teaching Secondary Math with Academic Safety, Quality Tasks, and Effective Facilitation by Geoff Krall. Copyright © 2018. Stenhouse Publishers.

Paleontological Dig

Congratulations! You've been assigned to a paleontological dig to dig up three ancient skeletons. Thanks to our fancy paleontology dig equipment, we've been able to map out where the skeletons are.

Your task: For each skeleton, sketch and write four linear functions that would surround the skeleton, so we may then dig along those lines and excavate it.

Check with your peers: Once you have your functions, compare them to your neighbors'. Their answers will probably be different. What do you like about their answers?

Optional: The technologically inclined may want to use Desmos (https://www. desmos.com/calculator/y1qkrfnsw2).

Challenge: What's the smallest area you can make with the four functions that still surround each skeleton?

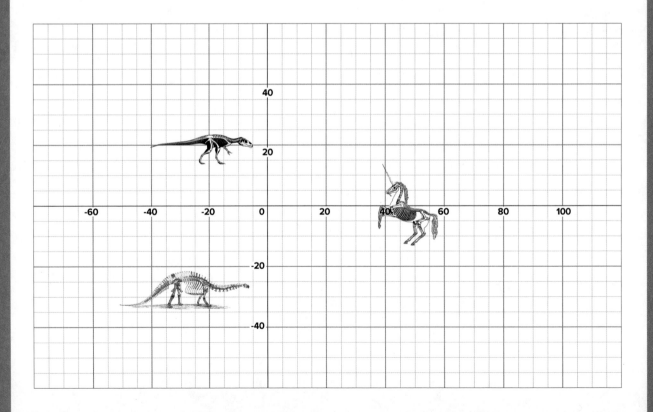

Necessary Conditions: Teaching Secondary Math with Academic Safety, Quality Tasks, and Effective Facilitation by Geoff Krall. Copyright © 2018. Stenhouse Publishers.

Work for Skeleton 1: Unicorn	Equations	Vertices

Work for Skeleton 2: Velociraptor	Equations	Vertices

Work for Skeleton 3: Brontosaurus	Equations	Vertices

Tell the diggers! You need to communicate with the diggers. Tell them where and how to start digging! Be sure to be as specific as possible and discuss your reasoning.

Necessary Conditions: Teaching Secondary Math with Academic Safety, Quality Tasks, and Effective Facilitation by Geoff Krall. Copyright © 2018. Stenhouse Publishers.

Reflection: What do you notice about the four functions for each skeleton?

Reflection: Describe the strategy you used to come up with the four functions.

Necessary Conditions: Teaching Secondary Math with Academic Safety, Quality Tasks, and Effective Facilitation by Geoff Krall. Copyright © 2018. Stenhouse Publishers.

Running from the Law

 ALERT!

Calling all units! Calling all units! We've just received notice that the notorious jewel thief Jimmy Slimfingers has struck again! A little while ago, he stole thousands of dollars' worth of jewelry and fled from the scene! We are looking for him and believe he could be in one of the following buildings.

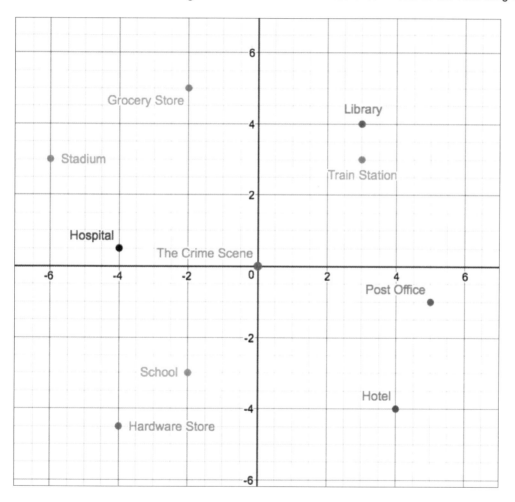

Given the amount of time that's passed and typical running speed, he could be as much as 5 kilometers from the crime scene.

Help us narrow down the location of Jimmy's hideout! Which of the buildings above could he be in? And can you help us establish a perimeter so we know the entire area that he might be in?

Necessary Conditions: Teaching Secondary Math with Academic Safety, Quality Tasks, and Effective Facilitation by Geoff Krall. Copyright © 2018. Stenhouse Publishers.

Work and Solutions

Without doing any calculations just yet, note where you think Jimmy could be and where you're certain he couldn't be, based on the information you've been given. (The table below may help you: check a box for each location.)

	I'm pretty certain he *couldn't* be here.	I'm pretty certain he *could* be here.	I'm not sure.
Grocery Store			
Library			
Stadium			
Train Station			
Hospital			
Post Office			
School			
Hardware Store			
Hotel			

Pause and compare answers with your group-mates.

Now, we know that Jimmy could have traveled *at most* 5 kilometers. How can we get more specific to determine your "not sure" answers? What *theorem* might we want to use here?

Look at your "not sure" answers. Use Pythagorean's theorem $(a^2 + b^2 = c^2)$ to investigate further and develop specific answers. Show your work below.

"Not Sure" Location 1

Location 1:	Work and Solution
Coordinates:	

"Not Sure" Location 2

Location 2:	Work and Solution
Coordinates:	

"Not Sure" Location 3

Location 3:	Work and Solution
Coordinates:	

Pause and compare answers with your group-mates.

Necessary Conditions: Teaching Secondary Math with Academic Safety, Quality Tasks, and Effective Facilitation by Geoff Krall. Copyright © 2018. Stenhouse Publishers.

Agenda: Running from the Law (Equations of Circles)

CCSS.MATH.CONTENT.HSG.GPE.A.1

Derive the equation of a circle of given center and radius using the Pythagorean theorem; complete the square to find the center and radius of a circle given by an equation.

Hand out Entry Document: Running from the Law. Ask students to read, annotate, and highlight the document. Suggested facilitation:

- Underline important information.

- Circle items you have questions about.

Facilitate the Know/Need to Know (or Notice and Wonder) process. Be sure to elicit the following:

Know (or Notice)	Need to Know (or Wonder)
The thief is *at most* 5 km away from the crime scene. • For further discussion/clarification: What do you mean by "at most"? What would an appropriate symbol look like in an equation? The crime scene is at the origin of the graph. We can rule out a few of the locations. We want to establish a perimeter. • For further discussion/clarification: What would the perimeter look like? (circle) Prior knowledge: To find the distance between two points, we can use the Pythagorean theorem.	Which direction did the thief go? And does that matter if we're going to set up a perimeter? For further discussion/clarification: What would the perimeter look like? (circle) How do we make a circle on a graph?

- Hand out student worksheets.

- In groups, have students discuss which of the locations the thief could be in, ones he couldn't be in, and ones they're not sure about.

- For the items under "not sure," have students calculate manually, using the Pythagorean theorem, to see if the location is 5 km or farther. Have them compare their answers.

  - Optional: Consider using this time to hold a small-group or whole-class workshop on the Pythagorean theorem, as needed.

Necessary Conditions: Teaching Secondary Math with Academic Safety, Quality Tasks, and Effective Facilitation by Geoff Krall. Copyright © 2018. Stenhouse Publishers.

- As you're monitoring groups, encourage them to draw the perimeter. It should be a circle about the origin with a radius of 5.

  - However, some students may note that there would be additional buildings and obstacles, preventing a straight line path. Be sure to acknowledge and honor such thinking. Ask how it might change the answers. Perhaps some of the borderline answers will move into the "no" category.

- Once every group has identified the locations where the thief could be and drawn a perimeter, host a whole-class lesson on writing the equation of a circle.

$$(x - a)^2 = (y - b)^2 = R^2$$

- Be sure to note that in this problem, *a* and *b* are (0,0) and therefore wouldn't appear directly.

- Also be sure to highlight the connection between the equation and the Pythagorean theorem.

- Consider doing a few examples or practice problems.

- So that students can get used to the vertical and horizontal translation of the circle equation (i.e., *a* and *b*), assign each group a different location to start from to establish another perimeter. Here are some examples:

  - Group A: Write the equation of the circle if the thief starts from the hospital.

  - Group B: Write the equation of the circle if the thief starts from the school.

  - Group C: Write the equation of the circle if the thief starts from the train station.

  - Group D: Write the equation of the circle if the thief starts from the hotel.

  - Group E: Write the equation of the circle if the thief starts from the stadium.

Necessary Conditions: Teaching Secondary Math with Academic Safety, Quality Tasks, and Effective Facilitation by Geoff Krall. Copyright © 2018. Stenhouse Publishers.

Facilitation Notes: PBL Unit
Bush v. Gore (The 2000 Election)

CCSS.MATH.CONTENT.HSS.ID.B.6

Represent data on two quantitative variables on a scatter plot, and describe how the variables are related.

CCSS.MATH.CONTENT.HSS.ID.B.6.A

Fit a function to the data; use functions fitted to data to solve problems in the context of the data. Use given functions or choose a function suggested by the context. Emphasize linear, quadratic, and exponential models.

CCSS.MATH.CONTENT.HSS.ID.B.6.B

Informally assess the fit of a function by plotting and analyzing residuals.

CCSS.MATH.CONTENT.HSS.ID.B.6.C

Fit a linear function for a scatter plot that suggests a linear association.

CCSS.MATH.CONTENT.HSS.ID.C.8

Compute (using technology) and interpret the correlation coefficient of a linear fit.

CCSS.MATH.CONTENT.HSS.ID.A.3

Interpret differences in shape, center, and spread in the context of the data sets, accounting for possible effects of extreme data points (outliers).

Necessary Conditions: Teaching Secondary Math with Academic Safety, Quality Tasks, and Effective Facilitation by Geoff Krall. Copyright © 2018. Stenhouse Publishers.

PBL Unit Process

Day 1	Days 2–3	Day 4	Days 5–6	Day 7
Entry Event Collect Knows/ Need to Knows. Establish group roles.	Workshops and Lessons Create a scatter plot and line of best fit. Identify what each group member brings to the table.	Project Benchmark 1 Groups present plotted data. Whole class: Update K/NTKs. In groups: Notice and Wonder about the data.	Workshops and Lessons Identifying outliers Creating residual plots	Project Benchmark 2 Conduct analysis of scatter plots. Review of current groupwork structures: What's working? What needs help?

Days 8–9	Day 10	Days 11–12	Day 13	Day 14
Workshops and Lessons Writing workshop Check in with groups to identify progress. Additional workshops on outliers and residuals	Project Benchmark 3 Turn in write-up of analysis.	Peer-edit analyses. Begin creating final product.	Present final product.	Post-PBL Unit Reflection Highlight positive group interactions and mathematical "smartnesses."

Necessary Conditions: Teaching Secondary Math with Academic Safety, Quality Tasks, and Effective Facilitation by Geoff Krall. Copyright © 2018. Stenhouse Publishers.

To the students of Akins New Tech High School:

The US presidential election of November 7, 2000, was one of the closest in history. As returns were counted on Election Night, it became clear that the outcome in the state of Florida would determine the next president. When the roughly 6 million Florida votes had been counted, George W. Bush was shown to be leading by only 1,738 votes, and the narrow margin triggered an automatic recount. The recount, completed in the evening of November 9, showed Bush's lead to be fewer than 400 votes.

County	Buchanan Votes	Bush Votes
ALACHUA	262	34062
BAKER	73	5610
BAY	248	38637
BRADFORD	65	5413
BREVARD	570	115185
BROWARD	789	177279
CALHOUN	90	2873
CHARLOTTE	182	35419
CITRUS	270	29744
CLAY	186	41745
COLLIER	122	60426
COLUMBIA	89	10964
DADE	561	289456
DE SOTO	36	4256
DIXIE	29	2698
DUVAL	650	152082
ESCAMBIA	504	73029
FLAGLER	83	12608
FRANKLIN	33	2448
GADSDEN	39	4750
GILCHRIST	29	3300
GLADES	9	1840
GULF	71	3546
HAMILTON	24	2153
HARDEE	30	3764
HENDRY	22	4743
HERNANDO	242	30646
HIGHLANDS	99	20196
HILLSBOROUGH	836	176967
HOLMES	76	4985
INDIAN RIVER	105	28627
JACKSON	102	9138
JEFFERSON	29	2481
LAFAYETTE	10	1669

County	Buchanan Votes	Bush Votes
LAKE	289	49963
LEE	305	106141
LEON	282	39053
LEVY	67	6860
LIBERTY	39	1316
MADISON	29	3038
MANATEE	272	57948
MARION	563	55135
MARTIN	108	33864
MONROE	47	16059
NASSAU	90	16404
OKALOOSA	267	52043
OKEECHOBEE	43	5058
ORANGE	446	134476
OSCEOLA	145	26216
PALM BEACH	3407	152846
PASCO	570	68581
PINELLAS	1010	184312
POLK	538	90101
PUTNAM	147	13439
ST. JOHNS	229	39497
ST. LUCIE	124	34705
SANTA ROSA	311	36248
SARASOTA	305	83100
SEMINOLE	194	75293
SUMTER	114	12126
SUWANNEE	108	8014
TAYLOR	27	4051
UNION	26	2326
VOLUSIA	396	82214
WAKULLA	46	4511
WALTON	120	12176
WASHINGTON	88	4983

Meanwhile, angry Democratic voters in Palm Beach County complained that a confusing "butterfly" ballot used in their county had caused them to accidentally vote for Reform Party candidate Pat Buchanan instead of Al Gore. See the ballot on page 330.

We have provided you the county-by-county results for Bush and Buchanan (https://tuvalabs.com/mydatasets/dedf373dbfcb4f0793aef1641afcaf51/). We would like you to assess the validity of these angry voters'—and therefore Al Gore's—claims. Based on these data, was the "butterfly" ballot responsible in some part for the outcome of the 2000 election? What other questions do the data bring up for you? And what can we do to ensure this doesn't happen again?

We look forward to reading your analyses and insights no later than May 5.

Sincerely,

Your county clerk

REFERENCES

Abiola, Oduola, and Harkirat S. Dhindsa. 2011. "Improving Classroom Practices Using Our Knowledge of How the Brain Works." *International Journal of Environmental and Science Education* 7(1): 71–81.

Baron, Andrew Scott, and Mahzarin R. Banaji. 2006. "The Development of Implicit Attitudes: Evidence of Race Evaluations from Ages 6 and 10 and Adulthood." *Psychological Science* 17(1): 53–58. doi:10.1111/j.1467-9280.2005.01664.x.

Beaton, Albert E., and Laura M. O'Dwyer. 2002. "Separating School, Classroom, and Student Variances and Their Relationship to Socio-Economic Status." In *Secondary Analysis of the TIMSS Data*, ed. David F. Robitaille and Albert E. Beaton, 211–231. New York: Kluwer Academic.

Becoates, Jocelyn B. 2009. *Determining the Correlation of Effective Middle School Math Teachers and Math Student Achievement*. University of North Carolina at Greensboro. libres.uncg.edu/ir/uncg/f/Becoats_uncg_0154D_10285.pdf.

Blackwell, Lisa S., Kali H. Trzeniewski, and Carol S. Dweck. 2007. "Implicit Theories of Intelligence Predict Achievement Across an Adolescent Transition: A Longitudinal Study and an Intervention." *Child Development* 78(1): 246–263. doi:10.1111/j.1467-8624.2007.00995.x.

Boaler, Jo. 2009. *What's Math Got to Do with It? How Parents and Teachers Can Help Children Learn to Love Their Least Favorite Subject.* London: Penguin Books.

———. 2016. *Mathematical Mindsets: Unleashing Students' Potential Through Creative Math, Inspiring Messages, and Innovative Teaching.* San Francisco, CA: Jossey-Bass.

Bourassa, Mary. *Which One Doesn't Belong?* wodb.ca/.

Cai, Jinfa, and Frank Lester. 2010. *Why Is Teaching With Problem Solving Important to Student Learning?* Reston, VA: National Council of Teachers of Mathematics.

Calamur, Krishnadev. 2014. "Math's Highest Honor Is Given to a Woman for the First Time." NPR, August 13, 2014. www.npr.org/sections/thetwo-way/2014/08/13/340086786/maths-highest-honor-is-given-to-woman-for-the-first-time.

Case, Bettye Anne, and Anne M. Leggett, eds. 2016. *Complexities: Women in Mathematics.* Princeton, NJ: Princeton University Press.

Cherng, Hua-Yu Sebastian, and Peter F. Halpin. 2016. "The Importance of Minority Teachers: Student Perceptions of Minority Versus White Teachers." *Educational Researcher* 45(7): 407–420. doi:10.3102/0013189x16671718.

Cody, Rachel Graham. 2013. "Expel Check: Portland Public Schools Has Spent Millions to Help Stop Racial Profiling of Students in Discipline Cases. The Problem Is Getting Worse." *Willamette Week*, September 24. http://www.wweek.com/port-land/article-21197-expel_check.html.

Coffey, David. 2014. "Do You Have a Boring Worksheet That You Want to Make More Interesting?" *Delta Scape*, April 18. deltascape.blogspot.com/2014/04/do-you-have-boring-worksheet-that-you.html.

Cohen, Elizabeth G. 1994. *Designing Groupwork: Strategies for the Heterogeneous Classroom.* New York: Teachers College Press.

Cohen, Elizabeth G., and Rachel A. Lotan, eds. 1997. *Working for Equity in Heterogeneous Classrooms: Sociological Theory in Practice.* New York: Teachers College Press.

Complete College America. 2012. "Remediation: Higher Education's Bridge to Nowhere." Washington, DC: Complete College America. www.completecollege.org, eric.ed.gov/?id=ED536825.

Dale, Edgar. 1969. *Audio-Visual Methods in Teaching.* New York: Dryden.

Danielson, Christopher. 2016. *Which One Doesn't Belong? A Teacher's Guide.* Portland, ME: Stenhouse.

Dar, Yehezkel, and Nura Resh. 1986. "Classroom Intellectual Composition and Academic Achievement." *American Educational Research Journal* 23(3): 357–374. doi:10.3102/00028312023003357.

Darling-Hammond, Linda, and Frank Adamson. 2010. "Beyond Basic Skills: The Role of Performance Assessment in Achieving 21st Century Standards of Learning." Stanford, CA: Stanford University, Stanford Center for Opportunity Policy in Education.

Day, Hy I. 1982. "Curiosity and the Interested Explorer." *Performance and Instruction* 21(4): 19–22. doi:10.1002/pfi.4170210410.

Dee, Thomas S. 2005. "A Teacher Like Me: Does Race, Ethnicity, or Gender Matter?" *American Economic Review* 95(2): 158–165. doi:10.1257/000282805774670446.

Dembo, Myron H., and Timothy J. McAuliffe. 1987. "Effects of Perceived Ability and Grade Status on Social Interaction and Influence in Cooperative Groups." *Journal of Educational Psychology* 79(4): 415–423. doi:10.1037/0022-0663.79.4.415.

Desmos. *Polygraph*. https://teacher.desmos.com/polygraph/.

Desmos. 2015. "The Desmos Guide to Building Great (Digital) Math Activities." *Des-Blog*, September 15. blog.desmos.com/post/150453765267/the-desmos-guide-to-building-great-digital-math.

Durlak, Joseph A., Roger P. Weissberg, Allison B. Dymnicki, Rebecca D. Taylor, and Kriston B. Schellinger. "The Impact of Enhancing Students' Social and Emotional Learning: A Meta-Analysis of School-Based Universal Interventions." *Child Development* 82(1): 405–432. doi:10.1111/j.1467-8624.2010.01564.x.

Dweck, Carol S. 2016. *Mindset: The New Psychology of Success*. 2nd ed. New York: Ballantine.

Eames, Charles, and Ray Eames. 1978. *Powers of Ten: A Film Dealing with the Relative Size of Things in the Universe and the Effect of Adding Another Zero*. Santa Monica, CA: Pyramid Films.

Eccles, Jacquelynne S., Janis E. Jacobs, and Rena D. Harold. 1990. "Gender Role Stereotypes, Expectancy Effects, and Parents' Socialization of Gender Differences." *Journal of Social Issues* 46(2): 183–201. doi:10.1111/j.1540-4560.1990.tb01929.x.

Edwards, L., and P. Torcellini. 2002. *A Literature Review of the Effects of Natural Light on Building Occupants*. Golden, CO: National Renewable Energy Laboratory. doi:10.2172/15000841. Available at http://www.nrel.gov/docs/fy02osti/30769.pdf.

Ellenberg, Jordan. 2015. *How Not to Be Wrong: The Power of Mathematical Thinking*. London: Penguin Books.

Frome, Pamela M., and Jacquelynne S. Eccles. 1998. "Parents' Influence on Children's Achievement-Related Perceptions." *Journal of Personality and Social Psychology* 74(2): 435–452. doi:10.1037/0022-3514.74.2.435.

Fuligni, Andrew J., Jacquelynne Eccles, and Bonnie Barber. 1995. "The Long-Term Effects of Seventh-Grade Ability Grouping in Mathematics." *The Journal of Early Adolescence* 15(1): 58–89. doi:10.1177/0272431695015001005.

Goldring, R., Lucinda Gray, and Amy Bitterman. 2013. *Characteristics of Public and Private Elementary and Secondary School Teachers in the United States: Results from the 2011–12 Schools and Staffing Survey (NCES 2013-314)*. U.S. Department of Education. Washington, DC: National Center for Education Statistics.

Graves, Ted, and Nancy Graves. 1985. *Broken Circles* (game). Santa Cruz, CA.

Grissom, Jason A., Emily C. Kern, and Luis A. Rodriguez. 2015. "The 'Representative Bureaucracy' in Education: Educator Workforce Diversity, Policy Outputs, and Outcomes for Disadvantaged Students." *Educational Researcher* 44(3): 185–192. doi:10.3102/0013189x15580102.

Haran, Brady. 2017. "Mathematics—Beauty vs Utility." Blog entry, January 20. www.bradyharanblog.com/blog/mathematics-beauty-vs-utility.

Hardy, Godfrey H. 2004/1940. *A Mathematician's Apology*. Cambridge, UK: Cambridge University Press.

Harel, Guershon. 2013. "Intellectual Need." In *Vital Directions for Mathematics Education Research*, ed. Keith R. Leatham, 119–151. doi:10.1007/978-1-4614-6977-3_6.

Headden, Susan. 2014. *Beginners in the Classroom: What the Changing Demographics of Teaching Mean for Schools, Students, and Society*. Carnegie Foundation for the Advancement of Teaching. www.carnegiefoundation.org/wp-content/uploads/2014/09/beginners_in_classroom.pdf.

Henningsen, Marjorie, and Mary Kay Stein. 1997. "Mathematical Tasks and Student Cognition: Classroom-Based Factors That Support and Inhibit High-Level Mathematical Thinking and Reasoning." *Journal for Research in Mathematics Education* 28(5): 524–549. Available at https://www.nctm.org/publications/article.aspx?id=17762.

Horn, Ilana Seidel. 2012. *Strength in Numbers: Collaborative Learning in Secondary Mathematics*. Reston, VA: National Council of Teachers of Mathematics.

Humphreys, Cathy, and Ruth E. Parker. 2015. *Making Number Talks Matter: Developing Mathematical Practices and Deepening Understanding, Grades 4–10*. Portland, ME: Stenhouse.

Illustrative Mathematics. "A Linear and Quadratic System." https://www.illustrative-mathematics.org/content-standards/tasks/576.

———. "Track Practice." https://www.illustrativemathematics.org/content-standards/tasks/82.

Kaplinsky, Robert. 2014. "Why Does Depth of Knowledge Matter?" www.robertkaplinsky.com, March 17. robertkaplinsky.com/why-does-depth-of-knowledge-matter/.

Kerckhoff, Alan C. 1986. "Effects of Ability Grouping in British Secondary Schools." *American Sociological Review* 51(6): 842. doi:10.2307/2095371.

Leinwand, Stevens. 1994. "Four Teacher-Friendly Postulates for Thriving in a Sea of Change." *Mathematics Teacher* 87: 392–393.

———. 2015. "SMP #3: Arguably the Nine Most Important Words in the Math Common Core." www.steveleinwand.com/presentations.

Lewin, Tamar. 2012. "Black Students Face More Discipline, Data Suggests." *New York Times*, March 6. http://www.nytimes.com/2012/03/06/education/black-students-face-more-harsh-discipline-data-shows.html?_r=0

Lockhart, Paul. 2009. *A Mathematician's Lament: How School Cheats Us Out of Our Most Fascinating and Imaginative Art Form.* New York: Bellevue Literary. "

———. 2014. *Measurement.* Cambridge, MA: Belknap Press of Harvard University Press.

Loewenstein, George. 1994. "The Psychology of Curiosity: A Review and Reinterpretation." *Psychological Bulletin* 116(1): 75–98. doi:10.1037/0033-2909 .116.1.75.

Loveless, Tom. 1999. *The Tracking Wars: State Reform Meets School Policy.* Washington D. C.: Brookings Institution.

Lyfe, Ise. 2012. "Kicking Black Boys Out of Class, Teaching Black Girls a Lesson." *Huffington Post*, September 19. http://www.huffingtonpost.com/ise-lyfe/kicking-black-boys-out-of_b_1894719.html.

Martin-Kniep, Giselle O., and Joanne Picone-Zocchia. 2009. *Changing the Way You Teach, Improving the Way Students Learn.* Alexandria, VA: Association for Supervision and Curriculum Development.

Math Union. 2014. "The Work Of Maryam Mirzakhani". https://www.mathunion. org/fileadmin/IMU/Prizes/Fields/2014/news_release_mirzakhani.pdf.

Mathematics Assessment Resource Service. "Mathematics Assessment Project." map.mathshell.org/index.php.

Means, Barbara, and Michael S. Knapp. 1991. "Cognitive Approaches to Teaching Advanced Skills to Educationally Disadvantaged Students." *Phi Delta Kappan* 73(4): 282–289.

Meier, Kenneth J. 1993. "Representative Bureaucracy: A Theoretical and Empirical Exposition." *Research in Public Administration* 2(1): 1–35.

mrmeyer.com/2011/the-three-acts-of-a-mathematical-story/.

Meyer, Dan. 2010. "Math Class Needs a Makeover." TED Talk, March. https://www .ted.com/talks/dan_meyer_math_curriculum_makeover?language=en.

———. 2011. "The Three Acts of a Mathematical Story." *Dy/Dyan*, May 11. blog. mrmeyer.com/2011/the-three-acts-of-a-mathematical-story/.

National Governors Association Center for Best Practices, Council of Chief State School Officers (NGA/CCSSO). 2010. Standards for Mathematical Practice. Washington: D.C: NGA/CCSSO.

National School Reform Faculty. 2014. "Compass Points Activity." http://www .nsrfharmony.org/wp-content/uploads/2017/10/CompassPoints-N_0.pdf.

Nguyen, Fawn. *Finding Ways* (blog). fawnnguyen.com/.

———. 2014. "First Two Days of School." *Finding Ways*, August 30. fawnnguyen.com/first-two-days-school/.

Oakes, Jeannie. 2005. *Keeping Track: How Schools Structure Inequality*. New Haven, CT: Yale University Press.

Organization for Economic Co-operation and Development. 2013. *PISA 2012 Assessment and Analytical Framework: Mathematics, Reading, Science, Problem Solving and Financial Literacy*. Paris: OECD. http://dx.doi.org/10.1787/9789264190511-en.

———. 2012. "Does Homework Perpetuate Inequities in Education?" *PISA in Focus* 46. Paris: OECD. http://dx.doi.org/10.1787/5jxrhqhtx2xt-en.

Pfeiffer, J. William, and John E. Jones. 1970. *A Handbook of Structural Experiences for Human Relations Training*. Vol. 1. Iowa City, IA: University Associated Press.

Pitts, David W. 2005. "Diversity, Representation, and Performance: Evidence About Race and Ethnicity in Public Organizations." *Journal of Public Administration Research and Theory* 15(4): 615–631. doi:10.1093/jopart/mui033.

Pólya, George. 1944. *How to Solve It*. Princeton, NJ: Princeton University Press.

Prince, Michael. 2004. "Does Active Learning Work? A Review of the Research." *Journal of Engineering Education* 93(3): 223–231. doi:10.1002/j.2168-9830.2004 .tb00809.x.

Ray-Reik, Max. 2011. "Why 2 Is Greater Than 4: A Proof by Induction." NCTM Annual Conference, April 15. Indianapolis, IN.

———. 2013. *Powerful Problem Solving: Activities for Sense Making with the Mathematical Practices*. Portsmouth, NH: Heinemann.

Ritchhart, Ron, Terri Turner, and Linor Hadar. 2009. "Uncovering Students' Thinking about Thinking Using Concept Maps." *Metacognition and Learning* 4(2): 145–159. doi:10.1007/s11409-009-9040-x.

Rose, Todd. 2017. *The End of Average: How We Succeed in a World That Values Sameness*. London: Penguin Books.

Rowe, Mary Budd. 1974. "Relation of Wait-Time and Rewards to the Development of Language, Logic, and Fate Control: Part 2—Rewards." *Journal of Research in Science Teaching* 11(4): 291–308. doi:10.1002/tea.3660110403.

Schwartz, Daniel L., and John D. Bransford. 1998. "A Time for Telling." *Cognition and Instruction* 16(4): 475–522. doi:10.1207/s1532690xci1604_4.

Slavin, Robert E. 1987. "Ability Grouping and Student Achievement in Elementary Schools: A Best-Evidence Synthesis." *Review of Educational Research* 57(3): 293–336. doi:10.3102/00346543057003293.

Spencer, Steven J., Claude M. Steele, and Diane M. Quinn. 1999. "Stereotype Threat and Women's Math Performance." *Journal of Experimental Social Psychology* 35(1): 4–28. doi:10.1006/jesp.1998.1373.

Stadel, Andrew. Estimation 180. www.Estimation180.com/.

Steele, Claude M., and Joshua Aronson. 1995. "Stereotype Threat and the Intellectual Test Performance of African Americans." *Journal of Personality and Social Psychology* 69(5): 797–811. doi:10.1037//0022-3514.69.5.797.

Stevens, John. Would You Rather . . . wyrmath.com/.

Stinnett, Anne M. 2013. *Implications for Ability Grouping in Mathematics for Fifth Grade Students*. Master's Thesis, University of Tennessee. http://trace.tennessee.edu/utk_gradthes/2462.

Strogatz, Steven H. 2014. *The Joy of x: A Guided Tour of Math, from One to Infinity*. London: Atlantic Books.

Swan, Malcolm. 2005. *Improving Learning in Mathematics: Challenges and Strategies*. Sheffield, UK: Teaching and Learning Division, Department for Education and Skills Standards Unit.

Thanheiser, Eva, and Amanda Jansen. 2016. "Inviting Prospective Teachers to Share Rough Draft Mathematical Thinking." *Mathematics Teacher Educator* 4(2): 145. doi:10.5951/mathteaceduc.4.2.0145.

Tsay, Chia-Jung, and Mahzarin R. Banaji. 2011. "Naturals and Strivers: Preferences and Beliefs About Sources of Achievement." *Journal of Experimental Social Psychology* 47(2): 460–465. doi:10.1016/j.jesp.2010.12.010.

US Department of Education, National Center for Education Statistics. 2016. *Digest of Education Statistics, 2015* (NCES 2016-014), Chapter 3. Washington, D.C.: US Department of Education.

Webb, Noreen M., Philip Ender, and Scott Lewis. 1986. "Problem-Solving Strategies and Group Processes in Small Groups Learning Computer Programming." *American Educational Research Journal* 23(2): 243–261. doi:10.3102/00028312023002243.

Weiher, Gregory, R. 2000. "Minority Student Achievement: Passive Representation and Social Context in Schools." *Journal of Politics* 62(3): 886–895.

Wilkinson, Alec. 2015. "The Pursuit of Beauty: Yitang Zhang Solves a Pure-Math Mystery." *New Yorker*, February 2.

Woollett, Katherine, and Eleanor A. Maguire. 2011. "Acquiring 'the Knowledge' of London's Layout Drives Structural Brain Changes." *Current Biology* 21(24): 2109–2114. doi:10.1016/j.cub.2011.11.018.

YouCubed. *Leo the Rabbit*. Stanford Graduate School of Education. www.youcubed.org/tasks/leo-the-rabbit/.

Yuki, Hiroshi. 2011. *Math Girls*. Translated by Tony Gonzales. Austin, TX: Bento Books.

INDEX